Beavertail Light Station

On Conanicut Island

Its Use, Development and History

From 1749

By Varoujan Karentz

Beavertail Light Station
Its Use, Development and History from 1749

BookSurge Publishing
7290 B Investment Drive
Charleston, SC 29418.

ISBN: 1-4196-8847-2
ISBN: 9781419688478

Printed in the United States of America

Cover design by Author
From an undated painting of Beavertail Light
Original located in Redwood Library and Athenaeum, Newport, RI

Photo by Author
Beavertail Light Station 2008

Contents

Chronology

Preface

Chapter 1.............Narragansett Bay and the Evolution of Beavertail
                     Light to 1800
Chapter 2 ....The Next 100 Years

Chapter 3 ....Keepers....1749 to 1972

Chapter 4............ Management and the Lighthouse Services

Chapter 5 ....Sound Signals at Beavertail

Chapter 6.............Charts, Piloting and Navigation

Chapter 7.............Shipwrecks

Chapter 8............ Lightships and the Light Tower

Chapter 9.............The 1749 Foundation

Chapter10.............The Organizations

Afterword

Appendix:
> *Appendix I*   *References and General Sources*
> *Appendix II*   *Narragansett Bay Lightships*
> *Appendix III*   *US Lighthouse Board Station Changes 1873-1905*
> *Appendix IV*   *US Lighthouse Board Reports*
> *Appendix V*   *BLMA Executive and Board of Directors*

Chronology and Events

1705	First navigational aid operated at Beavertail. (Open pitch fire built and manned by Indians)
1712	Request by Newport merchants to establish a permanent navigation aid on Beavertail
1719	Fog warning cannon periodically fired during poor visibility
1731	Colony order to raise funds for lighthouse construction on Beavertail
1749	Committee appointed to build lighthouse named "Newport Light". Wood tower completed in September of the same year
1753	Lighthouse burned and rebuilt with stone
1779	British troops burn lighthouse and remove light equipment when evacuating Newport
1789	George Washington approves transferring lighthouse to the Federal Government
1817	David Melville invents gas method for lighting lamps at Beavertail
1829	A 600 lb fog bell installed on the site
1852	Beavertail becomes experimental station to develop fog signaling devices
1856	Brick Keeper's house and granite light tower replace stone lighthouse
1898	Brick Assistant Keeper's house constructed
1930	First electric light beacon installed
1938	The Great Hurricane of 1938 destroys fog whistle house and uncovers original 1749 foundation
1939	USCG assumes responsibility of Beavertail Light Station

1972	Light beacon automated
1981	Beavertail State Park opens
1988	Fog signal upgraded
1989	Museum opened. Joint efforts of RI Parks Assoc, DEM, Town of Jamestown and USCG
1991	Fresnel lens removed, rotating beacon installed
1993	The Beavertail Lighthouse Museum Association assumes museum responsibility

Preface

The Navigation Problem

It was often called a "devil's voyage" by both captains and crews. Some vowed they would never go to sea again to be tossed and battered day after day and always burdened with constant trepidation that they knew not where they were. They feared the unknown rocky shoal just beneath their keel which always led to disaster. It grounded their ship, often taking lives or losing valuable, irreplaceable cargo. They looked for safe passage through rocks and shoals for some feature of land which could guide them to safe harbor and home. It was the lighthouse, either by its night lantern or its visible prominence during the daytime, that answered the sailor's prayer.

"We know now where we are"

This book covers the history of the lighthouse and the light station at Beavertail on Conanicut Island in Rhode Island. It is a story of brick, mortar, lighthouse evolution, the sailors who used the light and the generations of people who lived there. It's not easy writing a book about a 250 year old artifact that is still in use today. Much has happened and much has been written by historians who have found Beavertail noteworthy. There have been hundreds of articles, books, newspaper items plus thousands of letters and documentary papers which paint the colorful history of the light station. This book provides another glimpse of its past using material previously published, but from the perspective of how and why the light station was used; giving the reader a better understanding of its significance to the coastal and economic industry for which it was built. Its incidental contribution to Rhode Island's beauty, with its rocks awash by the sea, makes the site unparalleled anywhere south of Maine. While Beavertail's 250 year history is colorful and somewhat romantic, the reader should never forget the purpose of the lighthouse.

It is for the vessel at sea that searches restlessly through the dense fog and at other times, through cloudless nights for that loom of light which tells its master his navigational position and allows him to pilot his ship and his crew safely to port. This is the true reason for the light. It will never be known how many lives and cargos it has saved.

Intertwined in the story of Beavertail's first 100 years is the lack of technical innovations, of embarrassing technical development of America's lighthouses and the traumatic, sometimes political, interferences that plagued its growth. The effectiveness of Beavertail's light was impeded by both incompetence of early administrators and the inability of innovators to convince lawmakers of superior lighting systems other than those fueled by whale oil. America's lighthouses in general were technologically outdated and embarrassingly mismanaged until 1852 when the U.S. Lighthouse Board was established. The important lighthouse lamp, the light itself, suffered from technological inferiority during all those early years. Although this book does not dwell nor highlight those issues, the reader will gain an understanding of the changes at Beavertail that were impacted by them.

More importantly, when reading the 250 year history of Beavertail Light, the reader should let their imagination place themselves on the deck of their own imaginary vessel navigating the waters in the mouth of Narragansett Bay. It is only then, one can appreciate and understand Beavertail's contribution to navigational safety and how changes and improvements impacted the navigation methods of the times.

At the turn of the 18th century, navigation was still not an exact science nor did the practical ship's navigator have the tools to place their vessel's exact position on a chart. Even the charts of the day were suspect of inaccuracy and the cartographer often made assumptions when joining lines of shore features. It was the dilemma of the ship's master, the navigator, the crew, the Navy's Commandant or the merchant ship owner who wondered if the ship laden with cargo was safe or soon to flounder on an uncharted rocky shoal or shore. Not withstanding ocean storms, exploration through the ages by masters of the sea left countless tragedies of shipwrecks and loss of life. Families would pray for the safe return of their loved ones knowing some would never return. On top of the human toll was the loss of goods never to see their destination because of fundamental navigation flaws which placed ships where they were not supposed to be.

Although the heavens had been mapped and celestial algorithms created by the *Galileo's* and *Newton's* of the world, once the sailor had lost sight of land, every mile traveled was an estimate. The ability to determine latitude by angle measurements of the sun and some celestial bodies had been learned and practiced. These lines of equal distance from each other, from the equator to either pole were parallel. One could plot and advance that latitude line accurately by measuring the highest angle of the sun ("noon sight") at the position from the equator to either the North or South Pole; but where they were on that line to the east or west was denied. It was those meridians ("longitude"), the looped lines from pole to pole, which changed in distance at any width as does on an orange peel. Time converted to distance between these lines was necessary and no one knew how to measure it. The precise knowledge of the difference in time between the place the navigator was sighting a celestial body and another location was the prerequisite and unattainable. The navigator of that day had only one choice. They used their latitude sighting as a single line and coupled to it their practice of good seamanship as to how far and in what direction they may have traveled. That accepted navigation method of the day was and still is called "dead reckoning." The term "dead" for this type of navigation was actually a derivative of the word "deduced," meaning presumed. It later took on a more parochial meaning which emphasized the risk and the end result if the navigator "reckoned" wrong or carried their presumed position plots too far without a navigational fix of a known landmark.

Approaching land carried much fear and apprehension until the navigator recognized a land feature. When unrecognized land was sighted, a second decision had to be made. In which direction along the shore should they sail? The dead reckoning plots could place a vessel as much as 100 miles from its actual position and if they did not have a celestial fix for days because of weather, they were very much concerned that land fall could become catastrophic. There is an old saying of ship masters that holds truth even today; "The safest place for a ship is at sea." In our modern world, the analogy is; "the most dangerous segment of an airplanes' flight is the landing." For a ship, it is "making a landfall."

Essentially, the ocean sailor was guessing where they were. It took both skill and luck to arrive safe and sound to their harbor of refuge or destination. The coastwise sailor, on the other hand, cruised from landmark to landmark. They learned from their apprenticeship to recognize a hilltop, a rocky crag, the feature of the island, the safe opening into the harbor, the carrying of the tide and current to steer the vessel safely. It was local knowledge they gained from the years of making the same passages. When they ventured from their familiar course it was from other local mariners that provided them with the "do's" and "don'ts" peculiar to the coastal features. Night time passages were another thing. The safe course was well offshore, away from rocks and shoals, and their prudence was based on dead reckoning skills to arrive back in sight of recognizable land marks at daybreak. This type of coastal navigation was called "piloting" as in "piloting or plotting a course."

The toll of shipwrecks and lost lives throughout the history of maritime voyages is immeasurable. However, one fatal incident did result in a most significant development to help the navigator pinpoint his location at sea.

On 22 October, 1707, four homebound British warships from Gibraltar miscalculated their position and ran aground on the "Sicily Isles," a group of rocks at the southwestern end of England. The four ships were lost and with the exception of two seaman, all 2000 members of the crews, including their Admiral, *Sir Clowdisley Shovell,* died. So distraught was the British Admiralty, not only of this catastrophe but also because of experiencing three centuries of ships and men lost due to positional longitudinal errors, the British Parliament framed the famous "Longitude Act of 1714." This Act promised a prize of 20,000 British pounds for the solution to the longitude problem. It took another 80 years to test and develop a timepiece which adjusted itself for temperature and humidity variations, gravitational effects, including harsh rolling and pitching and was reliable enough to be accepted and used by mariners.

The longitude problem was solved in 1761 by *John Harrison,* a Scottish watchmaker who was constantly challenged and abused by the astronomers and mathematicians of the world who were advocating a celestial solution as the only viable option. *Harrison* finally received his prize twenty years after he made his working model of a time piece called a chronometer. It was not until the late 1790's that the mechanical chronometer coupled with celestial tables and the navigational sextant was accepted as the best device to calculate one's longitude. For the next one hundred eighty years, the chronometer became the navigator's crutch and time measurement continued to be refined.

Every ocean going ship carried at least one. Many carried three and used them to calculate even smaller errors by comparing their rate loss or gain against the other two each day. The chronometer was refined and made even smaller and more accurate with invention of the quartz movement along with electronic navigation systems such as LORAN (Long Range Radio Aid to Navigation) and GPS (Global Positioning System).

The problem of knowing one's position was not unique only to the Europeans of that early era. The fledging colonies, established along the New England coast of America, were founded as seaports. As they grew with development, the needs of goods, supplies and materials surged to be moved between ports. Shipbuilding took hold in New England; mixed with vessels arriving from Europe to the colonies with new immigrants and families. Coastal trading had begun and with it the problems of safe navigation among rocks and shoals demanded better methods including the centuries old solution problem of longitude.

It did not take very long for local merchants, ship owners and those who sailed in them to see the need of protecting their investments from wreckage due to inadequate coastal navigational aids. The first crude coastal light fires were established by ship owners when they expected their ship to reach port. But estimates of when they were to arrive were never reliable because of the effects of weather, winds, tides and currents. Ships sailing to the colonies from Europe or Africa would send notice ahead of their estimated arrival date with a ship that left before they did. Many times the ship with the message aboard was bound for another port and the information arrived via overland. Adding all the variables, notification of arrival was only an estimate and it could be weeks or even months different from the actual arrival date.

The lighthouse has been in existence as a navigation aid as early as 285 BC and was used by the sailors of the Mediterranean. It solved the longitude problem by being a fixed point just as if it had been located in mid ocean. The navigator knew where he was and it marked the hazards he feared or the entrance to a safe haven. It was both a point of arrival and departure. It was the first and last reliable navigation aid arriving from the sea or sailing out of sight of the land. It was the most important landmark searched for, coming and going, either day or night. Its importance can not be overemphasized. The lighthouse was the beacon of safety and life. Next to God there was nothing of more importance than that which assured the safety of the ship and its crew arriving from the sea.

One must imagine the relief of the captain and crew upon seeing the light.

"At last....... We know now where we are".

Acknowledgements

As with any historical essay, much credit must be given to all those preceded this book with their own writing and research of Beavertail Light. There are many too numerous to mention. The writings in this book are based on excerpts of those early writers and without them, 250 years of history which is so well documented in hundreds of archives would not be available today. I am much indebted to them for illuminating me with information from their writings and to be able to weave their stories into this book.

I am thankful to the Beavertail Lighthouse Museum Association (BLMA) without whose collections and use of their archives this book could not have been written. The wealth of information scattered among their files was startling. I marveled at the insight of those persons who diligently recognized the value of news clippings, letters, organizational records and other documents knowing that years later they would be of value to a researcher.

On a personal note, I wish to thank the following for their patient tolerance in answering my questions and providing material which filled in gaps and voids of data collection:

Linda Warner, a BLMA member, officer and past President for many years who today I consider the foremost historian about the light. Her husband George, President of BLMA who assisted me in recording much information and for his independent research on Beavertail which he shared with me. Richard Sullivan, another officer who also has been associated with the BLMA almost from inception. He read and commented upon the manuscript of each chapter and his contributions appear throughout the book. My sister Anahid Varadian for her editing corrections and my daughter Sona Andrews for her reviews and revisions. Edward Spinny, who graciously allowed me to excerpt direct passages from his unpublished manuscript on "Piloting in Narragansett Bay." The Jamestown Historical Society and their President, Rosemary Enright, who not only provided many of the photographs found

*between these covers and never hesitated in fulfilling any request I
had for information. Lanette Macaruso and her student team for use
of her extensive study of early fog signal development at Beavertail.
Sue Maden for sharing her Beavertail documentation files and
notifying me of Beavertail related topics she came across. The
Jamestown Philomenian Library for use of their outstanding
collection of reference material about Beavertail and the early
history of Colonial Newport, Jamestown and Conanicut Island. U.S.
Coast Guard Academy Library, New London, Connecticut for
unrestricted use of their U.S. Lighthouse Board archives as well as
the National Archives Records Center, Waltham, Massachusetts for
copies of lighthouse records. Frank Meyer, a past Board member of
BLMA, for his uncanny ability to answer and provide detailed
reference data to many of my questions. Richard Chellis, who was
born at the lighthouse; George Light, a Coast Guard Petty Officer
stationed at Beavertail; Sandra Driscoll, a direct descendent of a
Beavertail "Keeper" and Dan Goguen who wrote of his experience
as a crew member on the Brenton Reef Lightship.*

Their help and contributions of information put this book together.

Chapter 1

Narragansett Bay and the Evolution of Beavertail Light up to 1800

Beavertail Light Station, synonymously called "Beavertail" or "Beaver Tail Light", with it gray granite light tower and almost two identical white painted brick keeper's houses is located on Rhode Island's Conanicut Island in the middle of lower Narragansett Bay. It is officially termed a "Light Station" by the U.S. Coast Guard. Its location on Beavertail Point is situated south of the village of Jamestown at the very southern tip of a peninsula connected to the main island by a narrow two lane causeway road named "Beavertail Road." Once the causeway has been crossed the entire 2.6 mile long peninsula's correct designation is "Beaver Neck," although over the years the name has erroneously evolved to being called "Beavertail." When the peninsula's orientation on a map or chart is viewed horizontally, its shape takes on the appearance of a beaver. The northern end, "Beaver Head" resembles a beaver's head and the southern end pinched by the waters of Hull Cove on one side and Austin Hollow on the other resemble that of a beaver's tail, hence "Beaver Tail." Beavertail Point at its most southern point where the light station stands is a popular visitor destination. The light's exact geographic location is 41 degrees 26.967 minutes North Latitude and 71 degrees, 23.966 minutes West Longitude.

The story of the "Beavertail Light" or "Newport Light" as it was first called, begins in Newport, Rhode Island 75 years before the beginning of the Revolutionary War. Less than two miles to the east of Jamestown, on the other side of Narragansett Bay's East Passage, sat colonial Newport. Since its founding in 1639, Newport rapidly transformed and focused on maritime commerce. By 1682 a naval officer was assigned to register all "deck vessels" in and around the port. Newport had developed into a vibrant seaport near the end of the 1690s with its deep natural harbor protected by a barrier island ("Goat Island") and a sheltered anchorage formed inside "Brenton Cove." It took only a few more years for Newport to establish itself as the seaward connection to the other colonies competing with Boston, whose vessels had to contend with the longer difficult passage around the scimitar arm of Cape Cod.

Coupled with a safe seaport, fertile land, successful farming and an abundance of fish it was only a matter of time that Newport's transportation of products by sea would lead to building of ships, establishment of supporting chandleries, merchants, ship owners and tradesmen.

By 1739, Newport merchants operated more than 100 large ships. In 1749, 160 ships were cleared for foreign voyages and by 1769, throughout the Narragansett Bay area, over 200 vessels were engaged in foreign trade and another 300 to 400 used in coastal traffic.

The risks associated with the sea were a way of life. Shipwrecks were common along the coast. There were no navigation aids. Local knowledge of the rocks, shoals and reefs were learned only after loss of life, cargo and the ships themselves. Night time passages were even more notorious and the prudent captain would wait off shore until visibility provided identifiable land marks. Shipwreck losses were devastating to the owner's investments of vessel, crew and cargo. With accumulating losses of vessels and cargo, the marine insurance business took hold and well known wealthy colonial businessmen including *Moses Brown, Stephan Hopkins, John Gerrish and Joseph Lawrence* began underwriting "risks at sea." *William De Wolf* of Bristol also took up the business of underwriting the risks that ships took. Although insuring ships and cargo against "the dangers of the sea" was profitable, the losses and delay suffered by merchants, ship owners and underwriters overwhelmingly led to the recognition by all for the need to provide a navigation aid to help guide their vessels entering Narragansett Bay.

The Approach and Hazards of Narragansett Bay

The approach to Newport and Narragansett Bay is represented by a wide body of water identified as "Rhode Island Sound." It stretches for 33 nautical miles from the eastern side of "Block Island" to a little known island off the western coast of Martha's Vineyard called "Nomans Land." Just off center of an imaginary line between these two islands and perpendicular to it, 16 miles to the north, lies the entrance to Narragansett Bay and Newport. The depth of water gradually decreases from about 150 ft to 75 ft and while measuring depth to determine position was and still is a significant navigation method, the rock hazards around the Bay's entrance rise abruptly and give no warning until it is too late.

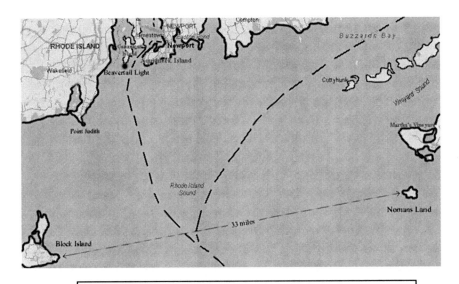

Seaward Approach into Rhode Island Sound

Today, as a vessel enters Rhode Island Sound and the low landscape comes into view, there is no visible distinction or breaks along the shore line defining the entrance into Narragansett Bay. Point Judith and the western shore of Narragansett take shape, but both the "East" and "West Passages," split by "Beavertail Point" meld into an unbroken strip of land. Beavertail Point bisects Narragansett Bay and remains as the principle point of land a navigator uses to lay course for safe passage. Except for the present entrance buoy "NB" situated 3.9 nautical miles south of Beavertail Point, it is not until the navigator is two to six miles offshore that the first visual references takes shape. The Newport (*Pell*) and Jamestown (*Verrazano*) bridges lie low on the horizon and the Beavertail

Lighthouse, with its 24 hour a day rotating 9 second flashing white light, immediately identifies Beavertail Point both during the day and night.

From the period 1863 to 1963 four different lightships *(see Chapter 8)* supplemented Beavertail Light to guide ships safely into the East Passage. The last ship, "Brenton LV 102," equipped with fog horn and a radio beacon transmitter, was replaced by a "Texas Tower" rigid platform. The unmanned tower remained on location until 1989 between Beavertail Light and Brenton Reef. The safe passage into Newport and beyond, via the East Passage, was to keep the Brenton Reef lightship, and later the tower, to starboard (on the right hand side) and the Beavertail Light to port (left hand side) of the entering vessel. Both the lightship and the "Texas Tower" were discontinued with the advance of electronic navigation aids, particularly Loran and an early Global Positioning System (GPS) called "NAVSAT" and the high costs of maintaining the lightship.

Although during the time both aids (Beavertail Light and Brenton Lightship) were operational, navigators from time to time have been fooled by the wide mouth of "Mackerel Cove" on Conanicut Island. After passing both the lighthouse and the lightship, Mackerel Cove appears as another opening into the upper bay. The causeway road at the head of "Mackerel Cove" connects Beavertail to the main part of Conanicut Island. It is a low narrow road indiscernible from the sea. The tendency, however, is for the navigator to see an apparent passage which in reality is blocked. Once identified as an obstruction, the tendency is to steer the vessel to the right toward Newport, placing the ship on a dangerous course to "Kettle Bottom Rock."

The loss of ships entering or leaving Newport from or to the sea was due to many factors, but the primary threat, were the dangerous rocks identified as "Brenton Reef." This underwater cluster of rocks that stretches out to the southwest from "Brenton Point" for ¾ of a mile and in calm weather is noticeable only by a mild swell or heaving of the sea. During a strong south easterly gale, water breaks over the reef and a mile of white water exposes the line of rocks. The reef was named after a survivor from a British ship bound into

Newport that sunk on the reef. She was a little girl, too young to know her own name, adopted by the *"Jahleel Brenton"* Royalist family in Newport.

Less than a mile to the east of "Brenton Reef" is "Seal Ledge," an underwater hazard with only 12 ft of water above it. Two miles west of "Brenton Reef," just to the south of Beavertail Point, lies another underwater hazard; the fabled "Newton Rock" with less than 6 ft of water over it. It too has been the downfall of mariners attempting to cut short the passage around Beavertail Point. During the summer months, from April to October,fog developing over the entrance to Narragansett Bay adds another hazard. Brought in by winds from the east to southwest, moist air condenses with the seasonable cold water forming fog. Once it arrives, fog usually prevails anywhere between 4 to 12 hours, but also periods of 4 to 6 days are experienced with only short clearing intervals brought on by dry northerly and westerly winds.

To the captain of a ship approaching Newport in the 1700s, however, it was a bleak view of non identifiable land and much guesswork as to where the shielded opening of the East Passage was located. By today's standards it is amazing that ships propelled only by the wind could navigate through the hazards and safely bring to shore both their passengers and cargo. Some ships came up along the southern coast of the Narragansett land mass to enter the Bay, passing Point Judith with treacherous rock ledges standing off to the west of the point. In the late 1700's, a day beacon marked the tip of Point Judith and it was not until 1810 that a lighthouse was actually constructed there.

At this point, it is worthwhile to interject a note regarding handling of large sailing vessels entering Narragansett Bay in order to give the reader an appreciation of the seamanship and navigation skills involved and particularly the risks of groundings. Handling big square rigged sailing vessels required both daring and skill. The limitations of sail power required professional experienced seafaring men. The attention to navigation and ship handling was extremely demanding. Wind shifts, tide and current changes all affected maintaining control and staying off the rocks. Maneuverability decisions were not given a second chance in shallow or restricted bays. *William Low* provides a good example of this in his 1936 "Short History of Beavertail Light" where he cites the Revolutionary War movement of *Commodore Sir Peter Parker's* entire British fleet entering Narragansett Bay and its shallower West Passage. "Hence around the northern end of Conanicut Island, and then south, brought to anchor in a "workman-like fashion" along the shores of Portsmouth down to Coddington Point." This feat was even more remarkable since *Parker's* fleet consisted of seven (7) multi deck "warships of the line", four (4) frigates and seventy (70) transports containing six thousand (6000) troops. Rightly so, *Low* doubted if seaman could be found today to repeat this feat.

(Thirteen (13) of these British transporters were later sunk deliberately by the British to act as a barrier against the French ships invading Newport. This was to protect their stronghold in Newport in July and August of 1778. One of the sunken ships was the "Discoverer" renamed the "Lord Sandwich", the ship that famous explorer "Captain James Cook" used on his first voyage to the South Pacific in 1768.)

Low further recounts his boyhood vision of the multi-sail three masted frigate "Constellation," sister ship to the "USS Constitution," "beating" [tacking] out, under full sail through the East Passage against a moderate breeze and states "anyone who has seen this will understand."

Early navigation charts of the area were both crude and inaccurate. Depth soundings recorded by transiting vessels were also unreliable since navigation methods themselves were only as good as the navigator's estimate of their location by use of instruments of questionable accuracy. Most navigation charts of that era had no corrections for magnetic variation, and terrain topography was skewed by visual distortion as a function of the curvature of the earth and the observer's height above sea level. It was not until 1816 that a reliable chart was available covering the entrance to the East Passage and Newport. This is not to say that sailing directions were non existent. Under direction of the American Congress, in 1796 the 1st "American Coast Pilot" written by *Captain Lawrence Furlong*, was published and made available to mariners. Remarkably it covered recommended sailing routes and passages from Maine to the Virginia Capes. Its sailing directions were endorsed by local

captains and it provided the first compiled set of navigation
guidance for the northern east coast of the country.

From *Point-Judith* to *Rhode-Island* harbour,
your courfe is N. E. and the diftance about 5 Leagues. The
Light-Houfe muft be left on your larboard fide ; it ftands
on the South Point of *Conanicut-Ifland* : This Point is called
the *Beaver's Tail*, and is about 3 Leagues diftant from *Point-
Judith*. After leaving the Light-Houfe on your larboard
fide, you muft take care to avoid the Rocks which lie off
South from *Caftle-Hill*, fome of which are above water :—
Caftle-Hill is on the Eaft fide of *Rhode-Island* harbour. If
you fteer N. E. you will have 20 Fathoms water ; the fhore
is hard and rocky. A little within the harbour, and near to
the fhore on the Weft fide, there is a rock called the *Kettle-
Bottom*. There is alfo a Cove on the Weft fide, called *Mac-
karel Cove*, the entrance of which is fhoal and dangerous.——

> **Excerpt from America's First Coast Pilot published 1796**

For the 18th century master of a sailing vessel prior to 1749,
however, the navigation problem of entering Newport after nightfall
was multiplied because the faint glow of oil lamps and candlelight
from Newport's residential lights could not be seen at any great
distance. The safe course to steer was always in doubt. The captain's
navigation uncertainty was compounded during bad weather plus
they had to guess the effects of the vertical and horizontal
constituents from tide and current. The time of the turning of the tide
at an estuary was an important decision parameter for the sailing
vessel's ships master. The continuation of the 6 hour changeable
ocean tide wave along the shore line becomes distorted by
underwater hydrographic features. Current sets of up to 1.6 knots
takes place as the tide ebbs out of the Bay and cross currents from
Buzzards Bay or Long Island Sound carry shipping off course.
Unless compensated by the vessel's navigator, the current sets
contribute directly to unfortunate shipwrecks. Often as not, standing
offshore until daybreak when safe passage could be made was the
decision of the prudent navigator.

The shipwrecks and delays on entering port with valuable cargos as
well as shipments on shore awaiting forwarding to other ports took a
heavy toll on the profits of the Newport merchant. As commerce

grew, the demands of safe passage into Newport became an economic priority. The reality and solution of this issue resulted in the need to locate a lighthouse on Beavertail Point.

The Slave Trade and Beavertail Light

In early 2006 the Providence Journal published a series of articles written by Paul Davis outlining the extent of the slave trade by Rhode Island ship owners and captains. The exposé titled "Unrighteous Traffick" was enlightening not only by the number of ships and merchants involved, but also because of the economic significance. Without question, the ramifications of slaving resulting in increased shipping and its importance to the safety of those ships dictated the need of a navigational aid at the entrance of Narragansett Bay and spurned the colony to establish the light at Beavertail.

By 1710 Newport had turned itself into a dominate maritime regional center, becoming one of the five major ports in the America along with Boston, New York, Philadelphia, and Charleston. Maritime commerce began to boom. Its growth spilled over into surrounding towns on Narragansett Bay. Trade and the export of rum, candles, fish, furniture, silver, and other value-added goods were the main engines of economic growth during the 18th century. Activities inextricably linked to Newport's participation in the slave trade and widespread ownership of slaves by families throughout the city were fueled by the shipping magnates. Newport was populated by English settlers with the strong religious beliefs of both Puritans and Baptists. The Quakers soon dominated the port city, but religious diversity kept Newport secular even in early times.

Although the slave trade's famed "Trade Triangle" had a focus point in Europe, mainly with English ship owners, Newport's entrepreneurs jumped right into this lucrative trade. Slavery was legal and morally acceptable and ships were readily modified to carry human cargo. Traders bought enslaved Africans in exchange for goods shipped from Europe and the American Colonies. From Newport, rum, candles, dried fish, furniture and silver products were shipped to Europe and Africa. The second part of the triangle was the voyage of human beings from Africa across the Atlantic to the Caribbean and the America's. Those Africans who often survived a terrible journey were sold to work on plantations. The third part of

24

the triangle was the return voyage to Europe or to the American Colonies with slave labored crops of coffee, rice, tobacco, sugar and molasses. The triangular trip could take up to a year to complete.

The origin of Beavertail Light was tied directly to the slave trade. The protection and safety of ship traffic into Newport Harbor aligned itself to this 18th century economic engine as surely as why Rhode Island ships ruled the American slave trade traffic for more than 75 years. In 1730 half of the wealthiest residents of Newport and Bristol were involved in the slave trade. The safety of ships and preventing their loss translated to profit and the influence of the wealthy made the demands of a light at Beavertail impossible to ignore.

The first recorded departure of a slave ship from Newport was in 1709, but by that time over 100 vessels had been built in Rhode Island and most were engaged in trading ranging to the southern colonies and to Africa. It did not take long to add a "slave voyage." By 1725 regular slave voyages from Newport around the "triangle" and back were being recorded. There actually was competition between English based slave ships, whose owners had larger vessels with greater sized crews, and the colonists. Some estimates claim Rhode Island ships made over 1000 voyages during the period from 1725 to 1807 carrying over 100,000 human chained cargo even though slavery trading was outlawed in Rhode Island in 1787. At its peak, Newport was the home port of 184 slave ships doing business via the trade triangle. Including ships of the families of *John and Moses Brown* from Providence and *Aaron Lopez,* the largest taxpayer in Newport.

Newport was the hub of New England's slave trade, and at its height, slaves made up one-third of its population. Business was so good that in February of 1707 the colony laid down an impost tax of 3 pounds for each negro imported. By 1774 the waterfront bustled with activity with over 150 separate wharves and hundreds of shops crowded along the harbor between Long Wharf and the southern end of the harbor. Some reports considered Newport as the fourth richest city in America. As Newport's trade throughout the Atlantic basin grew, the city became an epicenter in the development of modern American capitalism.

Almost half of Rhode Island's entire slave voyages occurred after trading was outlawed. Rhode Island law was enacted in 1789 to end slave trading but it had little effect. As late as 1805 a political quirk had established a separate customs district in Bristol and slave trading was again an open business with 50 ships or more from Rhode Island sailing for the African coast. Even before the end of the 18th century, Bristol surpassed Newport as the busiest slave port in Rhode Island. *The DeWolf's* family of Bristol, the largest slave trading family in the US history, had financed almost 100 slaving voyages between 1784 to 1807.

The counter trade that developed from the slave trade was enormous in the formation of new businesses within the colony. The manufacturing of rum fueled the slave business. Prior to 1754 eighteen (18) vessels were carrying hogsheads of rum and twenty two (22) distilleries were operational in Newport boiling molasses into rum for export. Rhode Island ships carried barrels of it on the "first leg" of the triangle buying the African slaves. One estimate claims over 11 million gallons eventually reached the "Gold Coast.' The slaves in turn were shipped to the West Indies as the "second leg" and traded for molasses which, on the "third leg", was returned to Rhode Island to make more rum As the profits grew, so did the local businesses. New goods, both grown and manufactured, passed onto more ships leaving Narragansett Bay and then on to other colonies on the east coast.

Not only was Rhode Island in the forefront of the slave trade, it had its share of slaves as well. Newport, "The Kings County," which encompassed the lower half of western Rhode Island and Jamestown was populated with slaves. They worked in both households and in the fields. The 1730 census records of Jamestown show eighty (80) Negro slaves living on Conanicut Island plus nineteen (19) Indians. The Negro's represented 36 % of the island population. The highest concentration per capita of any county in the New World. Only South Carolina and later Mississippi exceeded this ratio. By 1747 the number of Negro slaves on Conanicut Island had increased to one hundred ten (110). Across the Bay in Newport one family alone, *Abraham Red,* father of the founder of "Redwood Library," owned two hundred thirty eight (238) Negroes in 1766. Slaving was big business and only South Carolina surpassed Rhode Island in the practice of buying and selling slaves.

Earlier, in 1774, the arrival of the HMS Rose, a twenty (20) gun frigate did much to stem illegal slave shipping including smuggling of taxable goods which had been much ignored by the colonists. She was a frequent visitor into Narragansett Bay. Although illegal slaving continued, other sources of shipping commerce began to intercede. The orient had opened up and demand for New England products began to find their way around Cape Horn. A series of fast and large ships were constructed. The *Brown* family owned dozens and many sailed from Narragansett Bay to Canton, China. A record breaker at the time was the *Ann & Hope* who sailed to Canton in four (4) months and one day including a stop in Australia. On a return trip to Rhode Island she floundered on shoals of Block Island and was wrecked.

The 1807 Congressional abolition of the slave trade, along with the end of the "War of 1812", helped put an end to the seventy five (75) year Rhode Island market. The slave trader *De Wolf* of Bristol apparently wanted some revenge for the loss of his business. He outfitted one of his ships, the "Yankee", as a privateer, loaded her with a crew of one hundred twenty (120) men and went hunting for British merchant ships. In three years, "Yankee" captured prizes valued at $5,000,000, and returned $1,000,000 in profits to the people of Bristol.

The war of 1812 changed much and affected other economic opportunities. The slave trade was over for all practical purposes and the railroads had begun their expansion. Newport began to slip into a depression that ended its vibrant center for business. Changes began to take place in the shipping business as well. Manufacturing of goods by New England tradesmen and entrepreneurs took over. Rum distilling went south to Kentucky and Tennessee and was replaced by whisky and bourbon and Newport began to lose more of its luster. Through all this evolution, shipping demanded better navigation aids and improvement of these aids became a constant ongoing task that had the attention of the Colonial government and then the Federal government of the United States.

1712 Beavertail Light ... The First Light in North America ?

> *For reasons unknown or not documented, any claim to being the first of anything, especially the first lighthouse in America remains as such, "only a claim", until challenged and backed up with acceptable proof. The assertion is not verifiable and only conjecture between known facts can be assumed, yet credible arguments have been established.*

Jamestown was settled in 1639 and established as a town in the year 1678. These early settlers under a form of land ownership council retained "Proprietors Records". These Jamestown records are still in existence. One record dated April 1705 stated the following: "Ordered and made by the authority of this present Council that there shall be a *chimney* built to the "Watch House" (*Beaver Tail*) at the discretion of *Captain Stephen Remington.*" This chimney could have been attached to the watch house, which one record states as being built in 1667. *Remington,* in genealogy records created by *Lois Sorenson* (a modern day descendant), is reported to be both a ship captain and captain in the Jamestown militia. He is buried in "Friend's Cemetery" off Eldrid Avenue in Jamestown. He lived from 1661 to 1739 and according to Jamestown "Proprietors Records" many of the meetings of the "Proprietors" were conducted in *"Remmentun's"* house. He apparently ran a house of entertainment and was exempt from any taxes because the town held meetings there. In 1703 he was chosen to be the foreman of the Jamestown Town Council.

Not much is known about the "Watch House", its purpose or its new chimney. Beavertail was a favorite observation point for "watching" vessels of any type entering the Bay via either the "East" or "West" passage. The West passage was much shallower where around the northern portion of Conanicut Island twenty one (21) ft of water discouraged ships of deep draft to use it. The East passage on the other hand was a shorter run into Newport and carried much deeper water. For those reasons, the East passage was favored by mariners. In either case, the Watch House was strategically situated to observe traffic going or coming. Perhaps its use also became a landmark for vessels at sea. The question and answer of the term "chimney" and its meaning as light or a traditional fire flue is moot. It is readily assumed that the Watch House was constructed earlier. Was it a chimney to be used in the conventional way as part of a fireplace in the Watch House or was it a navigational beacon? Was the Watch House used to look out for friendly vessels and ships that were overdue or as a watch for French privateers, which at that time were sailing along the entire New England coast ? Ten years earlier on 12 July 1690 French privateers entered Newport after taking possession of Nantucket, Martha's Vineyard and Block Island. The flamboyant era of piracy continued into the next decade. There was also fear that the French and their indigenous Indian tribes,who in 1704 attacked and destroyed Deerfield, Massachusetts less than 100 miles away, would sail into Narragansett Bay.

If *Captain Remington*, the person placed in charge was a militia officer, it would seem logical that the watch tower was used for military observation purposes. Numerous questions arise as to its use and also of its practicality. Assuming that it was indeed a watch tower built and manned to sight a vessel still at sea or entering the East Passage, what actions took place after a ship was sighted? Was another signal or warning sent to Newport or to the ship that was sighted and if it was, what type of communication was passed? Could flags have been used? Any overland communications would take nearly two hours to deliver from the Watch House on Beavertail Point to the village of Jamestown and then by sail or rowboat to Newport. By that time a ship first sighted off Beavertail Point would be entering Newport harbor.

In the early days of flag signals (vexillology), challenges were exchanged requesting the name and hailing port of the vessel. But prior to 1750 there was no protocol. (The British notably used a flag, "blue pierced with white" called the Blue Peter and it was used in the British Navy from 1777 as a general recall flag. In a quarter of a century the term "blue peter" was used by all to designate this flag. Civilians knew its significance, for merchant ships and convoys

*in the French wars would not sail until the escorting man-of-war
hoisted the blue peter for passengers to come aboard. Captain
Frederick Marryat's "Code of Signals for the Merchant Service"
first appeared in 1817 and was reportedly quite popular, going
through several editions before being supplanted by the
International Code of Signals in the mid 1800's*

This Watch House theory (that of the 1705 order to build the
chimney) could be plausible since, three years earlier, Briton with
her American Colonies had entered a war with France (Queen Ann's
War 1702-1713). Ships coming in and going out of Newport had
increased considerably and more attention was paid as to who and
what they did. Over time, other watch houses were also built at
"Point Judith", "Castle Hill", "Sachuest Point" and "Brenton Point".

Susan Franklin, the sixth generation descendant of *Able Franklin*
(the first keeper of the Beavertail Light), herself a careful
researcher/historian and student of Rhode Island history,equates the
practical interpretation of a lighthouse as defined by "Websterion"
dictionaries. Her contention is that "there certainly was a light on the
south tip of Conanicut Island as early as 1712, four years before
Boston Light was kindled" in 1716.

While the possibility of the French attacking Newport existed,
uncontrolled piracy along the east coast was also a threat. As early
as 1699, *Lord Bellomont,* the Royal governor, had cautioned that
Rhode Island was "a place where pirates are ordinarily too kindly
entertained". By 1705 the entire east coast from Canada to the
Carolinas was under control of French privateers and nightly patrols
were established along the sea coast. It was not only the French who
preyed on shipping. American privateers from the Colonies,
including those from Rhode Island, found relative ease in
victimizing unarmed enemy merchant ships along the Atlantic coast
and Caribbean islands. For a number of years there was much
activity of bringing prizes of captured ships into Newport. Merchant
ship owners actually modified their ships into gun carrying vessels
and as privateers collected commissions paid by Rhode Island for
the capture of French flagged shipping. There is a distinction
between "privateering" and "piracy" but it was very vague and many

captains of the day crossed over and back as determined by the prize they sought or captured.

There were no punishments for piracy at the time. Rhode Island and Newport were prime locations for pirates to recruit crews and the likes of *Captain Kidd, Blackbeard* and *Thomas Tew* were acceptable as residents. Stories and legends about *Captain Kidd* abound in Jamestown including his buried treasure at various locations on Conanicut Island. His close association with another pirate, *Captain Paine* of Jamestown led to further belief that treasure was left on the island.

The "Queen Ann" war was over by 1713 but privateers now turned pirates continued capturing unarmed vessels. Situations gradually changed and by 1718 Newport's merchants were losing more than they had gained by the hands of the pirates. It was a new era and pirates of the 1720's were now being hanged for their deeds. In 1723 twenty six (26) pirates were hanged in the same day in Newport. Nevertheless, shipping and vessels entering Newport and transiting further up Narragansett Bay continued. All of the activity, good and bad, further increased the supporting arguments that indeed a guiding light needed to be established.

The Birth of the Light at Beavertail

The theory of this 1705 light at Beavertail being the first lighthouse gains even more credibility because of a meeting of Jamestown Council Members on 9 June, 1712, seven years after the building of the chimney at the Watch Tower and four years before Boston Light was constructed. The council "ordered" *Gershom Remington (age 22)*, the son of Stephen *Remington*, first an Ensign of the Militia for Jamestown and later promoted to Lieutenant, was " to warn the Indians to build a beacon as soon as possible at Beavertail." They further ordered that *Benedict Arnold (this Arnold was the son of the past Governor of Rhode Island who was the first owner of the land at Beavertail and great grandfather of the famous Revolutionary war traitor of the same name)* "look after the watch and see that it be faithfully kept". There must have been tremendous pressure and influence on Jamestown's Town Council from Newport's colonial government, its ship owners and wealthy merchants. To the decree, the Town Council added a fine of three (3) shillings on anyone who neglected their duty in keeping the watch at Beavertail and in addition threatened a number of local residents who were to build the tower a forfeiture of three (3) shillings each if they did not build the beacon. It is this beacon that is imagined by many being a navigation light.

It is clear at that period of time there was much priority and importance to create a beacon, repair the watch house and man a regular standing watch at Beavertail. *William Low* postulates that at no time prior to the Revolutionary War had a hostile vessel actually entered Narragansett Bay, nor was there any record of purposeful destruction of shipping or property. He reasons that the purpose of the beacon, watch house and the scheduled watches were for the purpose of guiding vessels into Narragansett Bay, therefore filling the functions of the present day lighthouse. While not in the accepted form of a lighthouse constructed of brick and mortar, nevertheless it was established purposely to look seaward and recorded as first known for this use.

This beacon, most probably an open pit fire, was tended to by local Indians. Over the subsequent years, local historians and artists have taken the liberty of describing this beacon as a fire brazier on top of a pole. While no such record of its actual configuration exists, it is likely that a beacon was constructed next to the "Watch House" and on top of stone rubble as high as practicable at the time. This light beacon and watch house were also equipped with a fog cannon in 1719, about the same time one was installed at Boston Light.

Arnold, the owner of the land at Beavertail, per order of the Council, "kept and administered the watch faithfully". All this activity took place 4 years before the lighthouse on Boston's "Little Brewster Island" was constructed. Accordingly, the 1712 light at Beavertail certainly can profess to be the "first tended" navigation light in America. The delineation between it and the Boston Light, being that it was not a lighthouse structure but a beacon, remains controversial and most likely will continue to be so for generations to come.

Although confusing, records show that improvements continued to be made in the light beacon after 1712. In 1740, *Abel Franklin* was ordered to build a beacon and a *John Wilson* tasked to finish the chimney in the "Watch Tower". The order, from the "Proprietors Records", seems to indicate that the beacon was a new one and the old chimney was never fully finished. In 1741 and again in 1744, funds were voted by the Jamestown Council to add a gate, repair the doors and install better locks to the "Watch House" doors. The "Watch House" must have been a respectable size since the building contained both south side and north side facing doors.

1716 Boston Light *(the accepted first lighthouse in America)*

There is no argument based on Colonial records that "Boston Light" on "Little Brewster Island" was built in 1716, thirty three (33) years before the 1749 lighthouse at Beavertail and eleven (11) years after *Remington's* "Watch Tower." (*Boston Light while being the oldest, is not the oldest in continuous service. That distinction belongs to "Sandy Hook Lighthouse" in New Jersey built in1764*). Boston was the largest seaport at the time and with its sheltered inner harbor teaming with chandleries and shipyards, it was a favorite port. The light was a welcoming beacon and constructed at such a height that its "loom" on a clear night could be sighted 27 miles away. Located on Little Brewster Island in Boston Harbor it was rebuilt with a 75 foot rubble stone tower in 1783 and raised in height in 1859 when a large second order Fresnel lens was installed. Boston's inner harbor lies west of a cluster of 20 surrounding barrier islands and numerous shoals and rocks. Currents caused by the 9 to 12 ft tides flow around these islands, set vessels off course and when the wind died, the captain had no choice but to anchor the vessel or be set upon the shoals of the barrier islands. The approach to Boston from Massachusetts Bay, similar to Rhode Island Sound, was confusing to early mariners. The horizon was simply a line of land and no breaks could be seen between the islands until they were very close at hand. Navigation through and around the islands at night was impossible. The light on Little Brewster, one of the outmost islands, was the guiding beacon from the sea and its height above the sea provided the land mark the navigator desperately needed to set course for entrance into the outer harbor. Dangers still persisted with the approach around the light, particularly "Shag Rocks" and "Harding Ledge", both in close proximity to the light. Once the navigator passed the light close aboard on their starboard (right hand side), they then had to find an 8 mile long twisting channel passage between other islands and shoals to enter the inner harbor. A local pilot was certainly necessary and available to take onboard and guide the vessel safely into the harbor.

The Newport Tower

The distinction of Boston Light being the first in the Americas has also been questioned in a quasi historical book titled "*1421 The Year the Chinese Discovered America*" published in 2003. The British author claims the first lighthouse in North America was built by the Chinese around the year 1421. The light allegedly was constructed by a crew stranded from one of the ships of a large Chinese fleet that supposedly were sent out by the Ming Dynasty to explore the "ends of the world." The site coincidently is located in Newport, Rhode Island. As far fetched as this story may be, the author contends that a window of the structure was aligned so that a fire in the tower could be seen from the ocean, guiding ships north into Narragansett Bay. The fire would then be shielded until another window came into view to the vessel, directing it to the east and into the harbor cove of Newport. This stone and mortar structure still stands on a hill in Newport.

Photo by author
Newport Tower

Much controversy surrounds the origin of this structure. For centuries it has been called the "Newport Tower," "Viking

Tower" or "Mill Tower". Volumes of suppositions as to its use or purpose have been written by scholars, historians and archeologists but a gray layer of the unknown haunts even the experts. There is no record of ownership or any consensus by historians of its purpose. While the Chinese origin claim of being the first lighthouse could be a hoax, it casts a shadow of doubt on the Boston Light declaration of being America's first and allows the second postulation, the "1712 Beavertail beacon" to surface as a challenge to this claim.

The 1749 Lighthouse at Beavertail

The merchants and ship owners in Newport were undoubtedly the force that persuaded the Jamestown Town Council to provide the pre-1705 watch house and later its 1712 associated beacon. It was their gain or loss that a navigation aid was placed or not placed into operation at Beavertail Point. The land owners of Beavertail at that time were mostly residents of Newport and their interests and futures were tied to the economic conditions manifested by shipping directly related to the slave trade. At the time, Conanicut Island to them was an agricultural development opportunity, but Beavertail Point specifically was the ideal location for a navigational aid to protect their ships and maritime interests.

It is assumed that the early watch tower and beacon was operational for 30 years or at least intermittently based on the 1740 "Proprietors Records" of funding repair work. It is also possible that after the threat of pirates had subsided the need for the watch house was diminished, but strong demands by three Newport ship owners for a navigation aid resurrected the need that Beavertail Point be provided with a reliable light. Some money was raised beginning in 1738 and tariffs from vessels were diverted to help pay for the labor and materials. The building of the new light did not start at that time because of the interruption of another war, this time between England and Spain.

It took another nine (9) years when, in 1749, the Newport town records state: " a committee was appointed to build a light house at Beavertail on the island of Jamestown, alias Conanicut, as there appears a great necessity for a lighthouse as several misfortunes *have happened recently for want of a light."* They further went on to say, *" whereas there is a necessity of building a Light house at Beavertail, which will be of singular service for vessels coming into the harbor in the night season and prevent great damage which is occasioned for the want thereof".*

With that directive, a committee was formed to manage the construction of the new lighthouse. The builder and architect selected was *Peter Harrison* and with his brother, *Joseph Harrison* who was a member of the committee, undertook the task of employing tradesmen and carpenters from Newport and Jamestown. The lighthouse was built at the very southern tip of Beavertail on a rock ledge less than 50 feet or so from the edge of the sea.

The design of the structure must have been perplexing to *Harrison*. He had never built a structure such as this, nor were there any designs available other than Boston Light located on Little Brewster Island. But *Harrison* had much insight as to what requirements a

lighthouse should provide. He was a ship captain prior to becoming a self taught architect and could relate to sighting objects over the horizon's curvature and night time light intensity at sea. Obvious considerations such as material of use, accessibility and design of the lantern works, location and configuration had to be selected and designed in such form as to be able to be built by local tradesmen and stand up to the shore line environment. The design height of the light itself was somewhat ambitious as described below.

Photo Courtesy of BLMA
Model of Original 1749 Lighthouse

The height of the light tower from the ground up was a total of sixty nine (69) feet, with the lantern itself standing eleven (11) feet. The stone base was twenty four (24) feet in diameter tapering to eight (8) feet at the top of the lantern. Below the lantern a "gallery" is described which most likely also served as a lookout. The circular timbered structure was sheathed in wood and internally a wooden platform staircase was constructed for access to the lantern room. Exact details as to the design of the lantern are non existent. It is only known that whale oil was used to fuel the lamps. A Keeper's House was located next to the light which perhaps could have been the old "Watch House." By the end of the year the light was lit.

There must have been much delight and celebration that such a light was finally built. It was a land mark that stood as the highest structure in the vicinity. Newport now had a real navigation aid and those on Conanicut Island showed pride in having the lighthouse on Beavertail. Ship owners relaxed as to their vessels arriving at night and navigators took heart that a reliable bearing line could be drawn on their charts either during day time or night, miles distant from entering port.

Unfortunately, its life was short lived. Four years later in July 1753, the total structure was destroyed by fire. The cause was never explained but apparently it was not inattentiveness by keeper *Abel Franklin* who lived next to the lighthouse. He was the same man who in 1740 was ordered to build a beacon *(he remained at Beavertail as the keeper for 21 years)*. After the fire disaster, no time was lost by the General Assembly and in August they voted to erect a new light using stone or brick. The material was gathered from the Colony's "Fort George" *("Goat Island")* which over the years had, on and off, been fortified as threats appeared from Briton's foreign enemies. In 1739, Fort George was completely re-designed, fully repaired and fitted with thirty five (35) guns and garrisoned *(the designer was no other than Peter Harrison who built the Beavertail light 10 years later)*. After the construction at Fort George was completed there remained much unused material suitable for building the new lighthouse. *Peter Harrison* designed the new structure which was built by *William Reed*. The new light took some time to complete and during its construction *Keeper Abel Franklin* diligently displayed an ordinary lantern to help ships identify the point. Undoubtedly the lantern was much subdued for use as a reliable navigation light and fixed lower to the ground than the original light. There is no information how effective it was as an interim light. However, *Franklin* was commended for fortitude and responsiveness to his duty as a lighthouse keeper.

Model of 1783 Lighthouse

The tower was rebuilt and fitted with a respectable light composed of 15 individual lamps, each with a conical reflector. The lamps must have been fairly rudimentary since the smokeless oil lamp designed by *Aime Argon,* the Swiss physicist, and popular for lighthouse applications had not yet been invented. Two (2) groups, one of seven (7) lamps and the other of eight (8) lamps were mounted on 3 foot diameter copper tables. The lower eight (8) lamps "illuminated every point on the horizon, while the upper seven lamp configuration, the vacant space towards the land". From a navigational point of view, why the land space was illuminated, is not understood but perhaps the description of the lighting arrangement was not accurately stated. In any case, *Franklin* the keeper must have had his hands full each night tending the 15 lamps that required filling, trimming of wicks and cleaning smoked up chimney windows.

Apparent from subsequent General Assembly records ten (10) or so years later this new lighthouse had its difficulties. Reference is made to it being "much out of repair" and revenue from duties imposed on shipping as not being sufficient to maintain the light. The solution was to increase the duty on every "Coasting Vessel" to the sum of three (3) pounds and to eight (8) shillings per ton on all other vessels. What was out of "repair' was not recorded but at the time there was a bitter land battle by *Josiah Arnold* who was not satisfied as to the settlement for his land taken for lighthouse use and the fact that the General Assembly was taking steps to punish him for not putting the lighthouse in good repair. Records also show that the General Treasurer of the Colony paid *John Stevens,* a bricklayer, 550 pounds for his work in building the lighthouse and in 1756 another general obligation was paid to *Joseph Jacob*, a merchant of Newport, for 1694 pounds towards "defraying the charge for building the lighthouse".

Another seldom mentioned activity which fostered additional shipping and vessel traffic in Narragansett Bay was its pre Revolutionary War whaling industry. Whales were abundant off shore during the summer seasons up along the Atlantic coastline as evident even today although not in the same numbers. Rhode Island, by 1775, had fifty (50) ships engaged in hunting of whales and prior to that time a large industry of candle making was established in Newport. The prize oil "spermaceti" from which candles were made came from "head matter" of the whale and was later acknowledged as the primary oil to be used in lighthouse lamps because of its high illuminating, clean burning features and its inherent ability not to thicken when cold. Again, another of the famed *Brown* family monopolies controlled the spermaceti market flourishing in both Newport and the Colonies. In addition to the Rhode Island owned ships, the whaling ships of Nantucket unloaded the valuable sperm oil separately from their other cargos of oil at Newport.

The importance of Narragansett Bay and Newport both as a commercial port and as a naval anchorage cannot be diminished. A principle navigation aid to get vessels in and out safely was mutually supported hand in hand by the two needs.

Robert Melville was engaged to conduct a survey on the feasibility of such a project. His findings were recorded in a letter sent from Newport, dated 16 January, 1764. Melville wrote:

> *I have been constantly engaged in obtaining the surveys and drafts of this harbor and Narragansett Bay...and the positions for docks, shipyards, hospitals, etc. The whole bay is an excellent man-of-war harbour...affording good anchorage, sheltered in every direction and capacious enough for the whole of His Majesty's navy...The vicinity of the ocean is such that in one hour a fleet may be from their anchorage to sea; or from the sea to safe anchorage, in one of the best natural harbours the world affords.*

The Revolutionary War

The Revolutionary War and demands of money elsewhere halted any major renovation or improvements to the light as the colonies had begun to resent the British dominancy because of imposed taxes and tariffs. American independence movements caused the British to send forces to the colonies to quell uprisings. Newport was a strategic port and one of the centers for pragmatic revolutionist sympathizers.

In 1776 the British landed 6000 troops in Newport to quell the uprising of the Colonials. They undoubtedly used the light at Beavertail for safe passage of their own vessels. How the British used the lighthouse during their occupation of Newport and Jamestown is not very clear. All the residents of Conanicut Island had fled. Beavertail light was important to the British. They remained in Newport for three years and numerous supplies and transports came and went.

British troops, including two (2) battalions of Hessian Troops, were stationed on Conanicut Island and artillery troops with cannons were located at Beavertail at the fortification on "Fox Hill," two (2) miles north of the lighthouse, now called the "Conanicut Battery,". It would seem likely they would have used the light during their occupation began in December of 1776 and lasted for almost three (3) years. That probability is re-enforced by the fact that when the French fleet of *Admiral Comte d'Estang* appeared off Newport in July of 1789 the British evacuated Conanicut Island and set fire to the light tower and removed much of the lighting apparatus. The British believed destroying the lighthouse could confuse the French fleet and impair merchant shipping. The British fled Newport after scuttling ships in the harbor as the French fleet approached. By 1784, Beavertail light was back in operation and remained in use until the present lighthouse tower was built in 1856.

The lighthouse Superintendent *William Ellery* some years after the Revolutionary war wrote:

" That among other articles of apparatus for illuminating the Light Houses which were taken by the British and sent to Bermuda, there were a number of those lenses that all the articles captured were sent to New York and there purchased by Mr. Lewis, on account of the United States, that some of them have been sent by him to the Light Houses at Point Judith, Watch Hill, Montauk Point, Gay Head, Tarpaulin Cove and Home's Hole and probably to other light houses."

This statement appears to lend credence to the fact that privateers of the day captured British ships and cargo and sold the prizes back to the Federals.

Unlike the burning incident by the British on Conanicut Island, the harbor in Boston was controlled solely by the British. American troops in 1775 were sent to burn down part of the lighthouse on "Little Brewster Island" so as to deprive its use by the British. The British immediately rebuilt the lighthouse and later as they left Boston, set off a gunpowder charge that demolished the entire structure. It was not until 1783 that Boston Light was rebuilt.

Early Descriptions of the Lighthouse

Only three known artist sketches of the tower at Beavertail are known to exist. All are undated and somewhat crude but show a circular gallery and a dome shaped lantern room. A later one was sketched by a French naval officer *(Ozanne)* in 1779 who participated in *Admiral D'Estang's* fleet encounter with the British who had manned the fortification now known as "Conanicut Battery". This drawing was discovered in the "Louvre" in France. The torn sail in the drawing is believed to illustrate the great storm that forced both the British and French ships to break off an engagement and retire to safe ports for repairs.

Another drawing, 35 odd years later shows "*David Melville's* "Gasometer" house (Chapter 2) near the keeper's house and was probably drawn after 1817.

Sketch courtesy of BLMA
1778 Drawing of Newport Light

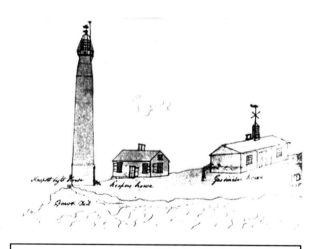

Sketch courtesy of BLMA
David Melville's Early 1800's Sketch

A fourth rendition, a painting estimated to have been painted in the decade preceding mid 1800 by an unknown artist is replicated on the cover of this book. The original now resides in the archives of the Redwood Library and Athenaeum in Newport.

The light was initially known as the "Newport Light" and identified that way for many years. Some also called it *"Harrison's Light"*

42

after the builder/designer. When later notations on nautical charts were made showing the light located at Beavertail Point, it began to assume the name *"Beaver Tail"* in the same manner of the point itself. *George Putnam,* Director of the US Lighthouse Service at one time referred to the light as "Conanicut Light". The stone and mortar foundation ruin located in front of the present granite faced light tower is all that remains of the lighthouse built in 1749. (Chapter 9 of this book devotes itself to the documentation of the 1747 lighthouse ruin.)

Creation of the US Lighthouse Establishment.

The Colonial Congress of the new United States wasted no time in recognizing the importance of lighthouses and the economic role they played in the safety of shipping. The ninth law passed by this new congress addressed the need of bringing lighthouses under the umbrella of the Federal Government to provide for repair and maintenance to provide safe and easy passage of vessels into and out of harbors. The 1789 law created the "US Lighthouse Establishment" and took over the jurisdiction of America's twelve (12) lighthouses then in existence. Beavertail previously under administration of the Newport Colony was with that group transferred in 1790 and approved with a specific note from *President George Washington* to *Alexander Hamilton, Secretary of the Treasury.*

However, the State of Rhode Island fearing a loss of revenue and the inability of the new government to maintain the light hesitated with the formal transfer and did not officially deed the property to the United States until 1793. Other early historical documentation indicates;

"that if the United States shall at any time hereafter neglect to keep it lighted and in repair, the grant of said lighthouse shall be void and of no effect".

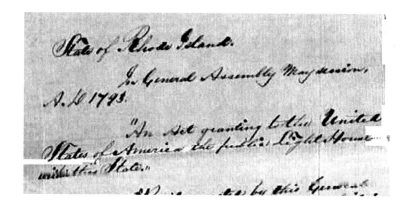

Rhode Island General Assembly Transfer Deed

The Lighthouse Establishment became the forerunner of four successive federal agencies over the period from 1789 to the present who managed and controlled the nation's navigation aids. The actual day to day administration was undertaken at the local level by the "Collector of Customs". For Rhode Island lighthouses this responsibility was located in Newport for many years.

(As a note of interest, the original twelve (12) lighthouses grew dramatically to seventy (70) in 1822, and by 1852 over three hundred thirty (330) lighthouses were operational in the country.)

Chapter 2

The Next Hundred Years and Beyond

The 19th Century saw many innovations implemented at Beavertail. The industrial revolution had begun. Inventors, engineers and manufacturing tooling brought new ideas and improvement to lighting and mechanical equipment of navigation systems. The importance of navigation aids for safety and commerce called for organization and reorganization of lighthouse related agencies at both local and government levels. They all retained the same objectives of improving lighthouses, lightships and the nation's waterway buoy systems.

With Beavertail Light as part of the seaward looking "first line" of lighthouses, its priority and role was always in the forefront. Narragansett Bay and its ports had become the frequent home of the fast packet boats and large passage-making, ocean-going, "square riggers". The smaller sloops were criss-crossing in and out of the bay to nearby ports including New York and by 1821 paddle steamers were commonly seen along the Bay. A few years later regular service by steamboat companies began operating from Providence to New York and ports along the Long Island coast. Steam power came slowly to the bay and as its popularity rose commercial sailing packet boats were gradually phased out. When steam ships took over, the change overwhelmed the existing navigation systems since tide, current and wind were no longer major handicaps.

Although steam operated vessels were becoming common, the large sailing ships still were the ones that moved heavy cargo and undertook the longer coastal runs and the trans-Atlantic trips. "Coastal Schooners", as they were known, carried the movement of bulk cargo and the steam ships concentrated on carrying passengers. More vessel traffic appeared when the US Navy committed itself to the lower bay and expanded its operations at Newport. Day and night ship traffic increased and placed higher demand on Beavertail

Light to remain operative and reliable. One of the worse nightmares to be had by a master of a ship was to make a night landfall expecting to see Beavertail Light, not finding it and hearing the surf on the rocks somewhere ahead.

Two other factors added even greater numbers of vessels over the years. Fishing, which had always been a mainstay, grew as the population increased and the other was the rapid popularity of recreation boating. Both disciplines were ocean going and while most of the recreation boating was confined to the bay, many ventured out to "Block Island," "Buzzards Bay," the "Elizabethan Islands", "Martha's Vineyard", "Nantucket" and "Long Island Sound." When the "Cape Cod Canal" was completed in 1940, it saved much time from rounding the outer cape. As a result, vessel traffic passing by Beavertail increased dramatically and the light was used as a major fixed reference and as a piloting "bearing line" by navigators.

The growth and demand for improvements at Beavertail and other lighthouses was continual and the evolutionary changes through the decades mandated that Beavertail Light Station be kept operational at all times. The details are not consolidated or retrievable as to why and when the many changes, including the sound signals, took place at Beavertail in both its physical form and its light characteristics. This chapter gathers what is known from snippets of notes and miscellaneous records.

Hurricanes

The original 1749 Beavertail Light stood very close to the sea on a rock ledge. The present light tower and its surrounding buildings sit nearby, a hundred feet or so away. All are exposed without any buffer to storms and hurricanes. In some ways it is miraculous that they still stand, although the ravages of the sea from time to time have destroyed some ancillary structures. The rage and seas that build up from storms are so attractive that literately vehicle traffic jams have occurred by the curious who drive the perimeter around the lighthouse road to view and gasp at the thunderous waves building and crashing upon the rocks. During major storms the road is closed by police for obvious safety reasons, yet people will park in a safe area and walk to the light station hypnotized by what nature beholds to them.

Only four major hurricanes classified as "Category III" have crossed the lighthouse location peninsula or brushed nearby with a NE sector swath. Rhode Island has never experienced a higher category storm. The "Great Storm of 1938" is the reference bench mark for the other storms only because it was so well documented. Those that preceded it are compared by "similar intensities."

Intense Historic Hurricanes Strikes in New England

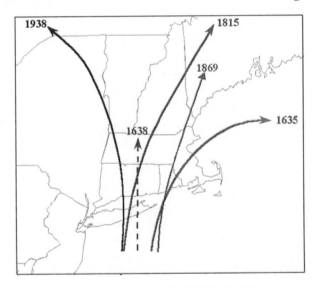

| Category III Hurricanes |

The earliest hurricane was recorded in 1635 by Massachusetts Bay Colonists and called the "Great Colonial Hurricane of August 25, 1635." It centered in Narragansett Bay and then veered northeasterly. Storm surges of 13 feet were noted in journals written by *Governors William Bradford* and *John Winthrop* in Massachusetts. Three years later in 1638 another storm of equal intensity slammed into the tip of Long Island and entered central Connecticut. Extensive damage to the forests suggested similarities of the 1938 hurricane. Of course neither of these two 1600 era storms had any effect on Beavertail since there was no light established until the 1700s. The third significant storm that followed was the "Great Gale of 1815" which destroyed the original Beavertail Keeper's house. That house was located close to the water "on a bad foundation". A stone replacement house was built within the year. The same hurricane totally destroyed the lighthouse at Point Judith built in 1810. The year 1869 brought another furious storm just west of Narragansett Bay but the strong winds in the Northwest quadrant were only offset by an outgoing tide and kept the surge down. Other hurricanes such as "Gloria" in 1985, "Donna" in 1960 and "Bob" in 1991 caused considerable damage with lesser intensity.

The 1938 hurricane was devastating by many standards. "Whale Rock" lighthouse sitting 1 mile WSW of Beavertail was toppled over and assistant keeper *Walter Eberle* lost his life. "Plum Beach" lighthouse 5 miles due north of Beavertail experienced seas so high that the two keepers had to climb up to the lantern room to safely ride out the storm. At Beavertail, the fog signal building sitting on top of the 1749 lighthouse foundation was totally

Photo Courtesy of USCG
Destroyed Fog Signal Building 1938

destroyed. *Edward Donahue,* the assistant keeper, was in the fog signal building when it began to fall apart. He threw himself into the raging seas. He and his son, who went to his aid, were washed back and forth and finally escaped the storms wrath. Inside the living quarters, four feet of water was sloshing back and forth. Windows and doors were broken through and the basements of both houses were completely flooded and remarkably the forgotten stone foundation of the original 1749 lighthouse was uncovered.

Carl Chellis, the keeper at Beavertail, lost his daughter who was among 7 others in a school bus that was caught by seas at "Mackerel Cove" three miles north of the light station. The bus driver and *Chellis's* son were the only survivors.

Hurricane "Carol" in 1954 collapsed the chimney of the Keepers House and blocked the entryway. *Keeper Turrillo* helped his children through a window into the other house for safety.

The Melville Gas House

Much has been written about the experimentation at Beavertail by *David Melville* and his partner *Winslow Lewis* regarding lighthouse illumination using gas in the early 1800s. *Melville,* a Newport resident, was the first person to use gas lighting in his home in this country and gave Beavertail the distinction of being the first lighthouse to be illuminated by gas in the United States. Interested readers are recommended to read the details in many of the references identified in *Appendix A.*

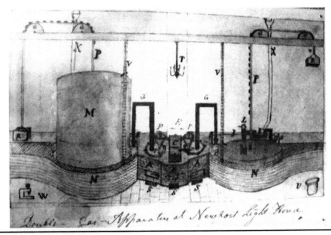

Sketch courtesy of BLMA
1817 Melville Gas Illumination System at Beavertail

Under a Government contract in 1817, Melville built a gas house on the site of the present fog signal building now used as an aquarium. The process of manufacturing the gas (a variant of hydrogen concentrated coal gas) was done by heating tar and resin in a confined vessel and passing the gas vapors through water for purification into storage tank type cisterns. The gas was hence distributed by underground piping from the gas house and up through the lighthouse to the lantern room. Dual 1600 gal "gasometer" tank containers were constructed at Beavertail. The apparatus was primitive in nature. The tank/cisterns were made of wood and the piping from tin and copper. Tight seals were difficult to make in that era and leakage of gas throughout the distribution system added to its inefficiency. Clay and sand were the primary sealants and neither held up very long under the heat and pressure. The 1817 experiment continued for over a year and the illuminated gas light could be seen as far away as Block Island, 15-16 miles away. The gas light burned cleaner and brighter than the whale oil lamps and generally simplified the keeper's task since the gas was piped up to the lantern room eliminating the need to carry oil up the tower.

The project failed only because *Melville's* partner *Capt. Winslow Lewis,* who had interest in the whale oil industry which fueled his oil lamp system of reflectors, saw his business threatened by this new lighting system. The whaling industry was also concerned since any alternative to catching whales and processing sperm oil was a threat to their way of life. Whale oil was not necessarily the only oil used to light lamps. Raw and refined oils of animals and vegetable origin oils were also used, but whale oil proved to be far superior since it burned brighter. *Lewis* also had support of the fledging US Navy who stated that whaling ships provided the training and recruitment of men directly into naval service. Acting as the de facto "Superintendent for Lighting for United States Light Houses", *Lewis* forced *Melville* to drop the project the following year.

The Oil Lamps

Winslow Lewis played an important part in lighthouse illumination although his involvement was criticized by many. He was a former ship captain from Cape Cod and had developed his own version (later to be controversial) of the popular *Argand* Lamp used worldwide. He had obtained a patent and successfully sold it to the US Government. His device was simple, using a reflector in back of the lamp and a lens in front. The intensity of the lamp was much subdued because the lamp used one half the amount of oil of other lamps. It was, however, adopted by the "Secretary of the Treasury" and ordered that all American lighthouses be equipped with *Lewis'* innovation, some say because of political pressure applied in congress for the adoption of its use. *(It should be noted that his solution did not solve the problem of the need for many lamps clustered to achieve acceptable light.)* By 1817 the transition of using Lewis' lamp began including Beavertail. For the next 40 years, although difficult to maintain and acknowledged as a poor lighthouse illuminant, the *Lewis* lamps, inferior to *Argand* lamps, were endured by the US Lighthouse Service.

Additional modifications to the Beavertail Light were made in 1827. *David Melville,* who ten years earlier experimented with gas illumination, was contracted to modify the top of the lighthouse, reducing its height and installing a new lantern configuration described below. He also installed a wooden circular staircase complete with "rest stops" every tenth step.

In 1838 an inspection by *Lieutenant George M. Bache* reported that Beavertail Light was 64 feet high and 98 feet above sea level, with the light visible for 15 3/4 miles. *Lt. Bache* described the lighting apparatus:

"The lanterns contain fifteen lamps, with reflectors, arranged around two circular copper tables, each three feet in diameter. The lower table supports eight lamps, which illuminate every point of the horizon; on the upper table there are seven lamps, the vacant space being towards the land... Several of the reflectors are bent from their original forms, which is probably owing to their great lightness, their diameters being 9 inches, and weight from 7 ounces to 1 pound; two of them being very much worn and cracked. The light-keeper informed me that they had been furnished by the contractors on their last annual visit."

Bache also criticized the construction of the keeper's dwelling:

"The present dwelling was erected in 1816; the walls are of rough stone of small size, and are badly laid. A portion of the masonry, being supported solely by the frame-work of the cellar windows, is cracked... The house originally contained five rooms; a brick addition of two rooms was made in 1834. A stable and wood-house are also on the premises."

One artist's rendering previously mentioned does provide a sense of the light station's building configurations. The painting is undated and could have been painted in the 1840s.

Copy courtesy of BLMA
**Undated (pre 1856) Painting of Beavertail Light
(artist unknown)**

Time certainly took its toll on Beavertail Light. An 1851 report stated that all the buildings at the Beavertail Light were in deplorable condition. The light tower was reported as the "worst built tower yet seen". Repairs were much overdue and the new

52

"Lighthouse Board" was committed to improve lighthouses nation wide. Furthermore, because of its location, Beavertail offered opportunities to begin experimentation of sound signals which had mystified investigators and challenged them to explore more practical equipment. With those demands, Beavertail Light Station was ready for a major change in both look and function. It definitely became a prime candidate for one of the new lenses.

1856 The New Building and Tower at Beavertail

The *Fresnel* lens had become popular in Europe as early as 1830 and some testing had been done by the US Lighthouse Service, but its management continued to favor the inefficient *Lewis* lamp. It took a major organizational change via establishment of the new US Lighthouse Board in 1852 to wrestle the *Lewis* lamp out of the hands of the now defunct US Lighthouse Service. The new board immediately adopted the efficient, low fuel consuming, single lamp miracle lens that was 400% more intense than the *Lewis* lamp. With the new lens, a new era of construction and improvement throughout America was undertaken by the US Lighthouse Board. By 1859, all US lighthouses were fitted with *Fresnel* lenses. This transition was not accomplished without problems. Many of the older wooden lighthouses could not withstand the heavy weight of the *Fresnel* lens. The heaviest weighed up to 5 tons and in some cases new buildings were required.

For Beavertail, congressional action appropriated $14,500 for a new lighthouse with a modern lens including a new fog signal apparatus. Construction started during 1855 and by the end of 1856 the new granite stone light tower was completed. The old lighthouse was torn down once the new tower was finished and operational. A new fog signal building was built nearby. Construction of the adjoining Keeper's House was started shortly thereafter and completed in 1859.

The light tower was built exceedingly strong. Granite blocks, 10 feet long and varying in girth, were set one upon another in a 10 foot square "log cabin" fashion 27 rows high to a height of 54 feet. The total weight of the granite alone is estimated at over 180 tons.

Inside the granite tower, a circular brick facing was laid along its total height extending past the granite blocks up to the watch room ceiling. The bottom of the lantern room rests on top of the brickwork. Crushed stone rubble was added between the interior of the granite blocks and the brick facing giving the tower structure a thickness of about 2 feet. There are only three windows, one on each of three sides in the tower before reaching the cap. The cap includes the watch room on one level and the windowed lens or lantern room turret above it. The inside of the watch room is lined with vertical wood panels. The outside of these two rooms and the associated external circular catwalk galleries are constructed of both cast iron and steel plate. Access to the outside gallery of the lantern room is by an iron ladder from the watch room catwalk.

A cast iron spiral staircase comprising 65 steps extends from the ground level up to the watch room. Each step interlaces with the step above and below and in turn is fastened into the circular red brick internal facing of the granite tower. The center of the staircase was kept open to haul heavy items up, including oil to the cap via an overhead pulley, as well as to provide the "tunnel" for the lantern clock operating mechanism weights. A door below the lens room is available to go out onto the circular iron railed watch room gallery deck to view and log shipping traffic on both the horizon or coming into the east and west passage. In addition, a steel trap door overhead opens up into the lantern room via a steel ladder extending upward. The ladder provided the access to the lantern deck itself which contains the light and the lens. The light is protected from the elements by the external glass framed turret.

Above the lantern room, on the very top of the structure, is a "vent ball". Its purpose was to rid the tower from moisture, heat, and exhaust smoke from the lantern. The design of the vent ball enabled the device to act somewhat like a venturi. The ball had large diameter vent holes drilled in its base in such a way that rain or spray could not enter the vent. For many years a large wind vane was attached to the top of the ball. This wind vane also acted as a lightning protection device. Today the configuration is a spiked pointed rod on top of the vent ball. Its base has an attached heavy copper cable/strap leading down and fastened to the side of the granite tower to a copper ground-rod driven into the earth at the base of the tower.

When the tower was built in 1856, it had a rotating 3rd order *"Fresnel"* lens to account for the group flashing characteristic. The design of the *"Fresnel"* lens, a dioptric beehive shaped configuration, was a discovery that changed the use of lighthouse lamps throughout the world. *Henry Fresnel* and his French invention did away with the multiple reflectors of the type used at Beavertail and substituted highly efficient, aligned and properly angled glass prisms with the lamp at the center of the lens structure.

Henry Fresnel's bee-hive layers of prism glass bent the light into a narrow beam. At the outside center, the lens was shaped like a magnifying glass so the concentrated beam was even more powerful. Tests showed that while an open flame lost nearly 97% of its light, a flame with reflectors behind it still lost 83% of its light. The Fresnel lens was able to capture all but 17% of its light. Because of its amazing efficiency, a Fresnel lens could easily throw its light 20 or more miles to the horizon. By rotating the optic array, myriad possibilities of flash patterns could be obtained through the installation of bulls-eye panels around the circumference of the array. Also, by placing colored glass panels in front of the bulls-eyes, a single light could not only be made to flash in a readily identifiable characteristic, but could be made to flash different colors within the sequence.

Hundreds, if not thousands, of technical papers, books and reports have been written about these prism lenses and the above is a very simple description of the principles of its design. Variable configurations and multiple sizes were built based on their use and illumination source.

Rather than a fixed light, a flashing light characteristic was chosen for Beavertail to differentiate its location from the other lighthouses in view. This first 3rd order *Fresnel* lens design incorporated flash panels or "bulls-eyes" arranged around the center of the lens structure and placed at the distance calculated to the focal length of the illuminating source. Above and below the bulls-eyes were the circular prisms which collected and bent the available light out in the horizontal plane. The lamp contained inside the lens itself consisted of two circular wicks, the outer burner wick having a diameter of 1 7/8 in.

The number of bulls-eye panels determined the flashes and as the lens turned, the rotational speed of the lens determined its timing characteristic. The lens used the hollow wick lamp system invented in 1782 by *Aime Argand,* a Swiss physicist, until the perfection of the oil vapor lamp at the turn into the twentieth century. *Argand's* hollow wick allowed a greater amount of air and enabled an almost smokeless and brighter flame which burned at a constant rate. The heavy glass 3rd order *Fresnel* lenses floated in circular trough of dense mercury with ball bearing features along the rim that kept the lens friction free and centered in the mercury pool as it turned. The mercury bath was common at all lighthouses which required a rotational light sequence. The heaviest of all lamps, including the 5 ton 1st order lenses, could be turned with very little rotational force. Most could be turned with finger pressure. It was the clock mechanism that maintained the timing of the flash and the keeper periodically would check the clock mechanism to assure that the lens rotation was accurate.

The 3rd order lens at Beavertail weighed about 2000 pounds. The weight corresponded with the combination of the heavy individual glass prisms and the robust bronze castings frame required to fasten and hold the prisms in place. At one time, over 65 US lighthouses were equipped with 3rd order lenses. The Beavertail lens was about 4 feet 8 inches high and 3 feet in diameter. It was this light in 1862, according to a Jamestown history essay, that "exhibited a 14 mile range, powered by a 19,000 candle power lamp 12 feet high 6 feet diameter". (The size stated is inaccurate, probably referencing another measurement in the lantern room)

As other lights came on line, including a stronger light on the Brenton Reef lightship located a short distance away from Beavertail light, a smaller 4th order "bee hive" lens was installed

56

in the Beavertail light tower in 1889. The lamp in use was still fueled with kerosene but with only one burner and a wick diameter of 1 5/8 inches. There is also a notation in one document in 1907 that yet another 4th order lens was installed at Beavertail. Little is know about the Beavertail lens configuration for the next 60 years. Some time after 1973 the light characteristic was changed to a fixed configuration with a 4th order lens containing only circular prisms without bulls-eyes.

Not all *Fresnel* lenses were made in France. The last Beavertail 4th order lens was made by *"MacBeth-Evans"* as identified by the 1952 Coast Guard allowance report. *MacBeth-Evans* was an American company located in Pittsburgh, Pennsylvania and was the largest American producer of household and commercial lamp chimneys during the 1800's. It added a *Fresnel* lens manufacturing capability probably under license from the French manufacturer. In 1937, the company merged with *Corning Glass Works* of New York and 3 years later its name *MacBeth-Evans* was absorbed.

Photo by Author
4th Order Lens on Display in Beavertail Museum

To provide accurate rotational speed, Fresnel lenses were rotated by a hand wound clock mechanism containing a suspended weight that extended down through the inside of the spiral staircase to the ground. The "leaden" weights may have been 65-80 lbs and required cranking up on a drum to the level of the lens room floor every 4 hours. There is limited data available on the specific mechanism at Beavertail, however, records do state the 4th order lens used there was rotated by a "Clock Type D Lens Drive" and the 135 foot clock cord 3/16 inch diameter wire rope. It is assumed that most of the length of this wire rope was wound up on the drum and extra length was required to replace worn or frayed wire as needed. Records do indicate that as late as 1931 the Beavertail electrified light characteristic was two (2) flashes every 15 seconds rotated by a hand wound clockworks.

(Of the 31 light stations established in Rhode Island, only 9 of the Fresnel lenses are still in existence, of which 7 remain in Rhode Island. "Block Island Southeast Light" has the only 1st order lens.)

The Change to Fossil Fuel

After the installation of the *Fresnel* lenses, most lighthouses, including Beavertail, went through a series of lamp modifications. The most significant improvements were brought about by the availability of kerosene. Whale oil, universally used by the Lighthouse Service, was expensive. In the 1860's, whale oil cost about 55 cents a gallon. Due to declining pods of whales caused by over hunting and the increased demand of fuel, the price was up to $2.50 by 1800. The equivalent today of about $200.00.
Some experiments were conducted with natural gas and porpoise oil was tested with poor results. Both mineral oil and a colza (grape) oil were tested with poor results also. Lard oil from animal fat was used and found to be a fair substitute if preheated; but kerosene became the prevalent oil.

The fledging fossil fuel oil industry in the United States at the time was helping convert residential and industrial lamps and lanterns used for illumination to "kerosene" oil. Kerosene, also called "mineral oil", sold for only .07 cents a gallon. However, it was not until the late 1870's that kerosene began replacing whale oil at lighthouses and at Beavertail it was not until 1880 that the change was made. It took another 27 years, 1907, when all lighthouses had converted to kerosene. This was also the time when shipping and vessel traffic were at their height, before railroads and trucking

58

became popular. In 1907, 22,860 vessels were counted passing the Point Judith lighthouse in daylight hours. This traffic count was four times greater than the number of vessels entering New York Harbor at the time.

With oil readily available and cheap, new uses were found for many applications. A "kerosene vapor lamp" was perfected and, almost universally, lighthouses inherited a brighter more reliable light. A second innovation was to add a pressurized fuel tank which force fed the fuel into the lamp's burner as a fine vapor. While these improvements added much to the illumination characteristic, there were some disadvantages. Mainly, it required attentive watchfulness particularly if a mantle broke or burned up and it also required periodic hand pumping to maintain a level of acceptable pressure in the fuel tank throughout the night. Kerosene oil continued to be the primary fuel until such time as the conversion to electrical illumination took place.

Prior to the time Beavertail was electrified, a hand winch was used to hoist oil up though the center of the revolving staircase to the watch room. Here the oil was stored for lamp replenishment each evening as needed. Oil reserves initially were stored in the attached building between the tower and the Keeper's House where the present electrical switch gear and monitoring equipment are located and later in the small "Oil Shed", still standing, located behind the Keeper's House

Electricity Arrives

The first electrical device that arrived at Beavertail was a telephone. In 1905 the "US Government" connected a telephone to Beavertail and now direct conversation through the switch board in Jamestown, then via an underwater cable to Newport, could be had with the Lighthouse Superintendent in Newport.

It appears that when electricity was routed to Conanicut Island in 1931, the 4th order oil lamp lens was again replaced by a refurbished lens without a center beehive bulls-eye. At the same time the fog signal horn was modified to be powered by electrically driven air compressors. The new electrified lens included a 120 volt, 7000 candlepower lamp. The lamp holder assembly contained two 750 watt incandescent bulbs, one of which was a redundant lamp (back-up). The assembly incorporated a "current" sensing solenoid activator. If the operating lamp's filament burned out, the current sensor would detect the loss of current and energize the solenoid to rotate the spare lamp into the lens' center position and take over as the operating lamp, hence providing continuous light operation. It allowed time for the lighthouse keeper to replace the burnt out lamp from the supply of spares. This lamp holder, lamp changing mechanism and the 4th order lens are currently on long term loan from the Coast Guard and demonstrated to visitors at the Beavertail Museum. When the Bureau of Lighthouses transferred Beavertail Light Station to the U.S. Coast Guard in 1939, the 4th order lens was refurbished and converted to 240,000 candle power.

The site at Beavertail in front of the lighthouse structures has also provided an unrestricted non-RF interference test opportunity for the US Navy to conduct shipboard antenna calibration tests. In 1932, The Navy's "Naval Research Laboratory" (NRL) test trailer laboratory monitored and evaluated the effectiveness of radio installations by having ships transit specified patterns for measurement purposes. Power to the NRL trailer was provided by the light station.

World War II and Beavertail Light

From early colonial days to the present, the military importance of Narragansett Bay has always been significant and tied to the importance of Beavertail light in guiding military vessels as they approached land. Most notably were events of the Revolutionary War and the U.S. Navy's presence in the 1800's and 1900's. Rear *Admiral Ralph Earle, Sr.*, who at one time served as the Commander of the Naval Torpedo Station in 1924, was one of the strongest champions of Narragansett Bay. He advocated the use of many desirable features of the Bay stating:

...the Fleet can make, with advantage, a much greater use of this Narragansett Bay than has ever been the case in the past....A study of the needs of operating the Fleet as a whole, point to the increasing utilization of the deep water anchorage in Narragansett Bay as the years go on.

World War broke out in Europe in 1939 and at the same time the president of the United States, *Franklin D. Roosevelt,* reorganized the lighthouse administration throughout the country. The "Bureau of Lighthouses" was transferred to the Treasury Department and absorbed by the Coast Guard. Two years later the four year period between 1941 and 1945 was very dramatic at Beavertail as it related to harbor defense and the need to secure the entrance to Narragansett Bay against the Axis threat.

America was at war and the Rhode Island ports of Newport, Quonset Point and Davisville were strategic navy bases. A shipyard, "Walsh-Kaiser Shipyard", at the head of Narragansett Bay on the Cranston/Providence line was building "Liberty" ships, "Frigates" and large "Attack Transports". "PT" type Air/Sea Rescue boats and Torpedo boats were being built in Bristol by the "Herreshoff Manufacturing Company" and just to the south in Melville, Navy crews were training to operate them. Aircraft carriers with their escorts traveled in and out of "Quonset Point Naval Air Station" and supply ships into "Davisville Supply Depot". Newport was the "Fleet Headquarters" for ships of the line, particularly cruisers and destroyers headed for the European theater and for convoys acting as their escorts off shore. Thousands of recruits at the "Newport Naval Training Station" completed training and were assigned to ships of the fleet.

Almost overnight, Newport and Narragansett Bay had become one of the Navy's largest and most important bases of operation. By the war's end, more than 100 ships of the U.S. Atlantic Fleet were based in Newport

Beavertail Light Station indeed had become a military asset where arriving and departing vessels used the light as their primary

61

landmark to plot their arrival and departure "rhumb" lines on maneuvering boards and ocean charts.

At times of war, the operation of the US Coast Guard came under the jurisdiction of the US Navy. The Coast Guard continued to man and operate the light station but was subordinate to the U.S. Navy. Both the "Light Station" and "Brenton Lightship" reported to "Seaward Defense Command", the joint Army/ Navy operations at "Fort Adams" in Newport.

Adjacent to the north boundary of the light station, a new fortification, "Fort Burnside", was placed into operation by the "243rd Coast Artillery" of the "Rhode Island National Guard." A joint Army and Navy military command post was constructed and identified as the "Harbor Entrance Command Post" (HECP). This building is still visible today, north of the light station and identified by antenna towers placed there by the Navy after the war. The HECP controlled all the traffic entering and leaving Narragansett Bay. Mine fields and submarine nets were strung across both the East and West Passage and underwater detection cables entered the water on either side of the rocks in front of the light house. On the east side bank, below the road level next to the Fog Signal building, a large caliber rapid fire machine gun emplacement was constructed and shored up with sand bags. The purposes of the gun was to prevent an enemy attack boat presumably launched from a disguised German freighter from speeding into the harbor and attacking naval vessels readying to escort convoys to Europe. In addition, two 3 inch artillery cannons were emplaced only a few hundred yards north of the light tower to fire upon slower vessels. This location was designated as Battery Whiting. The remains of the bunker and the gun locations are visible today.

Directly in front of the Fog Signal station and on top of the 1749 original Beavertail Light base ruin, a concrete cap, 3 inches thick, was constructed. This cap acted as the foundation for an optical range finder and the base for a portable machine gun. Adjacent to the ruin on the westerly side, a large 24 inch "carbon arc" searchlight was positioned to illuminate any questionable shipping.

Beavertail During WW II, 1942-1945

During this time, several small summer cottages along the west side of the road just before entering the light station property, were taken over by the military for temporary housing until housing at "Fort Getty" was built at the north head of the Beavertail peninsula. Each cottage could sleep up to 4 people. In 1942, a severe blizzard closed the road to Beavertail and personnel were marooned for several days in the un-insulated cottages. Lighthouse residents, *Edward Donahue* and his family, helped supply the Army personnel with both food and necessities.

None of the logs reviewed during the World War period referenced the status of the lights of either the Beavertail Light Station or the Brenton Reef Lightship. There is no record of any reduced illumination as took place at Nantucket or Boston light which were unlit during the war years. During WW II, the Vineyard Lightship (LV 73) reduced its lamp brightness from a 1000 watt lantern to a 40 watt bulb to minimize the chance of an attack by a German U-Boat. It appears just the contrary at Beavertail. *Capt. William Buckner,* a Navy pilot and later a Jamestown resident who also flew in coastal surveillance blimps over Beavertail, never remembered any reduced illumination of the light. For him, Beavertail was always considered a "welcome" bright navigation aid from the air. The U.S. Coast Guard's historian *Scott Price* states " *according to my sources, the lightship remained on station and in service during the war, including operating her light, radio beacon, and fog signal* ". Why Beavertail and Brenton Reef lights both remained at full brilliance when other coastal stations operated at reduce illumination is not known.

Post World War II

The war had ended in 1945 and things began to get back to normal. Ft. Burnside was in the process of being dismantled and the U.S. Navy continued to develop and operate radio equipment on the property north of the Beavertail light station. At the same time, Jamestown residents and others were beginning to talk about a new park. In 1981 "Beavertail State Park" opened to the public. (See Chapter 10) The southern end of the park abutted the light station and with new roads leading directly to Beavertail Light Station, it became a popular visitor destination.

Automation arrived in 1972 and signaled the end of 223 years of manned lighthouse keeping at Beavertail. *John Baxter* was the last keeper who had to attend the equipment. When *Baxter* and his assistant departed the light station, with them left the presence of any security, funding or support by the Coast Guard to maintain the buildings on site excepting the granite light tower which housed the light itself. For a period of time after automation, the light was monitored by the Coast Guard crew stationed at Castle Hill in Newport. They had visual sight of Beavertail and could dispatch repair personnel as needed.

A review of the 1952 Coast Guard inventory allowance list for Beavertail Light Station provides insight as to the number and type of equipment used. Inventory included kitchen appliances, brooms, shovels, rakes and garden tools, in addition to spare parts for the fog signal generators and the light itself. The lens installed at that time was the 4th order *Fresnel* bee hive described earlier, manufactured by "MacBeth- Evans". The main illuminant was the 750 watt "GE PS 52" lamp of which 36 of them were allowed on site as spares.

64

The fog signal was stated as being a 1st Class 6 inch diameter "Air Siren" manufactured by "H & H Co" apparently operated by a diesel engine driven generator rated at 3.45 KVA. The following year the 3 KVA standby generator was replaced by a new "Buda" 3 KW 120 volt diesel unit.

In 1955, over 400 cubic yards of fill were distributed around the seaward perimeter of the site, most of it over the eroded embankment on the SW side and 120 yards on the backside of the 1749 light tower foundation. Also during that year, the Coast Guard keepers were asked to provide weather information in support of the U.S. Navy radar facility (Building 19) just north of the site. Both MIT and Yale University were conducting experiments under contract with the Navy. Yale University's research project was called "Project Beavertail" and with the help of the light stations keepers, underwater wave action monitors were installed and tested.

In 1991, the 4th order *Fresnel* lens was replaced by a type "DCB 24" (Drum Contained Beacon) rotating Aero Beacon. While originally designed for airport use, it was typical of other replacements talking place in lighthouses nationwide. The DCB 24 uses a 1000 watt long life tungsten halogen lamp with the parabolic reflector mirror behind the lamp emitting a 2.5 million candlepower pencil beam. The rotating motor is mounted below the lamp canister drum and was adjusted to rotate the light to show as a characteristic flash every 6 seconds. In 2007 it was changed to 9 seconds . The light has two ear-like baffles on either side of the drum to minimize backward reflections off the lantern room glass panels as it rotates. The power to the beacon must be shut down for safety concerns when performing maintenance in the lantern room since the rotating baffles do not allow room for personnel. Beavertail light remains on continually 24 hours a day and as the drum rotates it appears to flash once in coincidence with its rotational speed.

The lamp generates intense heat. The Coast Guard currently warns guardsmen maintaining these lights to "Secure power, tag-out and then wait 15 minutes before servicing. Wear goggles, gloves and face shield. Lamp and mirror can explode if they come in contact with cold air from opening the door after light has been energized."

When the 4th order *Fresnel* lens was retired, a request was made by the "Rhode Island Parks Association" to the Coast Guard to display the lens on an on-loan basis in the museum established in the Assistant Keeper's house. This loan was approved until October of 2016 and is the centerpiece of the museum's artifact exhibits now operated by the BLMA. The agreement from the Coast Guard confirms that "the lens will be moved from the tower to the museum". Although the lens was first appraised at $10,000 by the Coast Guard, three years later its value stated on the loan documents was changed to $500,000. *Hugh Bucher,* the Beavertail Lighthouse Museum Association's first president, asked for a value reduction wavier back to $10,000 since the Association could not afford the $2000 annual insurance premium. The wavier was granted in 1994.

The lens itself has chips in various places of some glass prisms and is missing prisms on two of its quadrants. It has been rumored that the damage to the lens took place when it was being removed and lowered by rope tackle apparently colliding with the external granite wall of the tower.

At the time of automation the two tone automatic fog signaling device was installed across the perimeter road facing the sea. It is surrounded by a wire security fence with signs indicating it is Government property and a special warning sign for people nearby to be aware of penetrating blasts from the horn during fog conditions.

Beavertail was never without an emergency standby light as attested to by *Able Franklin* and his hand lantern after the fire of 1753. Later, when multiple whale oil and then kerosene lamps were in use, there was built-in redundancy; although failures of any of the lamps showed a light of lower intensity. When the light was electrified in 1931, solenoid switching incandescent bulbs provided a backup when one bulb burned out. Even with this feature, the Coast Guard did retain on site as a "Standby Illuminant", a portable 35 mm incandescent mantle type vapor lamp operated by kerosene in case of power failures. (*It was similar in operation as the kerosene system used in the Fresnel lens described earlier.*) The fuel was vaporized by a bicycle type hand pump building pressure through a vaporizer nozzle into the mantle surrounded by a lexon chimney.

During the 1950's, a battery operated emergency backup light was installed, mounted on a track pole bolted to the outside gallery deck of the granite tower. In the event that the emergency light has to be serviced, it is lowered via a sliding track controlled by a rope pulley system to the outside catwalk surrounding the watch room. This light extends above the top of the present lantern room and is operated automatically in case of a commercial power failure or loss of the utility poles supplying power to the DB 24 beacon. The battery supply bank and it's AC charger is located at the base of the granite tower in the old oil room now housing the automatic control switching and status monitoring systems.

This room also contains the only entrance into the tower where a door opening provides access to the spiral stairway. Because of all the electric switching controls and electronic monitoring system, the room is supplied with an automatic "Haylon" chemical fire extinguishing system. Until 2006, it also contained the automatic fog signal sensor which operated using a strobe light and a reflective receiver to detect fog. A small window in the room allowed the emitted strobe light and its detector to function and when fog was detected, it activated the electronic fog signal facing the sea located across the perimeter road. A new compact fog signal device, identified as an "atmospheric particle detector", is now in use. It is externally mounted outside this room and the window strobe light slot that was used by the old fog signal sensor is bricked up.

As of March 2007 (with the exception of the lantern room in the granite tower, the attached electrical switch/status control room and the fog signal) the light tower was added to the listing of all the other buildings which have been vacated by the Coast Guard. The entire site, with exception to the tower lantern room, has been turned over by license to the Town of Jamestown and the non profit Beavertail Lighthouse Museum Association for preservation purposes (See Chapter 10). The Rhode Island Department of Environmental Management operates a small aquarium in the vacated fog signal building. As of early 2008, the ownership of the property still remains with the US Government.

Chapter 3

The Keepers

Over the past two hundred and fifty eight (258) years, beginning in 1749, Beavertail Light's succession of keepers has been administered by five (5) different local and federal organizations. Even before the light was first authorized to be built by the Colonial Government in Newport in 1740, the Proprietors of Jamestown as early as 1705 ordered *Captain Stephen Remington* to build a "chimminy" to the "watch house" at Beavertail. On June 9, 1712, they ordered that a watch be set and a beacon established under the direction of *Gersham Remington.* They petitioned *Benedict Arnold,* the landowner of the site, to look after the watch and make sure that it was adequately kept. As described in Chapter 1, it remains somewhat ambiguous if the beacon was actually built or finished during that period or if the beacon was to be used as a lighthouse or as one of five (5) other watch houses along the coast that conveyed information or warnings of hostile vessels approaching. Later records in 1740 indicate that *Abel Franklin* was ordered to build a beacon at Beavertail and a *John Wilson* was appointed to finish the "chimminy". Sufficient documentation exists, however, to support the fact that a watch was in operation. But, as surmised above, it may have been for other means. In this sense, a light keeper, as we understand it, was not yet placed in charge.

It was in 1749 that the Rhode Island General Assembly acted to authorize the lighthouse and they requested that *Able Franklin,* as one of six committee members, oversee the construction and at that time become the first keeper of the light.

Franklin served a total of 21 years, including the period between July 23, 1753 and 1761 when the 1st wooden structure burned down and the 2nd lighthouse was built with brick and stone. During the time there was no structure. Franklin, in the spirit of the yet to be established "Light House Service", continued keeping the light lit with a hand lantern each evening. Most probably the lamp was hung from a pole at the ruins of the old structure.

The detailed records of keepers' assignments from the U.S. Lighthouse Board personnel archives at the Federal Records Center in St Louis, Missouri contain assignment information from 1845 to 1912. These records are on 35mm roll microfilm. They are organized by lighthouse districts with names of keeper assignment dates, rate of pay and reason for termination providing a vivid picture of personnel turnover and organization.

The names below and on the following pages of Beavertail Light Station keeper's and their assistants was complied from many references. It updates previous records and is believed to be the most accurate information available.

Beavertail Light Station Keepers 1749-1972

NAME	Dates of Service	Yr	Salary Per Yr	Reason of Termination and Comments
1749 Newport Colonial Government				
Able Franklin	1749-1770	21		Member of original Newport Colony Lighthouse Committee
John Bowers	1770-1790	2 0		
1789 US Lighthouse Establishment formed per order of President George Washington				
William Martin	1790-1803	13		Died on Station. Light Transferred to US Government 1793. Reported broken lens panes by sea fowl and driving winds
Phillip Caswell	1803-1818	15		Wife's health. Son-in law of William Martin. Survived the hurricane of 1815
John Remmington	1818-1818	1		Lantern lit by David Melville's experimental

70

Name	Years	Duration	Salary	Notes
				gas system
George Shearman	1818-1829	11		Past Ship Captain
Sylvester R. Hazard	1829-1844	15		Resigned First fog signal (bell) installed at Beavertail
Christopher A. Sweet	1845-1848	4		
Robert M. Weeden	1844-1848	4		Died 1848 Replaced by his wife Demaris upon his death
Demaris Weeden	1848-1857	9	$350	Resigned 1st woman light keeper at Beavertail with assistance from her son who filled the oil lamps and trimmed wicks each night
Joshua B. Rathbun	1857-1858	1	$350	Removed Cause unknown
1st Henry Rathbun	*1857-1858*	*1*	*$300*	*Removed* *Cause unknown*
Silas G. Shaw	1858-1862	4	$350	Removed Cause Unknown
1st E.E. Taylor	*1859-1859*	*1*	*$300*	*Resigned*
1st W.S. Spooner	*1859-1859*	*1*	*$300*	*Resigned*
1st W.H. Carr	*1859-1862*	*3*	*$300*	*Removed* *Cause unknown*
1st B.W. Walker				
William D. Weeden	1862-1862	1	*$350*	Removed *Cause unknown*
1st Albert Caswell	*1861-1863*	*1*	*$300*	*Resigned*
Peter Lee	1862-1863	1	$350	Resigned Wife and six children living in Keeper's quarters
Silas G. Shaw	1863-1869	6	$600	Removed Cause unknown
1st Christopher Austen	*1863-1863*	*1*	*$300*	*Resigned*
1st William Bactchella	*1863-1864*	*1*	*$300*	*Resigned*
1st Ann N. Shaw	*1864-1869*	*5*	*$400*	*Resigned* *Wife of Silas Shaw*

Name	Years	Tenure	Salary	Notes
Thomas King	1869-1973	5	$600	Resigned
1st Patrick McAssaran	1869-1869	1	$400	Resigned / Transferred to another station
1st Andrew King	1869-1873	4	$400	Promoted
W.W. Wales	1873-1895	2 / 2	$600	Died on Station / Previous Keeper at Dutch Island Light
1st Alex F. Fraser	1873-1875	2	$450	Resigned
1st Charles Lake	1875-1875	1	$450	Removed / Cause unknown
1st George Brown	1875-1876	1	$450	Permanent Appointment
1st George Brown	1876-1881	6	$450	Permanent Appointment
1st George Brown	1881-1885	5	$450	Resigned
1st John S. Wales	1885-1888	3	$450	Resigned / 2nd Son of W.W. Wales
1st George B. Wales	1888-1891	3	$450	Absolute / 1st Son of W./W. Wales
1st George B. Wales	1891-1895	5	$500	Promoted / Succeeded his Father W.W. Wales
George B. Wales	1895-1900	5	$600	Demoted / Unsatisfactory repair work at Beavertail
1st John S. Wales	1895-1910	15	$500	Resigned / Brother of George B. Wales
Joshua A. Overton	1900-1909	9	$600	Permanent Appointment

1910 US Lighthouse Service Established

Name	Years	Tenure	Salary	Notes
John A. Overton	1909-1915	6		Resigned
1st John S. Wales	1910-1915	5		Promoted
John S. Wales	1915-1919	4		Resigned
1st George T. Manders	1915-1919	4		Promoted / Retired sea Captain
George T. Manders	1919-1938	2 / 0		Retired / Total 24 years at Beavertail
1st Stanley B. Roads	1919-1920	2		Resigned
1st Edward A. Donahue	1920-1938	18		Transferred from US Light House Service into USCG

72

1939 US Coast Guard Assumes Responsibility of Lighthouses

Name	Years	#	Pay	Notes
Carl S. Chellis BM 1st Class	1938-1948	10	$85 mo	Lost daughter at Mackerel Cove during the 1938 hurricane. Transferred to Sabin Point Light RI
Asst. Edward A. Donahue	1938-1948	10		Promoted
Edward A. Donahue BM 1st Class	1948-1953	5	$126 mo	Deceased Served a total of 33 years at Beavertail. Raised 11 children on site
Asst. Dominic M. Turillo BM 1st	1951-1953	3		Transferred from Rose Island Light, RI
Dominic M. Turillo, CBM	1953-1966	11		Retired Transferred to USCG cutter Spar in 1958 and then to cutter Pt. Cypress before returning to Beavertail as Keeper in 1960
Asst. Ronald Bugenske MM 2	1962-1965	3		Transferred to Pt Judith
Asst. Calvin Hirsch ENG 2nd Cl	1965-1969	4		Transferred from Gull Rock Light, RI
John K. Martin CPO	1969-	unknown		Temporary Duty
George Light ENG 2nd Class	1969	3 mo	$350 mo	Transferred from Woods Hole.
John Baxter BM 1st Class	1970-1972	2		Light Automated Last USCG Officer in Charge at Beavertail
Asst. George Light ENG 2nd Class	1970-1972	2	$350mo	

Records from 1931 to 1972, the period that the U.S. Coast Guard operated and had personnel living at the light station at Beavertail, are less accurate. After 1972 the light was automated, giving Beavertail the distinction of being the second to last lighthouse in America to still retain a light keeper. *John Baxter* was the last official keeper.

The light station residences at Beavertail were abandoned for a period of time, but under license from the USCG to the Town of Jamestown, a succession of custodians were residents in the keeper's quarters primarily to discourage vandalism and unauthorized access to the buildings. The caretaker position was competitively advertised and the selected individual and his family were provided the keeper's quarters rent free under a renewable lease agreement. In addition, the custodian was required to pay the costs incurred for utilities and provide 20 hours per week of his services toward maintenance of the building and grounds.

Beavertail Light Station, Jamestown Appointed Custodians

Period on site	Name	Total years	Status	Appointed by;
1977-1992	Peter Anderson	16	Caretaker	Town Administrator
1993-1999	Clayton Carlisle	6	Caretaker	Town Council
1999-2007	Richard Shutt	6	Caretaker	Town Council

Clayton Carlisle's renewable lease extended to April 2001 was not used for the complete lease period
Richard Shutt' s tenure was contested because of eviction notification and he refused to leave in 2006 August

Operations Records

The "Department of Commerce Lighthouse Service", who operated all the nation's light stations prior to the U.S. Coast Guard, required keepers and their assistants to maintain detailed daily records of every aspect of their duties. These logs and journals eventually found their way into the "National Archives". The Beavertail records are only partially available at the New England Center in Waltham, Massachusetts. Others may be stored in the "National Archives Center" in College Park, Maryland.

Four series of journals were found at the New England Center dating back to 1880 in addition to U.S. Coast Guard inspection records dated during the 1950's. Fog signal records covering the period of 1882 through 1914 show the various signals that were tested or deployed, including sirens and steam whistles. Inspection reports cover the period of 1914 to 1945. Mysteriously, there are no entries or weather reports during the month of September 1938, the year of the famous "38 Hurricane".

The logs and journals at the "New England Archives Center" are not complete. Only a few of each type are on file. The Center does allow archives to be researched after an application to use the records is approved. Copies of pages can be reproduced, but they do not allow any of their records to be loaned to leave the archive repository.

Light House Keeper Duties

Keeping the lighthouse in operational order was a twenty-four hour job. Tasks included not only keeping the light lit from sunset to sunrise each day, but all the other work in maintaining the grounds, house and ancillary equipment. The workload was spread into shifts when an assistant keeper, (titled "No 1") was assigned. A more stringent requirement was that the keeper and his assistant had to alternate keeping watch, remaining in the "watch room" during the night or to climb down and up the spiral stairs as duties demanded. The family of the keeper was expected to help with attending duties at locations where there was no "No 1" assigned.

The lighting of the light usually took place ½ hour before sunset and was not extinguished until ½ hour after sunrise. During the evening vigil, the lens rotating clock works had to be wound and checked for accuracy, lamp wicks trimmed and mantles cleaned. Oil had to be replenished and pressurized periodically. If fog was present, the attention to the fog signal was relentless, particularly if the fog signal required steam. It took a great deal of effort to maintain steam depending on the boiler source. In later years the mechanical air compressors and oil engines required monitoring and service. Daytime duties never ceased. Keepers were tasked with cleaning the lens, polishing the brass and making repairs not only on the lighting equipment, but also in the living quarters.

When the U.S. Lighthouse Service was established, there was a need to formalize the duties and the responsibilities of the "Keepers" of lighthouses, and as such, in 1881 formal instructions were prepared. These instructions outlined the responsibilities of the keeper and his assistant(s) who were required to strictly abide by the orders of the keeper. Stringent reporting requirements were placed on the attendants at each light station. Meticulous records were made of virtually every action the keepers and their assistants preformed. Notations were required not only of daily activities, but also hourly, weekly and monthly events.

Severe rules and penalties were outlined to prevent theft, waste and economy of the supplies allotted to the light station. Inventory lists and the condition of equipment, supplies, usage and repairs were noted. Each station was allocated a finite allotment of operating and replacement parts. Each had to be accounted for regardless of consumption, repair or replacement, down to the number of knives, forks and spoons, lantern wicks, mantles and quarts of oil.

Inspections by representatives from the Light Station District were unannounced and frequent enough that keepers made sure reports were in order and entered onto logs in a timely manner.

Detailed accountability as to who was on site and the reason a light keeper was off station at any time was diligently recorded in a journal called "Absence Report" and made available for examining inspectors. Authorized absences included procurement of supplies, attending church on Sundays and visits to doctors. Otherwise, any other reason to leave the light station was discouraged and required detailed explanation. Keepers and Assistants were not allowed to leave the light station site at any time without entering their name, time they left and the time of return to the site. Journal entries included mundane tasks such as; "to get provisions", "to get haircut", "to go to church", "to get some clams", "to get the mail", "to get fresh milk", "to buy new shoes" or to get a pane of glass.

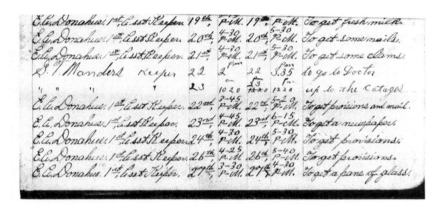

As the U.S. Lighthouse Service grew, so did its appetite for creating additional paper work. Keepers were required to summit monthly reports for every possible event that took place. These included detailed fog signal operations with expenditures of oil or coal as may be the case. Oil was a commodity that was both expensive and limited. Each quart of oil and its lesser measure the "gill" (about 4 ounces) had to be accounted for along with the daily consumption rate noted in the log book. Interestingly, the records of summer oil consumption clearly showed less oil use since the nights were shorter, whereas winter nights (sunset to sunrise) were longer and consumed as much as 10 quarts in one evening. The oil consumed for lighting the living quarters in the evenings was accounted for separately. The reports were compiled on a monthly basis and annualized for submission to the U.S. Lighthouse Board for their annual report to the Secretary of the Treasury. Neatness of entry written in ink was stressed and mandated to each keeper. A more detailed log was also required to identify the daily consumption of lamp oil, wicks and chimneys used in the light lens lamp. The 1888 Beavertail log book meticulously lists the exact minute of each day the light was lit, as well as the number of hours and minutes it remained lit. In addition to the oil consumption rate for each day, the log showed when wicks were trimmed or replaced. The log of December 1888 shows a total of 26 gallons of oil consumed during the month in the lamp of the 3rd Order Fresnel Lens and an additional 3 gallons of oil used in the quarters for illumination. The June 1887 log sheet graphically shows the reduction of oil use since the summer darkness hours were much less.

A regional "Superintendent of Lighthouses" was appointed and located in Newport. All the lighthouses in Narragansett Bay and Rhode Island reported first to him in all matters concerned with the operation of the light. Daily sunset and sunrise records, oil consumption rates, fog signal use, ship observations, supplies, shortages, defective stores, poor quality oil, malfunction of equipment, and absence from the station were required. Whale oil was expensive and as previously mentioned, it was very important to account for the quantity of oil on site. Exact amounts received and consumed each night and the quantity on hand had to be reported every three months to the Superintendent in Newport.

The reports were summarized by the Newport based "Superintendent of Lighthouses" who had collected similar reports from the other light stations and lightships in his district and forwarded the information to the "Light House Board". That board then amassed the supply information for logistical re-supply and compiled the formal report to the US Treasurer and Congress to appropriate funding for the next operational year. As envisioned, thousands of employees were involved and much paper work was exchanged.

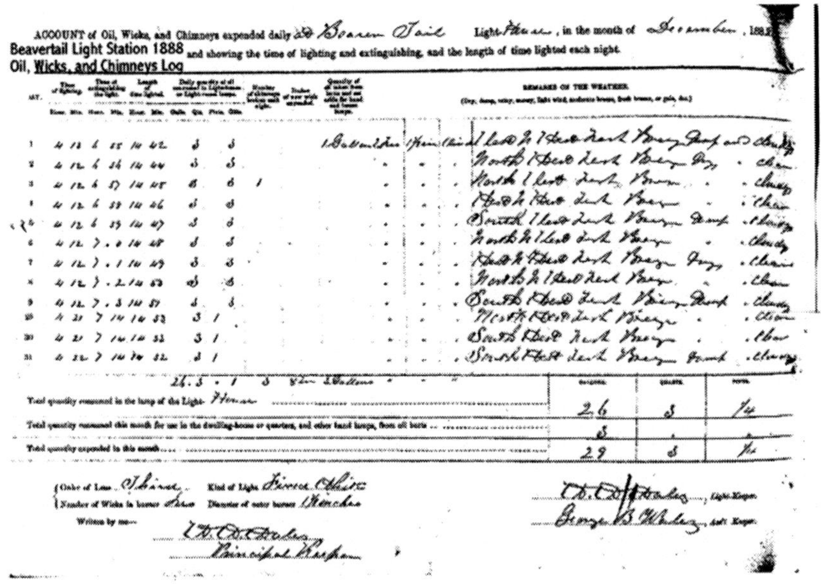

From USCG Archives

1888 Oil, Wick and Chimney Usage Log with Hours of Daily Light Operations Log

There was a fetish for cleanliness and orders stated that "All parts of the station, including bed chambers, were to be neatly kept. Untidiness will be strongly reprehended, and its continuance will subject a keeper to dismissal." In 1893, the Lighthouse Service prescribed that uniforms were to be worn while on duty to "maintain discipline, increase efficiency, raise its tone and add to the esprit de corps". The uniforms were adorned with cap ornaments and lapel rank insignia, including sleeve stripes for years of service. Unexpected and unannounced inspections were conducted frequently. Keepers had to remain in uniform while on duty and only when they were off duty or undertaking maintenance tasks not related to keep the light lit were they able to wear working clothes.

Detailed checks of the condition of the light station continued when the Coast Guard took control of the Beavertail Light Station. Its supplies and unit quantities of tools and spare parts were examined against the allowance tables established for logistical purposes. Interestingly, the February 11, 1952 report shows the inclusion of two Standby Illuminant lamps, one incandescent and one oil-vaporized in case the main light malfunctioned. When the Coast Guard took over, lighthouse record keeping took on different names and some previous requirements were modified. For example, the Coast Guard "Allowance List" identified items by stock number, units of quantity allowed on the light station and descriptions of each item to be maintained and accounted for. In the case of Beavertail, these lists provided additional insight as to how the station was equipped.

TITLE	CLASS OR STOCK NO.	UNIT OF QUAN-TITY	ALLOW-ANCE	NAME, DESCRIPTION, AND REMARKS ITEM	ITEM
				ALLOWANCE LIST U.S.C.G. ......BEVERTAIL L/S...... Part 1 of 1 Page 1 of 6 Group name LENS AND ILLUMINANT Group	
B	17	ea	1	LENS - 4th Order Mfg. - MacBeth - Evans	
C	59	ea	2	STORM PANES - 20-3/8" x 21-3/8" x 3/4"	
B	27-0	ea	1	LENS COVER - CG-27-0-3243	
C	17	ea	36	MAIN ILLUMINANT, LAMPS General Electric, PS 52 Mazal Bulb .750 watts - 120 volts Filiment C7A	
B		ea	1	LENS DRIVE - Clock Type C	
C		ft.	135	CLOCK CORD (spare) size 3/16"	
B	21	ea	1	STANDBY ILLUMINANT - 4th Order Kerosene Lamp	
C	21	ea	2	WICKS - round wick	
C	21	ea	3	CHIMNEYS - lox-on-type	

From USCG Archives
Excerpt From USCG Allowance List,
Beavertail 1952 Report

A daunting level of vigilance was demanded of lighthouse keepers charged with unfailingly keeping the lanterns lit and sounding the fog alarm at the immediate appearance of the murk and for its duration. When Castle Hill light was established across the East Passage, it was used by both light stations (Beavertail and Castle Hill) as a visual reference to gauge the density of fog. The fog horn was sounded when neither keeper could see the other's light. This

80

occurrence was logged and inspectors could check the times the fog signals were sounded compared with the log of each station. In later periods the lights of Castle Hill, Whale Rock and Brenton Reef lightship were used as ranges to determine when the fog signal at Beavertail should be activated.

Keeping the light in order and insuring it would be lit as required was of the uppermost priority. The lamp and lens maintenance came first and excuses for the lamp being out of order were not tolerated. Directives and instructions were expected to be adhered to without question. Consider *William Henry Davenport Adam's* 1870 account of the introduction of the Fresnel lens to understand how this vigilance was ensured even with advancing instruments for producing more efficient light and sound.

"The only risk in using the Fresnel lamp, says Mr. Stevenson, arises from the liability to occasional derangement of the leathern valves that force up the oil by means of clockwork. Several lights on the French coast, and more especially, the Tour de Corduan, have been extinguished by the failure of the lamp for a few minutes; this is not allowed to occur here.

During daytime hours a vessel identification watch was also set. All vessels that transited within sight of the Lighthouse at Beavertail were logged onto a daily journal of the "Passing Vessels Log." As an example, on a single day, August 10, 1881 a total of 56 vessels were logged. This log included the time of the sighting, a description of the vessel (Full Rigged Ship, Bark, Brig, Schooner, Sloop or Steamer) and its direction, coupled with the weather conditions at the time. The log mandated keepers to maintain a sharp lookout while doing other chores around the light. Logging the vessels in sight interrupted their maintenance routine or other general tasks, but the vessel count at the end of the year supported the annual request for fund appropriations from congress.

JOURNAL OF VESSELS which passed by or in the vicinity of the Light

DATE								Total number of vessels	REMARKS
Year and month	Day.								
1881.									
August	1		/	/	13	6	6	22	
"	2				9	8	17		
"	3				15	2	6	21	
"	4				16	1	6	23	
"	5				34	3	9	48	
"	6				14		6	20	
"	7				9	1	6	16	
"	8				31	3	6	29	
"	9				18	1	9	28	
"	10	2			48		6	56	
"	11	/		/	37	3	6	38	
"	12	/			35	1	8	35	

From USCG Archives
Light Keeper's Vessel Report Log, August 1881

The printed instructions for keepers at each lighthouse included a section devoted to the "Care of Lights and their Appurtenances". Lenses made of cast glass and heavy prisms of the Fresnel variety were common, however they required frequently cleaning from soot. Additionally, the lantern glass windows (that glass exposed to the outside weather) also required cleaning from salt spray and other contaminants. Insects were attracted to the light at night and further smeared the glass as they flew into it. Keepers were required to scrape and keep clean any residue remaining on the glass panes and keep the outside gallery walkway free from insect remains. Reports of birds that flew into the glass panes, breaking them and thereby requiring replacement of glazing panes were not uncommon.

Lens optics took on a reverse focal characteristic during the day, different from when the lamps inside were lit at night. The focal length from the lamp to the lens remained the same as the sun's light concentrated on the outside glass. The magnifying effect, now highlighted by the sun, focused a concentric beam onto the lamp source itself. Oil in the lamp under certain conditions could light or even explode and damage the lamp mechanism. As a result, keepers hung curtains each morning around the lens and cleaned the evening's soot off the optics. Keeper's from time to time reported burns on their hands from the sun coming through the lens and focused on there hands while cleaning the lamp if they neglected to shroud the lenses in the morning and instead cleaned them during the day. *George Light,* one of the last keepers at Beavertail tells of the scars he had on his hand from this inattentiveness.

Tom Tag, a noted historian of Fresnel lens, when asked if this was a common occurrence stated: *"It is true that the sun coming in reverse through the Fresnel lens will concentrate at the focal point of the lens and if a person's hand were in the focus he or she could be burned. Since the lamp normally occupies this position if it were full of fuel the sun could ignite the lamp in the same manner. It was common practice to place a linen bag over the lens during the day to prevent such ignition. There were canvas curtains that were placed on the inside of the lantern windows during the day which would allow the cleaning of the lens prisms without problems. The sun could not cause damage other than the two problems already mentioned."*

A more laborious and tedious task in the lantern room was the requirement that all brass work be kept stain proof, untarnished and bright. Most lights and bases were confined with heavy brass fittings. Keeping the lens clean was difficult to do in the salt water climate and required daily attention. The "Light House Establishment" and later the "Lighthouse Board" and the U.S. Coast Guard all required that only approved cleaning material supplied by its agency could be used.

Even with strict procedures in place and inspections conducted to enforce the rules and regulations the "Lighthouse Establishment" had no hard and fast rules regarding succession in the event of the death of a keeper. Women were often allowed to succeed a male keeper when they were deemed competent and experienced to undertake the duties.

Stephen Pleasonton, administrator of the Lighthouse Establishment from 1820 to 1852, had no qualms about appointing female keepers to replace related male keepers who died in service. In 1851, he wrote, *"So necessary is it that the Lights should be in the hands of experienced keepers that I have, in order to effect that object as possible, recommended on the death of a keeper, that his widow, if steady and respectable should be app't to succeed him."*

Such was the case of famous *Ida Lewis* of Lime Rock Light in Newport Harbor. She served for a lifetime performing deeds of courage and those of menial work in keeping the light operational. Over 30 women were appointed to these duties throughout the United States.

The only woman keeper ever at Beavertail was *Mrs. Damaris H. Weeden* who took over the keeper job with her son after her husband *Richard H. Weeden* died in 1845. There are conflicting records indicating her exact years of tenure, since a *Christopher Sweet* is also listed as a keeper from 1845 to 1848. Her son *William D. Weeden* is also listed as a keeper from 1848 to 1857 and again in 1862. *Damaris Weeden* remained as keeper for nine years, but it is believed she was replaced because of an 1851 inspection report describing the condition of the buildings as "in bad repair" and the tower "as the worse built tower yet seen". It had not been repaired in seven years.

The Assistant Keeper

The first Beavertail "Assistant Keeper" also identified as "No 1" (as were all Assistant Keepers) was *Henry Rathbun*. He first shows up in the 1859 personnel records. He must have been related to the keeper *Joshua Rathbun* who was removed for unknown causes after 6 months on duty. *Henry* resigned two months later. This is the same time period that the steam powered fog signal testing began and the new keeper's house was completed. The fog signal required constant attention in order to provide continuous steam from the boilers during fog.

It was not unusual to have a friend or relative of the Keeper assigned as the Assistant Keeper. While the Superintendent of the Lighthouse District interviewed and appointed the Keeper, the Keepers in turn were allowed to hire their own assistants. Salaries of both were paid by the local Superintendent.

The Assistant Keeper was also involved in the installation and modifications of the various signal equipment provided by the Lighthouse Board. There was a constant program of testing and evaluation and detailed records of the tests were kept. At Beavertail, as at other light stations, an Assistant Keeper was often added when the fog signal apparatus used steam or compressed air. There was considerable work involved in maintaining the boilers and later the oil fed engines that drove the compressors. Mechanical aptitude, plus in later years, electrical knowledge was required. When the fog was prolonged, constant attention was demanded of both the Assistant Keeper and the equipment. In addition, the Assistant Keeper was required to "assist" the Keeper as needed in standing a watch, tending the light and maintaining the grounds which added other burdens on "No 1".

The Assistant Keeper's house at Beavertail was constructed in 1898, but it appears that at one time he shared part of the Keeper's quarters. Some early photographs of the light station show other unidentified buildings on the site, but it cannot be determined if they were living quarters or buildings that housed domestic animals. The new quarters were almost identical and the same size of the Keeper's house without the expanded kitchen. The building was oriented 90 degrees from the Keeper's dwelling. A passage door was common into both kitchens, but has since been closed off. Both buildings are constructed from brick, but it is obvious that the brick work of the 1898 building is a bit more porous to moisture.

One overwhelming benefit of the Assistant Keeper's house at Beavertail is the unobstructed view from the seaside facing windows of both the first and second floors, whereas the Keeper's quarters have the granite light tower obstruction and fewer windows on the seaward side.

Salaries

The prerequisites for hiring a Keeper were not very stringent since the work was not technical nor required a trade-type discipline. Men had to be between 18 to 50 years of age with the ability to read and write and have enough mechanical talent to make repairs, paint and account for repair parts and supplies. Those who were to be stationed on a remote island did need to know how to handle a row boat or a sailing craft. Since watch keeping was the paramount job requirement, those with sea experience were preferred and selected first. Retired mates or captains were favored mainly because they were ones who could relate to having a reliable light for vessel navigation.

Pay at first was at the jurisdiction of the local Superintendent, but by 1867 Congress stepped in and established the annual salary at $600. This salary was fixed regardless of the location, even if the lighthouse or station was by itself distant from the mainland. Assistant Keepers were paid less and the scale ranged from $100 to $450 per annum. It appears that some lenience was allowed for supplementary income as both fishing and piloting was allowed during off duty hours. This is contradictory to the stated requirement that the light station be manned continuously, implying that Keepers and Assistants had to remain on site. Apparently at some locations it was not enforced as long as wives or other members of the family would tend the light.

By 1896, lighthouse service employees were classified and subsequently assimilated into the federal civil service system until the US Coast Guard took over lighthouse responsibility in 1931. New ratings were established and pay was related to the grade level of the "Petty Officer" rating which paralleled those of the US Navy.

Supplies and Uniforms

When the Lighthouse Board took over management of lighthouses, there was strict adherence to using lantern supplies and replacement parts from only one source. The "Messr. Morgan & Company" of

New Bedford, Massachusetts was the provider of oil and associated wicks and glass mantles. Sole source procurements by the government at that time were common and as expected, favoritism played a part. Any deficiency in quality or quantity of supplies, required to be on site, were required to immediately be reported to the Superintendent in Newport.

Instructions and manuals to the Keeper were written as the organization became more formalized and they were adhered to without compromise. The board established more disciplinary measures in the latter period of the nineteenth century to induce an "esprit de corps" among the Keepers. They provided uniforms in a dark blue indigo color with the lapels and caps embroidered with the letter "K", and for Assistant Keeper's "No 1". Separate clothes were provided for inside and outside work.

Photo Courtesy of Donahue Family
Beavertail Keeper Edward Donahue in U.S. Life Saving Service Uniform

The Other Residents of Beavertail Light (Ghosts)

"In March 2000, *Hope and Don Bucklin,* two frequent visitors to Beavertail were taking a picture of the Assistant Keeper's house from across the perimeter road. As they walked away, *"Hope"* said "Who was that man standing in the upstairs window gesturing?" She said it was an outline of a young man making strange

87

movements with his hands. *Don Bucklin* thought of *"Charlie Manders"*, the son of the keeper in the thirties who had "Huntington's chorea", a nerve disease that causes constant body tremors including hand movements. He stated, "maybe it's the ghost of *"Charlie Manders"*.

With that incident and after the photos were developed showing what could be a man in his twenties with dark hair, wearing a tan shirt and a dark vest outlined in the window, the *Bucklin's* and others were convinced that indeed *Charlie Manders* ghost was wandering around the unoccupied building. Others had noticed as well, a shimmering vague outline. *Manders,* whose reputation for the bazaar coupled with his storytelling, was the ideal candidate to take on the role of a ghost.

(Manders spent 24 years at Beavertail and was the most colorful of all the Keepers stationed there. Stories about him abound because some of his own generation who knew him are still living. He was noted for his stories, many of which were manufactured as the need

arose, telling tales to anyone who would listen. Manders, as a boy, ran away and signed on as a crew member on a whaling expedition. He later joined the U.S. Navy and served on square riggers in the China Sea.

Photo Courtesy of Jamestown Historical Society

Keeper Charlie Manders

As Keeper of Beavertail light from 1913 to his retirement in 1937, his exploits reportedly including the "Carnegie Medal for Heroism" never ended. But, in turn, this achievement may have been another one of his stories since no record of that award can be found in the Carnegie archives. Another of Mander's stories is that an admiral of the U.S. Navy told him that Beavertail Light had been seen a range of 40 miles. He died in 1954 in Jamestown at the age of 83.)

The Donahue Ghost

Margaret (Donahue) Halliday, daughter of *Keeper Edward Donahue,* was one who related the other ghost story at Beavertail that took place during the 1930's. Time and again over the years, she would relate the view she saw of "a woman with black hair and a white dress floating by". She would mention this to her daughter *Sandra Driscoll* and her son *John Driscoll*, but then it was said she didn't talk about it much to other people. Her parents were Irish and there is an Irish routine about denying the existence of ghosts.

Margaret Halliday grew up in the Beavertail Light Station, lived through the hurricane of 1938 and described how the waters of Narragansett Bay raged over the rocks surrounding the lighthouse almost washing the structure away. She moved furniture against the door to keep the water out and told how her father jumped into the water, rescued some people and then in trouble himself, how his son jumped in and saved him.

The Lighthouse Mouse

Stories abound about "church mice" and lighthouses themselves also seem to have their share. Beavertail is no exception. Surrounding the two major living quarters are a series of below ground level basement window casements. As far back as anyone can remember, there always was at least one mouse that could be seen in one of the casement wells. The most well known is the one often seen next to the entrance door of the museum at the Assistant Keeper's house. This mouse is so popular that return visitors to the museum often ask if the mouse has a name.

Chapter 4

Management and The Lighthouse Services

The Need for Organization

Beavertail Light and, for that matter, other lights were not conceived from the idea of any one individual. The need for navigation aids were well known and a necessity recognized by many. Ships and coasters were constantly lost along the entrances to many harbors of the New World. Furthermore, "time was money" and vessels forced to lay offshore with loaded cargo or spending the night at anchor until daylight were not profitable to business. Bad weather played its part as well. Every seaman knew the safest place for a ship was out to sea or in harbor; never to be caught grouping along a dark unidentified hostile coast in high winds and unknown currents. The "lee shore" was dreaded and ships sailed in the opposite direction until a safe passage could be seen after daybreak. It took, however, hundreds of years for navigation aids to evolve from the establishment of rudimentary private markers and lights to levels of sophistication and automation.

To bring these aids into American waters required planning, money and organization. From the very first beginnings, navigational aid evolution involved the participation of many disciplines. Ship owners, merchants, shipmasters and navigators, along with engineers, inventors, manufacturers, landowners, government agents, regulators and hosts of federal agencies were involved. Over time, large organizations were created where thousands of people were employed and worked to make the waterways safer for commerce, military and recreational use.

The light at Beavertail is a typical example where early need was recognized, debated and funded. Along with its construction, the light station required operation and maintenance and in subsequent years, upgrading, modernization and melding with other nearby aids. Every aspect of its design and use required considerable planning and commitments of manpower resources, money and material. Organizational responsibility started off with simple appointed committees. As more aids were established, the committees became overburdened, disorganized, mismanaged and resulting in unreliable navigation lights. Further complaints, mounting shipping losses and demands for better and reliable lights forced the need for central management. These lighthouse organizational and management structures evolved over the decades under the umbrella of various government agencies. Each succeeding organization made improvements in the nation's navigational waterways.

Colonial Management

Maritime services multiplied and navigation aids took more important meanings for both safety and economic growth as the colonial period evolved. The topic of shipping losses and lives in colonial Newport was the feed and fodder to many. Discussion and concerns related to its important trade affected the entire colony's economy. As early as 1730, Newport ship owners and merchants began petitioning the colonial government for a lighthouse to be built at "Point. Judith", "Beavertail" or "Castle Hill". With leverage from the wealthy ship owners, they and the merchants conceded that payments from arriving vessels could offset the costs of building and operating a lighthouse. The "Beaver Tail" light was finally authorized in 1738, but the war with Spain interrupted any plan for construction. With the war over and "peace restored", according to Rhode Island State archives, on "March 3, 1748, sixty (60) merchants (traders and ship owners) banded together and implored the Colonial government that a light be immediately established at Beavertail".

The first organizational committee of six (6) was formed by appointment. It included *Abel Franklin,* the first 'Keeper" of Beavertail light, and *Joseph Harrison,* whose brother *Peter Harrison* became the designer of the light structure. *Abel Franklin* appeared to be the overseer of the project. An accounting in August 1750 states the work of building the light began on May 8, 1749 and was completed on September 9 of the same year. *Franklin* distributed the paid funds of £1196 and 10 pence to the construction work force that at one period during the construction numbered 38 men. The building crew included a number of tradesmen including a window glazier and a painter. The final cost of the light was £5,213, 11 shillings and 6 pence.

From its initial operation in late 1749, the monies to pay for the cost of the light came out of a special fund called "Light Money" set up by the Colonial "General Assembly" in Newport. These funds were collected by the "Collector of the Port of Newport and Lighthouse Superintendent" (Customs Officer) from each vessel prior to its departure from Newport. The collector was *William Ellery*, one of the two Rhode Island signers of the Declaration of Independence. He was born in Newport in 1727, attended Harvard College and graduated at the age of 15. He later was a member of the Continental Congress in 1776 and under the new Federal Constitution, he was appointed to the Marine Committee and the first "Federal Customs Collector" of the Port of Newport.

For the next 40 years Beavertail Light was sustained under the direction of the Customs Collector, although not satisfactorily. Shipping had increased from 1761 to 1772 to seventy four thousand tons of foreign shipping and during the same period, 3508 coastal vessels had entered Newport. It is quite possible that many more came into the Bay bound for other ports such as Bristol, Warwick and Providence. This increase in shipping supports the arguments that Newport indeed was a major seaport destination in New England.

During Colonial management, there were complaints about poor light intensity at Beavertail and at times, that the light itself was not visible. In August of 1754, changes to the lantern were required and two additional acres of land were purchased north of the light in anticipation of added keeper facilities. By June 1761 and into 1762 a new committee undertook an investigation as to why the light was unreliable. It took, however, another two years before the committee determined what had to be done to provide better reliability of the light. Its main recommendation was to "alter the lantern". The reason being, that the earlier repair was not properly done and the present lantern construction did not emit light through the lantern

92

glass in stormy weather because of condensation buildup. While no details were given as to why moisture was collecting on the glass and/or windows, it is assumed they were not sealed from the weather. Salt spray coating the windows added to the poor illumination. This condition continued up to 1770 and contributed to rot and decay of the building, which in turn put the lantern in danger of possibly falling from its structure. A report made to the Customs Collector determined that insufficient air was circulating through the light tower thus preventing the wood support to dry adequately.

By 1785 the "Light Money" deficiency had reached a point where it was necessary to increase the duty to 8 pence per ton on any foreign flagged vessel, 4 pence per ton on any U.S. flagged vessel doing foreign trade and 2 pence per ton on all ship and vessels traveling between U.S. ports. The Newport Customs officer also required that any arriving vessel must report its arrival within 24 hours and provide a manifest of its cargo.

The Revolutionary War

The Revolutionary War with England and demands of money elsewhere halted any major renovation or improvements to the light. In 1776 the British landed 6000 troops in Newport to quell the uprising of the Colonials. Both British and Hessian troops were billeted in Newport and on Conanicut Island. The British had taken over the gun battery and revetments (now known as "Conanicut Battery") on Prospect Hill on the Beavertail peninsula. All the residents of Conanicut Island had fled.

Beavertail light was important to the British. They undoubtedly used the light for safe passage of their own vessels. During their stay in Newport, numerous supply and transports came and went. Nothing is known as to how they operated or maintained the light during that period, but as they fled Newport in July of 1778, as the French fleet approached, they scuttled ships in the harbor, dismantled the light apparatus and burned the light tower down. The lighthouse Superintendent, *William Ellery,* after the Revolutionary war wrote:

" That among other articles of apparatus for illuminating the Light Houses which were taken by the British and sent to Bermuda, there were a number of those lenses that all the articles captured were sent to New York and there purchased by Mr. Lewis, on account of the United States, that some of them have been sent by him to the Light Houses at Point Judith, Watch hill, Montauk Point, Gay Head, Tarpaulin Cove and Home's Hole and probably to other light houses."

This statement appears to lend credence to the fact that privateers of the day captured British ships and cargo and sold the prizes back to the Federals.

Captain *Winslow Lewis,* mentioned above, was a Boston based developer of lighthouse lenses who attempted to improve the famous *Argand* lamp design by adding spherical reflectors behind the lighthouse lamp. He convinced the Federal Government, after the war, to standardize lighthouse lenses with his design and sold his devices to the Government. Eventually, he became the "Superintendent" for lighting the United States light houses. Many of his critics, including ship masters, considered his design inferior to the original *Argand* lamp. By 1812, *Lewis* exemplified the true "conflict of interest" that can occur with a federal employee who has overextended his authority to benefit his own means.

U.S. Lighthouse Establishment

The new organization and standardization of lighthouses that finally arrived to the Colonies was a critical and important move although not efficient. The Revolutionary War had been won and the United States had taken its first steps as a union. Trade, transportation and movement of goods relied heavily on shipping and there was a recognition for the need of reliable navigation aids and some form of management to insure that reliability. Economical, safe navigation was paramount to the success of the new republic as the United States gathered the new states under its wing.

On August 7, 1789, President George Washington signed the ninth act of the United States Congress which provided that the States

94

turn over their lighthouses, including those under construction and those proposed, to the central government. This act created the "U.S. Lighthouse Establishment".

Ten lighthouses were turned over to the Federal Government including Beavertail light. The office of the Secretary of the Treasury was assigned as the overseer and managed lighthouse operations for many years. President *George Washington* signed the recommendations sent to him by *Treasurer Alexander Hamilton* and on October 12, 1790 *Washington* formally acknowledged that Beavertail Light was "agreeable to him and would receive his approbation".

However, all did not go well with this establishment. Communications were difficult and there was a lack of standard practices. In addition, many of the lighthouses lacked organizational logistics support and the local committees would defer to their own ideas. Funds were always lacking to pay personnel or provide for supplies and repairs. The lack of management direction at the federal level made matters even worse.

A dark period of technological stalemate endured for over 32 years under the direction of Commission of Revenue. In 1820, *Stephen Pleasonton*, an Auditor of the U.S .Treasury, was assigned to oversee the lighthouses in the United States. *Pleasonton* was so dogmatic about the deployment and use of Argand lamp and parabolic reflector system that he refused to recognize the 1822 invention of the French scientist *Augustin Fresnel* and the superior performance of the prism lens system. It was not until the 1840's that he was forced to test the new system. By that time, the Lighthouse establishment had deteriorated even further and complaints about poor and unreliable lights were commonplace. The cries of ship owners reached Congress and finally in 1852 a new organization, the "U.S. Lighthouse Board", was formed to fix the poor reputation of the country's lighthouses.

U.S. Lighthouse Board

This new organization, the U.S. Lighthouse Board, revolutionized the country's navigation system almost overnight. The new board began experimenting with new equipment and proceeded to design, build and install the best available at the time. By the beginning of the Civil War in 1861, all U.S. lighthouses had been converted to the use of *Fresnel* lenses. The U.S. Lighthouse Board existed for 58 years and during that time it built up the country's navigation aids, lighthouses and lightships into an organization unequaled anywhere in the world. Over 11,000 aids were deployed and attended to.

In addition to upgrading and installing new equipment, the board made great strides in personnel management. Keepers were selected and recruited because of their abilities and sea knowledge. Standards were developed as were rules and regulations, and orders were expected to be obeyed with stringent reporting requirements placed on the attendants at each light station. As mentioned in the previous chapter, meticulous records were required of virtually every action the keepers and their assistants preformed. Notations were made not only of daily activities, but also hourly, weekly and monthly events. Inventory lists and the condition of equipment, supplies, usage and repairs were noted. Each station was allocated a finite allotment of operating and replacement parts that had to be accounted for regardless of consumption, repair or replacement. The inventory meticulously included the number of knives, forks, spoons, lantern wicks, mantles and quarts of oil. A station "absentee log" was maintained indicating who was on station and off station. This listing had to indicate where the keeper or assistant keeper was going, the reason why and included the time of departure and the time of return. Inspections by representatives from the Light Station District were unannounced and frequent enough that Keeper's made sure reports were in order, accurate and entered into logs in a timely manner.

The strides in engineering, construction and board's learning cycle installing new lights set the stage for standardization in many of its lighthouses. Beavertail's granite light tower, for example, was replicated at many locations in the country. Close by at Watch Hill, the same granite construction and design was used and built in 1856. Its granite block design was strong and sturdy and the same configuration is found in lighthouses in the Great Lakes and other locations along the eastern United States.

U.S. Lighthouse Service

The next service that was established was the "U.S. Lighthouse Service" which in 1910 became an arm of the "U.S. Department of Commerce" known as both the "Bureau of Lighthouses" and the "U.S. Lighthouse Service". During its life, the Lighthouse Service doubled the number of navigation aids. New electronic and radio systems emerged and innovations in types of navigation aids greatly improved the effectiveness and reliability of equipment. Automation concepts were explored and tested and led the way for reducing manpower. It was the era of electricity replacing oil lanterns, batteries replacing gas lights in buoys and installation of radio transmitter beacons for radio direction finders and communications. All these innovations increased the safety to ships at sea and those vessels navigating the waterways. The U.S. Lighthouse Service stayed in existence until 1939 when it was then absorbed into the U.S. Coast Guard.

U.S. Coast Guard

The Coast Guard assumed responsibility for U.S. lighthouses in 1939. In doing so, a more militaristic approach to lighthouse management ensued. Although some of the former Lighthouse Service employees remained in a civilian status, others joined the Coast Guard Service. They manned lighthouses, went to sea or took on lifeboat life-saving station assignments. Beavertail's Assistant Keeper, *Edward Donahue,* who had been on site since 1921, transferred into the U.S. Coast Guard and eventually completed 33 years of service there.

World War II was imminent and by 1941 a wartime mission to guard the shores of America added further to the development of navigation aids and lighthouses. Fleets of ships supplemented the shore stations and as the war expanded, patrol frigates for convoy duty, weather stations and new radio navigational direction systems were developed. Electronic systems such as Loran and Shoran bridged the need of navigating in overcast weather with uncanny accuracy. Beach patrols and communications up and down the coasts of the United States were improved. By war's end in 1945, a modern organized and sophisticated organization had been built. With it came the need for more automation, increased navigation aid reliability and greater technical demands on the lighthouse keepers.

In the next 20 years, the Coast Guard began replacing the expensively manned and high maintenance lightships with sea buoys. The overriding need to reduce expensive manpower at lighthouses resulted in a major system upgrade program called the "Lighthouse Automation and Modernization Program" (LAMP). With this innovation lighthouses no longer needed on-site personnel. Shortly thereafter, lighthouse keeper's houses themselves were abandoned and only the lights themselves and foghorns were maintained. By the mid 1960's, drastic reductions were achieved and by 1990 keepers of lighthouses had vanished, ending a 270 year history of manned lights.

Navigation technology at the same time took a major step forward with deployment of the U.S. Navy's limited satellite system. It was in operation only a few years; but during that time, it provided highly accurate, wide area coverage by satellite and proved to be the forerunner of "NAVSTAR", the United States "Global Positioning System" (GPS). Although the system is operated and maintained by the U.S. Air Force, it brings precise navigation capabilities to anyone, any place on earth. The accuracy is so precise that any equipped vessel can navigate between the buoys in dense fog and if so programmed can do it automatically.

Meanwhile, the Coast Guard's abandoned lighthouses were rapidly deteriorating. Concerned historians and preservationists protested, then rallied and took their voices to Washington. It was not until the year 2000 when the U.S. Congress passed the "National Lighthouse Preservation Act" which recognized the historic significance of lighthouses and the men and women who had manned them. The Act enables municipalities, state agencies or non profit organizations to take title to lighthouse properties that were no longer of use to the Coast Guard and preserve them for public use. The turnover process is somewhat cumbersome involving a number of federal agencies ending up with the "National Park Service".

Beavertail Lighthouse Records

Beavertail Light Station records are scattered in many locations at various agencies and only by a through and detailed time consuming search will they be found. Early documents in Newport and Jamestown archives have references to the lighthouse as do many federal repositories. By far, the U.S. National Archives in Washington and Maryland, plus their regional offices, have acquired most of the agency files including those of the US Coast Guard. Most of these files are located under an identifier called "Record Group #26". Personal files are in a records center in St Louis, Missouri. The U.S. Coast Guard Academy Library in Groton, CT is another location as are organizational sources such as the lighthouse and lightship historical organizations.

During a search at the U.S. National Archives Regional Center in Waltham, Massachusetts, a wealth of records kept by Light Keepers who manned Beavertail Light Station were found.

The detailed daily records that the Department of Commerce's U.S. Lighthouse Service required Keepers and their Assistants to maintain eventually found their way into the National Archives. The Beavertail records are only partially available at the New England Center. Others may be stored in the National Archives Center in College Park, Maryland.

Four series of journals were found dating back to 1880 along with U.S. Coast Guard inspection records of the 1950's. One of the early journals included the "Passing Vessel Logs" where the Light Station Keepers entered the date and type of any vessel (Full Rigged Ship, Bar, Brig, Schooner, Sloop or Steamer) that passed in sight of the lighthouse. Vessel traffic on some days was quite heavy. As an example, a total of 56 vessels were logged on August 10, 1881.

As described in earlier chapters, Keepers and Assistants were not allowed to leave the light station site at any time without entering their name, time they left and the time of return to the site in "Absences Reports". They were also required to keep other detailed logs as previously described.

Site inspections were conducted unannounced. After 1939 the USCG took control of the Beavertail light station and continued detailed checks of the condition of the light station. Its supplies and unit quantities of tools and spare parts were examined against the allowance tables established by the USCG. Interestingly, the February 11, 1952 report shows the inclusion of two Standby Illuminant lamps, one incandescent and one oil-vaporized, in case the main light malfunctioned.

Fog signal records covering the period of 1882 through 1914 show the various signals that were tested or deployed at Beavertail, including sirens and steam whistles. Inspection reports cover the period of 1914 to 1945. Mysteriously, there are no entries or weather reports during the month of September 1938, the year of the famous "38 Hurricane".

The logs and journals at the New England Archives Center are not complete. Only a few of each type are on file. As previously mentioned, the Center does allow archives to be researched after application to use the records is approved. Copies of pages can be reproduced, but they do not allow any of their records to be loaned to leave the archive repository.

Reports from Beavertail Light were forwarded to the 3rd Lighthouse District located in Newport and subsequently passed along to the US Lighthouse Board. The Board annually provided a formal report to the Secretary of the United States Treasury under which the Lighthouse Service was organized. The chronology of activities reported to the Lighthouse Board provide a perspective of the changes and activities at Beavertail and includes the Brenton Reef Lightship.

The following were extracted from those reports:

1873   Considerable Repairs were made to the Daboll trumpet
        fog signals operated by the 24 inch Ericsson caloric
        engines. The duplicate engines were also repaired one at a
        time.

1874 $8,000.00 were expended for better accommodations (the
        Keeper's quarters were completed in 1856)

1876   *Beavertail Light Ship #11.* $21,620 was expended for
        repairs to include new ship frames, hosepipes, rails and
        rigging.

1880   Fog signal repaired.

1881   Dwelling repaired. Installed two 10 inch steam whistles
        with duplicate boilers and a large water cistern for
        collecting rain water. It was quoted: "the new signals will
        meet every want of the navigation".

1882   *Brenton Reef Lightship #11.* Hull is in good condition.
        Deck leaks, bell frame rotten, foremast decayed.

1888   *Beavertail Lightship #11.* New canvas, paint and
            medicines placed aboard.
        Lighthouse fog signal was operated for 504 hours, 67,456
        pounds of coal consumed.

1889   Purchased land for $3500. Repointed tower and replaced
        and refitted lantern glass.

1897   Brenton Reef Lightship #11. 12 years on station. Needs
            through repairs before   winter.
        *Hog Island Shoal Lightship #12. Vessel is old. No spare
        vessel is available. Needs $500.00 to repair. Received new
        main, jib, boat sails, cooking gear and stores.*
        Lighthouse fog signal was operated for 593 hours, 46
        tons of coal consumed.

1898   Light Station Addition (Assistant Keeper house) completed.
Hog Island Shoal Lightship # 12. Vessel not seaworthy and weak. $70,000 estimated to replace. Fixed lighthouse can be constructed for $35,000.

1899   Two 13 hp oil engines for fog signal to be installed. Light characteristic changed to flashing white. 8 flashes at 2 second intervals then dark for 15 seconds. Lens size changed from 3rd order to 4th order.

1900   Fog signal changed from 10 inch steam whistle to second class siren. Automatic duplicate 13 hp oil engines with two air tanks, two sirens and auto signals. Complaints that signal is not sufficiently loud enough. Added two large trumpets and sound deflectors on roof to deflect signal seaward.

Changed color of tower to white.

1901   Changed fog signal to conical siren by long continued experiments and tests. "Signal now seems to meet requirements of navigators."

1903   *Brenton Reef Lightship #39.* Built in 1875, 387 tons on station. Has chime fog   whistle signal. Two steam whistles (6 and 12 inches) Signal used for 614 hours. Consumed 89 tons of coal.

Light station. 2nd class siren, oil engines and compressed air. Signal used 583 hours and consumed 949 gals of fuel.

1904   Inspected the 2nd class siren in duplicate, worked by oil engines. Signal in operation for 497 hours and used 873 gal. of fuel.

1905   Inspected the 1st class compressed air siren in duplicate, worked by 13 horsepower oil engines. Siren signal in operation for 120 hours that and used 1032 gal. of fuel.

Chapter 5

Fog and Sound Signals

One must experience standing on the deck of a ship completely surrounded by fog. Not a single physical reference to be seen and unable to judge the depth of visibility. Fore, aft and abeam, a milky mist void of any dimension surrounds the vessel. Perception is incalculable. The surge of water at the heaving vessel's bow and the gurgle of her wake the only sounds. All hands are straining to hear the dreaded surf or a shipboard fog signal announcing a vessel somewhere, knowing that odds exist where they could possibly collide without having time to take evasive action. Add to this anxiety, straining an uplifted ear to identify the tone characteristic of a whistle buoy or gong or that of a lighthouse fog signal and then trying to determine its direction. Is the intermittent signal stronger or weaker; is the vessel bearing on or away? Does the sound characteristic coincide with the navigation aid on the chart? No other situation at sea is more perplexing or nerve rattling than voyaging in fog.

Fog at Beavertail

During periods of low visibility, rain, snow, and particularly fog, a light station takes on a new and different role from that of a prominent lighthouse casting a welcome glow to the offshore mariner. The light becomes obscured by unfriendly weather elements, and for the sailor trying to establish a navigational reference mark, navigation becomes a challenge and as mentioned, develops into a perplexing situation. The dense barrier of fog across the entrance of Narragansett Bay was a nemesis to the navigator and a cause for very accurate calculations being made as to his vessel's position. With visibility reduced, murky sightings or the worse situation, complete absence of any features 100 ft. from his vessel, any transit into the bay was perilous. The safe option was to stay offshore until the fog lifted, which of course was not a comfortable answer to the crew, master or shore based owner. This problem led to very early ideas of providing an audible warning for nearby hazards not visible to the navigator and identification of a position location.

Without entering the theoretical explanation of how fog occurs, it is sufficient to simply say that when moist warm air moves over cold water, the moist atmosphere condenses and fog forms. This takes place commonly in Narragansett Bay during the early spring through midsummer by onshore winds carrying moist air into Rhode Island Sound and into the approaches of Narragansett Bay. The density, extent of coverage and the time it remains depends on variable factors. Generally, fog will cover the area along the coast and thin out a few miles inland where it encounters warm air rising from the ground. It will linger along the coast until the sun's warmth dissipates the condensation and by mid morning the fog usually begins to lift.

It is not uncommon during the months of April, May, June and July to often find Beavertail Point and the waters from the east through to the west fogged in. At the same time, a mile or so north of the point, clear sunny weather can exist. Weather condition log books from the Beavertail Lightship, only a short distance from shore, consistently show its total hours of annual fog horn operation exceeded those of Beavertail Light Station confirming the fog persisted much longer and of greater density further out from the shore.

A wide host of sound signals were deployed when considering fog signal history starting with explosive devices such as cannon or explosive charges. It is noteworthy here to comment about the use of cannon since at one or more times, cannon had been used at Beavertail. The lighthouse in Boston harbor used cannon extensively as a fog signal in the sense that when fog occurred, it was fired periodically. It was not considered practical because it was unknown if a ship was actually within the sounding range. Gunpowder was both expensive and limited in supply and although cannon balls were not used, repeated firing deteriorated gun barrels. At some locations, the cannon was used only in response to a ship offshore that either through soundings (measurement of depth) or glimpse of land through the fog used it as a signal. The vessel fired its own cannon and waited for a response from shore which then gave the vessel's navigator a sound bearing to steer toward. In any case, it was not precise and only provided general bearing direction. Subsequent exchanges of cannon fire would reduce the error, and hopefully, the land station would appear and provide the navigator his visual position fix.

Beavertail has probably seen more types of fog signals than any other New England lighthouse station. At Beavertail, it evolved from cannon to a horse drawn treadmill powering a whistle to electronic tones. A fog bell and tower installed in 1829 lasted only four years. It was complex for its time, incorporating weights and mechanical gears adjusted to repeat a striking hammer hitting the bell, time controlled by the clock mechanism. The configuration was improved by the U.S. Lighthouse Service and commonly used in many lighthouses for almost 15 decades. Over the years, other signals were developed including bells, whistles, gongs, trumpets, diaphones, sirens, horns and electronic tones. All of these required power of some sort to operate. These too were developed to match the demands of the audio device including clockwork mechanisms, steam, compressed air and even wave motion. Almost without exception, the fog signal at any given light station was superceded by a newer development over the life of the light station and changes to the fog signal characteristics were also made. As late as 1945, the Coast Guard in their annual "Light Lists" showed there were over 100 different sound signal characteristics being used by light stations along the coasts and Great Lakes of the United States.

It was at Beavertail in 1852 where the U.S. Lighthouse Board (later named U.S. Lighthouse Service) determined the light station there be the principal base where they could experiment and improve on new ideas for sound signals. Fog signal equipment technology, as crude as it was in 1850, had much room for design improvement and the application of mechanical ingenuity. But the signaling equipment devices were not the only issue. The understanding of how sound was transmitted played an equal role in the development process as did the study of the best and proper location of the signal equipment. Parameters such as height above water, absorption, refraction or acoustical interference by land features all played into the equation. Earnest scientific research, testing and deployment of improved sound signals by the Lighthouse Board were undertaken and much was learned.

Certain phenomena, such as sound voids peculiar in specific geographical areas, perplexed investigators and were never fully understood. For 85 years, from 1852 to 1938, testing and experimentation continued at Beavertail and extended to other light stations as well. Tests were also conducted by observers located at light stations listening to ships purposely sailing on predetermined sailing tracks and sounding their signals at given intervals. Interesting enough, up until 1900, as technology evolved and new fog signaling equipment was developed, it was the human ear that was used as the instrument of measurement and effectiveness. In later years, sophisticated analytical sound level instrumentation meters and frequency measuring equipment were placed in use and helped develop the fog signal equipment deployed today. With thousands of hours of test and untold millions of dollars spent in development, test and installation of fog signal equipment, it is still the human ear that remains as the instrument of use by the mariner as it did hundreds of years ago.

Beavertail Sound Signal History

As recent as 2002, only fragments of fog signal history, deployment and experimentation was documented by lighthouse historians at Beavertail. For example, there is record of a bell tower in operation from 1829-1831 mounted in a 12 ft. high brick tower. The bell weighed 600 pounds and was controlled by a wind up clock mechanism hammer which struck the bell every ten seconds.

An unsigned and undated painting of Beavertail completed prior to 1856 does show the earlier light tower, a fog signal building and other structures on the site. The fog signal building has two twin whistles protruding through the roof and an attached shed. The twin whistles were probably operated by either steam fueled by coal stored in the shed, or by compressed air provided by horse power as described below.

More recent information was available from old Lighthouse Board records of the "Regional New England U.S. Records Center" in Waltham, Massachusetts. Some 16 log books of fog signal operations and maintenance information from 1914 to 1945 are available, but the evolution and detailed descriptions of the various sound signals and of the many experiments conducted at the Beavertail site were never collected for archival use. Only through excerpting the data from the log books and reconstructing information from other sources can some semblance of the equipment used be identified.

In 2004, *Lannete Macaruso,* a Beavertail Lighthouse Museum Association (BLMA) member and later a member of the BLMA board, had asked the BLMA for any suggestions for a topic to help her conduct a college level creative writing course at the "Community College of Rhode Island" for employees of "General Dynamic's Electric Boat Division". The students were participants in the firm's multi-trade associate degree training program.

She explained that the course objective required students to undertake research containing technical material with historical content and be of interest to a group of male students. It was suggested filling in the historical information void of fog signals used at Beavertail would be helpful to the BLMA and its docents. *Macaruso* and her small class of four students comprised of *Matt La Branch, Carl John, David McHale and Robert Riggi* enthusiastically undertook the study. *Macaruso* provided the guidance and direction, editing and rewriting much of the draft material.

As a result, a considerable amount of the following information was extracted from references used in the study and the writings of the class. The student collections and their summary included much information on sound physics, propagation of sound over water, and the problems with "sound shadows" or sound "multi-path" and the angles of reflection that played a role in the inconsistency and controversies at Beavertail.

Data was also extracted from some research undertaken by *Sarah Gleason* who in 1955 had written her findings in the BLMA quarterly newsletter, the "Lighthouse Log", and a substantial amount obtained directly from records of the "U.S. Lighthouse Board".

The Sound Problem

Some brief understanding that needs to be accepted by the reader is that sound propagation over water is not consistent because of air currents, atmosphere participation and temperature variations as a function of range. Velocity, surface effects and geometric spreading all play a part on the affect of sound propagation. It is a daunting problem that cannot be remedied by just installing "louder" signal devices. Much was unknown during the early days. The experiments at Beavertail were the first to prove these variables existed, along with other phenomena, even through they were suspected many years previous.

An example of the propagation problem comes from an 1881 report which stated: a "steamer" (steamship) about a half mile from the Beavertail fog signal reached a point where the fog signal could not be heard. Steam puffs from the stack pipes could be seen confirming that the signal was being blown. The blasts were previously heard by the same "steamer" from 10 miles away until it reached that point.

"Everyone strained his ear to hear the signal, but without success; and we had begun to doubt our position when, the fog lifting slightly, we saw the breakers in altogether too close proximity for comfort. When we passed the point as closely as was safe, and abreast of it and at right angles with the direction of the wind, the fog signal broke on us suddenly and with its full power. We then ran down the wind to Newport and had the sound with us all the way. The fog continuing during the next day, the signal kept up its sound, and we heard it distinctly and continuously at our wharf, though five miles distant. A report from a USN inspector says that signals may be heard through the densest of fogs and but that fog may have in-auditable spots from various directions."

Fog signals are heard greater when the wind is blowing with the fog signal. When the wind is blowing against or horizontal to the fog signal the signal is then dissipated and or not heard for required distances.

108

Prof. Stokes of England believes there are two great causes of these phenomena, non-homogeneity in the atmosphere, and movement of the wind. Homogeneity in the atmosphere is believed to be produced by precipitation, more so a heavy northeast snow storm. As read in a statement by the USN inspectors that a fog signal was heard clearly. These extraordinary conclusions are best heard when the observer is windward of the signal. (Sound signal packet USN inspectors LT. Comm. F.E. Chadwick and Capt. George Brown p733)

The most respected sound signal scientist of the era was *Joseph Henry* who previously was the First Secretary of the "Smithsonian Institution". He was appointed as one of 6 members to the U.S. Lighthouse Board, and for the first time, a highly competent scientist directed the development of sound signals and the studies of sound propagation nation wide. He remained on the Board for 25 years. It was he who approved and directed that Beavertail be the first location to test the famous "Daboll Trumpet Fog Signal". Beavertail was ideally situated as a testing ground. The light station was easily accessible by researchers and the equipment necessary to be transported to the site. Testing equipment required both apparatus and monitoring vessels. Also, the Beavertail peninsula bisected Narragansett Bay, whereby observer vessels could sail in a wide arc around the signal source for the test programs. Berthing in nearby Newport for the vessels was readily available as were supplies and support from the Navy. The other requirement called for fog and the early spring through mid summer weather foggy conditions in Narragansett Bay provided ample opportunities to conduct tests in low visibility.

Lighthouse Board records extracted from Keeper logs reflect that the fog conditions at Beavertail exceeded 500 hours a year. During the year 1897, the Station log indicated that the fog signal was used a total of 593 hours. Comparatively, Sequin, Maine in 1907 experienced a record, still unbroken, of 2,734 hours of fog. In 1916 the lightship stationed at the entrance of San Francisco Bay recorded 2,221 hours. On the low side, of below 90 hours per year, were stations located in Florida.

The log books at Beavertail also indicated the amount of coal or fuel was dispersed as a function of operating hours. The twin 10 inch whistles during 1881-82 were operated by steam and 81,000 lbs of coal were on hand. The 1906 First Class siren was operated with compressed air provided by a pump driven by an oil fueled engine.

The fuel storage capacity was limited to 1000 gallon capacity requiring refilling the tank when the supply went below 300 gallons.

LIGHT-HOUSE ESTABLISHMENT:

RECORD

OF THE

10 inch Steam Whistle

FOG-SIGNAL

At Beaver Tail Light Station,

Third District, from September 1st 1891

to July 31 &c., 1892.

RECORD OF FOG SIGNALS

At Beaver Tail Light Station. For month of September, 1944

DAY OF MONTH	LOW VISIBILITY				FOG SIGNALS Type First Cl. Air Siren				RADIOBEACON Type Transmitter ..... Freq.			
	Fog, Snow, Rain, Smoke, Haze, Etc.	TIME BEGAN	TIME CLEARED	TOTAL DURATION Nearest ¼ hour	TIME STARTED SOUNDING	TIME STOPPED SOUNDING	SIGNAL WAS SOUNDED Hours / Minutes	STEAM OR AIR PRES. lbs. / Pounds	TIME STARTED FOR THICK WEATHER	TIME STOPPED FOR THICK WEATHER	SIGNAL WAS OPERATED FOR THICK WEATHER Hours / Minutes	
1	Fog	0655	1945	13.30	0600	1945	13 / 45	45				
1	"	2010	2045	.35	2015	2045	/ 30	"				
1	"	2125			2130			"				
2	"		0045	3.20		0045	3 / 15	"				
2	"	0455	0545	.30	0500	0544	/ 45	"				
3	"	0755	1130	3.35	0800	1130	3 / 30	"				
8	Test	1000	1015		Test		/ 15	"				
12	Fog	2310			2315			"				
13	"		0000	.50		0000	/ 45	"				
13	"	0010	0045	.35	0015	0045	/ 30	"				
13	"	0755	1930	11.35	0800	1930	11 / 30	"				
13	"	2000	2015	.15	2005	2015	/ 10	"				
13	"	2340			2345			"				
14	"		0200	2.20		0200	2 / 15	"				
14	"	0210	1030	8.20	0215	1030	8 / 15	"				
14	"	1210	1245	.35	1215	1245	/ 30	"				
14	"	1855	2030	1.35	1900	2030	1 / 30	"				
14	"	2100	0030		2100	0030	3 / 30	"				
20	Fog	2125			2130			"				
21	"		0500	7.35		0500	7 / 30	"				
21	"	1205	1235	.10	1230	1235	/ 05	"				
21	"	1325	1515	1.50	1330	1515	1 / 45	"				
21	"	2130			2135			"				
22	"		0110	3.50		0110	3 / 43	"				
26	"	0525	0700	1.35	0530	0700	1 / 30	"				

110

Year	Notation
1873	First class Daboll Trumpet operative by 24 inch Ericsson caloric (heat) engines in duplicate. One engine at a time, need considerable repair.
1880	Fog signal repaired
1881	Installed two 10 inch steam whistles with duplicate boilers with large cistern for collecting rain water. System will meet every want of navigation.
1888	Fog signal operated for 504 hours, 67,456 pounds of coal consumed.
1890	New fittings, auto signal and smokestack installed. Engines overhauled. Fog Signal was operated for 496 hours and used 28 tons of coal.
1893	The fog signals operated for 433 hours and used 52 tons of coal
1895	Fog signals operated for 554 hours, using 57 tons of coal.
1896	The 10 in. steam whistles, operated for 520 hours and used 51 tons of coal. 1899
1897	Fog signal operated for 593 hours, consumed 46 tons of coal.
1900	Fog signal changed from 10inch steam to second class siren automatic with duplicate 13 hp oil engine, two air tanks, two sirens auto signal. Complaints received "not sufficiently loud". Added large trumpets and deflector on roof to deflect sound from trumpets to seaward.
1901	Changed to conical siren and continued experimental testing "Seems to meet requirements of navigators"
1903	Installed 2nd class siren, oil engines and compressed air. Fog signal operated 583 hours, consumed 949 gals of oil.
1904	Inspected the 2nd class siren in duplicate, worked by oil engines. In operation for 497 hours and used 873 gal. of fuel.
1905	Inspected the 1st class compressed air siren in duplicate, worked by 13 horsepower oil engines. Siren ran for 520 hours and used 1032 gal. of fuel.

The Daboll Trumpet

While other devices, such as a cannon and bell at one time or another were used at Beavertail, it was the 1851 installation of a new and somewhat radical device that moved fog signal equipment into a new technology sector. Devised by *Celadon L. Daboll,* a Connecticut experimenter/inventor of sound signals, his new invention brought rapid improvements and mechanization to sound signal systems. *Daboll* previously had designed a number of hammer struck bell systems that were deployed in New England but his new device was an air modulated trumpet. It was called a trumpet rather than a horn because it included a reed mechanism similar to a clarinet musical instrument. An earlier version had been tried aboard a lightship off the New London,

111

Connecticut coast, but results were not conclusive partially due to the inability to maintain enough air reserve to power the trumpet.

The new horn was installed in 1851. *Daboll* used his own funds for operational tests at Beavertail. He hoped to show his experiment as a success, eventually to collect payment for the equipment and testing costs and to build subsequent fog signals at other locations. Earlier, *James Henry* of the Lighthouse Board, being a strong advocate, argued the need of better sound signals. In 1850, he pressured the US Congress to appropriate $2500 for new fog signals. (*Some of the funds from this appropriation were later used to pay Daboll for his design and tests at Beavertail.*)

The new *Daboll* configuration consisted of a 17 foot long horn (trumpet) having a conical flaring lip 38 inches across its mouth. The horn then tapered down to 3 inches where the resonating reed, in this case a 10 inch long, 2 inch wide steel strip was rigidly fastened at one end. Air at 15 to 20 psi was forced through the orifice over the reed and modulated the free end by vibration. One report states that the trumpet produced at shrieking sound.

Photo Courtesy of US Lighthouse Society

Steam Driven "Daboll" Type Trumpet Horn Used at a Scottish Fog Signal Station

At Beavertail, the power to drive this system was unique. *Daboll* devised a horse driven air compressor pump system complete with reserve air tanks. One report read, *"fog seldom lasts all day. It will require about one-third of the time (during fogs) to work the horse, to keep up a regular series of signals"*. Arguably, it was the world's first truly one-horsepower machine. The horse was stabled in a shed behind the lighthouse and when needed led into the compressor shed and harnessed to a rotary treadmill. The treadmill was belted or geared through a rotary mechanism which in turn operated the air pump pistons forcing the pressurized air into a reserve container tank. From the tank through a control valve, the compressed air was fed via piping to the inlet orifice of the trumpet.

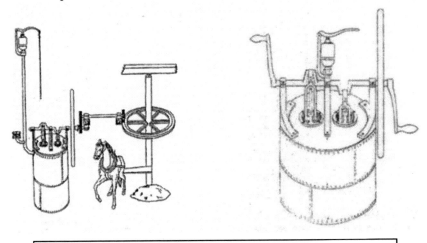

Sketches Courtesy of BLMA
Daboll's Horse Powered and Hand Powered
Compressed Air Configurations

The results of the first series of tests established that *Daboll's* trumpet was heard at great distances and was superior to the whistle. The 1851 experiment was also tried with an air whistle and an air trumpet, both operated by compressed air. The Lighthouse Board sent observers to Beavertail aboard the steamer "Empire City" from New York. Arriving at the coast between Beavertail and Brenton Reef, it encountered dense fog with *"navigation extremely hazardous"*. The fog signal *"sent its clear shrill notes far over the water, indicating the bearing of the point much more accurately than a bell or cannon would have done".* Even the Customs Collector in Newport, over 6 miles away, could hear the fog signal and had commented favorably as to its penetrating sound as did people at Fort Adams. This was not unexpected since Newport was downwind from the predominantly SW winds that blew across the Beavertail Point.

Regardless, the Board was impressed and recommended that *Daboll's* system be installed at other lighthouse locations. They did however recommend that hand power rather than horse power be used as it is *"very desirable in all cases that will admit it".* A sketch of the hand powered version showed two crank handles that required two men to rotate and seemingly appears awkward to operate, not to mention tiresome. *Daboll,* on the other hand, defended the horse power method with Congress claiming it would not cost more than what was being paid for manually ringing fog bells. How many horse operated trumpet type fog signals were eventually deployed is uncertain, but those that were, operated successfully.

The horse operated compressor was not long lived for various reasons, one of which was cost. One report stated *"the expense and inconvenience of maintaining a horse prevented its extensive use".* Nothing has been recorded on how the horse was kept moving and for how long. Also, about the same time, much success was being achieved with primitive fuel powered engines. Some, classified as "heat or caloric engines", used expanding hot air fueled by coal or gas to move pistons up and down. Other engine developments operating with oil began to look very attractive for powering mechanical pumps. *John Ericsson,* another inventor, had begun building incredible engines as early as 1833. He made many versions of the caloric engine which was suitable for use in lighthouses. A new era of energy conversion was in the making and other engineers leaped forward to use these devices. *Daboll* and Beavertail were not to be left behind.

In 1857, a conversion of *Ericsson's* caloric engine was fitted at Beavertail replacing the horse. The coal fed engine was more

114

reliable and while it needed an attendant to monitor and feed it fuel, it also provided a more consistent supply of air to the fog trumpet. *Daboll* used the new engine and ran more experiments including pairing up two trumpets. There were reports which also stated that the sound was more powerful although accurate measuring systems were not available to confirm its efficiency. Further testing continued resulting in the Lighthouse Board decision to install similar systems at other lighthouses and retire the horses to farms. The designer of the caloric engine, *Ericsson,* had continued to improve his design finalizing on a machine configured to using both a power piston and a supply piston which he then fitted with valves. There were many variations with cylinder diameters ranging in size from 8 inches to 32 inches one of which was also installed at Beavertail.

Three model variations of this *Ericsson* engine exists today at the "New England Wireless and Steam Museum" located in North Kingstown, Rhode Island. Also located in the museum is a *"DeLaVergne"* oil engine which probably drove the air compressor for a horn at Beavertail. This is supposition, but the *DeLaVergne* was a gift to the Wirless and Steam Museum from *Alan Davenport* whose family owned the Jamestown Water Company. Since the privately owned water company had limited funds, they may have aquired it used, from the Lighthouse Service. The same kind of engine was used by *Marconi* to make electricity for his pioneer wireless station at Wellfleet, Massachusetts. *Marconi* possibly acquired his as well from the Lighthouse Service. It was the standard compressor engine used by the Lighthouse Service.

It also appears that at the same time the *Daboll* trumpet was under evaluation at Beavertail, the Lighthouse Board also became interested in steam whistles. Beavertail was chosen as the test site and the first experiments in their use as fog signals also began in the fall of 1857 but very little information is available. A five inch *(diameter)* whistle was installed and with it a coal fired boiler that provided the steam to operate the whistle. At the time, railroad train whistles were common and the designs were relative easy to modify both in pitch and volume.

Photo Courtesy of New England Wireless and Steam Museum

Ericsson Caloric Engine

They worked by steam under pressure entering the bowl of the whistle and exiting through an orifice slot. Some of the steam passes into the whistle's bell and some passes outside of it. Differing pressure inside and outside of the whistle causes the bell to vibrate the air molecules which in turn generates the sound. The pitch, or tone, is dependent on the length/diameter of the whistle's bell and by altering the distance between the steam orifice and the rim of the drum. When brought close to each other, the sound produced is very shrill, but as the distance is increased, a deeper tone is generated.

Even *Daboll* began designing and building steam whistles, modifying them to be suitable in the fog environment. Steam boilers of that era, needed to power the whistles, were known to be unstable. There was hesitancy on the part of the Lighthouse Board to place potentially dangerous boilers in the hands of lighthouse keepers. On the other hand, reports from other locations claimed the steam whistle was superior to the trumpet horn and the Board noted that improvements in steam boilers had been made over the years. Accordingly, they decided to conduct further experiments notwithstanding the fact that the steam whistle did indeed sound like a railroad whistle and could confuse the mariner.

For the next 8 years, to 1866, experiments continued at Beavertail. A new reed modulated horn and a hot air engine to operate was installed. Testing continued not only with equipment but also by vessels that were engaged by the Lighthouse Board to traverse the seaward area and evaluate the effectiveness of steam whistles compared to the *Daboll* trumpet. The testing became very complicated due to atmospheric variables and it was at this time that sound blackout anomalies, or as the Lighthouse Board called them "ghosts or silence" areas were found in the geographic area. Tests, equipment modifications and improved engine installations continued for almost two decades. Volumes of data were collected and consensus was never achieved as to which fog signal apparatus were the best. Slowly and deliberately support for the *Daboll* trumpet began to subside as the steam whistle gained popularity. *Daboll* attempted to defend his trumpet system stating "it *required little fuel, no water and was perfectly safe*" but its inherent nemesis was its prone nature to malfunction. Unreliability, needs of repair and high costs contributed to its demise.

Then, in 1881, several controlled experiments were conducted that sounded the final days for *Daboll's* trumpet. *General James Duane*, head of the U.S. Lighthouse Board at the time, directed a series of experiments involving the *Daboll* trumpet and a 12 inch *Daboll* steam whistle. The results consistently stated that the whistle exceeds the first class trumpet. Also, a statement from an engineer in Canada where a *Daboll* trumpet had been in operation over four years stated: "*The expense for repairs, and the frequent stops to make these repairs during the four years they continued in use, made them [the trumpets] expensive and unreliable. The frequent stoppages during foggy weather made them sources of danger instead of aids to navigation. The sounds of these trumpets had also started to deteriorate.*"

The Steamship "Rhode Island" Disaster

Photo From the National Archives
SS Rhode Island

The unexplained 1880 shipwreck grounding and sinking of the steamship "Rhode Island" in dense fog off Bonnet Point, Narragansett, while Beavertail's fog signal was operating, prompted an extensive study and test program by the Lighthouse Board. The ship had left New York the day before with 170 passengers on board and over 750 tons of cargo. She grounded at 4:00 a.m. on 6 November with almost a complete loss of cargo. All passengers were safely rescued but the vessel was a total loss. Her master reported that the fog was dense and the ship stopped frequently to assure its position. The vessel passed Point Judith and unlighted Whale Rock safely and the signals from Beavertail were reported "heard and answered" during the approach to the West Passage. Passing Beavertail, the vessel somehow mistook its bearings and went aground so suddenly and with such force that both smoke stacks were toppled over and crashed through the upper staterooms. She soon began pounding on the rocks and began to break apart. Cargo was floating out from her broken hull and onto the shore. It was reported that many of the survivor "ladies were taken to a large boarding house in Jamestown". The *Daboll* trumpet on Beavertail was alleged to be the blame for the loss which exceeded $1,000,000. Bonnet Point was one and half miles from the fog horn, but pilots and crew of the "Rhode Island" claimed the fog signal was not heard aboard the steamer just prior to the grounding because *"the fog signal keeper failed to operate his machine"*.

A U.S. Navy officer was assigned to undertake the investigation. He first verified that indeed the fog signal was in continuous operation on the day and morning of the disaster by the fact it was heard in Newport and by other vessels who had taken action further out to sea than the "Rhode Island". The keeper at Beavertail, *William Wales,* who was first blamed for not operating the fog signal was cleared of any neglect. Ten days after the wreck had occurred, the Navy officer, in clear weather, had the fog signal at Beavertail placed in operation and sailed the course the "Rhode Island" had taken to its disaster point. The results were astounding and confirmed the testimony of crew members of the "Rhode Island" that the signal was not heard off Bonnet Point.

This single incident set in motion a major series of tests and experiments to understand the science of sound propagation, and more importantly, the development and test of sound signaling devices. The U.S. Lighthouse Board had now committed itself to improve and upgrade sound signals nationwide.

At Beavertail, a propagation anomaly was eventually discovered and the phenomenon exists to this day and yet is still not fully understood. However, the West Passage these days, up to the southern end of Dutch Island, in addition to the fog signal at Beavertail, has one bell buoy and two gong buoys to guide mariners during restricted visibility conditions.

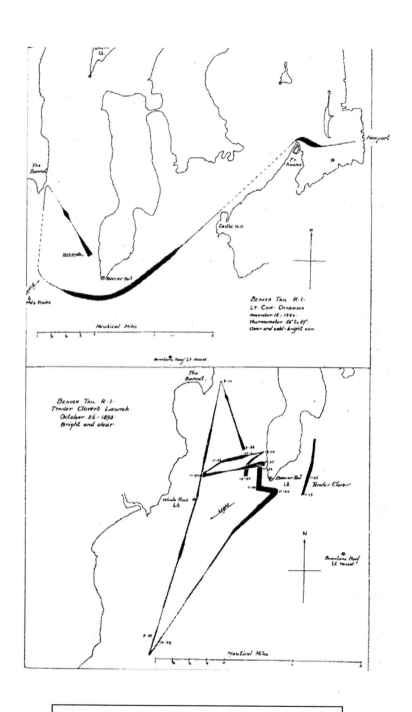

From US Lighthouse Board Report
**Test Tracks Conducted after SS Rhode
Island Disaster**

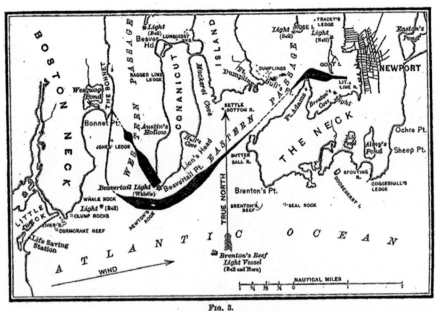

FIG. 3.

This diagram shows the result of observations made by Lieut.-Commander Chadwick, U. S. N., on Beaver Tail fog-signal, Rhode Island, made November 16, 1880, from a sail-boat. Thermometer at beginning, 58° Fahr.; ending, 67°. Wind, moderate, from the west. Weather, clear and cold, with bright sun. Time, beginning at 11.15 A. M.

Diagram From US Lighthouse Board Archives

1890 Sound Signal Tests at Beavertail Indicating Areas where Signal Could be Heard

---

In 1881 more tests were conducted under the direction of *Lieutenant-Commander F.E. Chadwick* of the 3rd Lighthouse District aboard another vessel and again in 1893, with a vessel equipped with atmospheric measuring instruments from the Weather Bureau and their on-board scientific observers. Beavertail Light Station was now equipped with new sound signaling devices, twin 10-inch steam whistles manufactured by "Crosby Steam Gage Company" of Boston, Massachusetts. These were driven by duplicate boilers with water provided by a rain water catch cistern supplemented by a small well. The Lighthouse Board was convinced that the twin whistle system would *"meet every want of navigation"* ignoring the "want" of fresh water needed in the boilers to turn into steam.

Photo's Courtesy of BLMA
Pre 1896, Twin 10 inch Steam Fog Signal Whistles

The new whistles that superceded the *Daboll* whistle could be heard at greater distances than its predecessors or so they believed. But the Lighthouse Board was still bothered by consistent reports from ships about signals emanating from Beavertail being heard, then fading away and again becoming strong.

Many assumptions were drawn from all the years of testing. Volumes of data, hundreds of reports, testimonies to the Congress, scientific papers presented at symposiums and reputations of participants questioned, praised or discounted. There were no definitive conclusions. The various hypothesis presented were confusing and led to more conjecture. Ultimately, mariners were continuingly warned about sound propagation anomalies when navigating in fog while newer, more reliable sound signal equipment, was developed and deployed.

Following the 1881 tests, Beavertail saw more upgrades. New fittings were installed, the fog signal engines were overhauled, a new smokestack replaced the old one and for the first time, an automatic fog signal controller device was tested. The device manufactured by "Crosby Company" made it possible to time the fog signal and saved or used less steam. It was eventually adopted by the Lighthouse Board to be universally used at other light stations.

Siren Signals

At Beavertail, the next generation of siren sound signals was installed. They were first experimented in the late 1860's with steam boilers at the light station in Sandy Hook, New Jersey. At this time sirens were thought to provide a balance of use between whistle and horns, but they gradually became a preference. Beavertail was used to evaluate sirens using air instead of steam. In 1900, a 2nd class siren with duplicate 13 hp oil fueled engines were installed. The tests were not conclusive because of complaints that the signal was *"not sufficiently loud"*. The Lighthouse Board experimented further and added trumpets to the output of the sirens complete with a large acoustical deflector on top of the fog signal house. The trumpets, similar in size and shape of *Daboll's,* were designed with a wide mouth and a narrow throat. Air, under pressure at the throat, was driven through a disk with radial slots and a high revolution revolving plate placed in its throat created the sound.

(It should be noted that the location of the fog signal house was located almost on top of the original 1749 colonial stone foundation which had been covered over with fill many years before. The fog signal house or building contained a coal bin in addition to the fog signal plus the engines that developed either steam or compressed air to operate the fog signals being tested or in operational use.)

Records show that siren modifications continued from 1900 to 1905 that included changing from a vane type siren to a conical device and upgrading from 2nd class sirens to the larger 1st class type. The configuration was comprised of parallel system which provided both redundancy to protect against a single failure and when combined into a louder signal. By 1905 compressed air had replaced steam power with its demands of boilers and water supplies. Oil (diesel) fueled engines had also gained popularity for efficiency, reliability and safety and begun to replace the older coal fired boiler systems. Electricity was the next logical improvement to run pumps, compress air and turn rotary equipment such as sirens; but the distribution infrastructure took time to route the power lines to many of the remote light stations.

An undated photograph of Beavertail Light Station also shows a large ground level rotary siren at the base of the granite light tower. It was installed sometime after 1900 since the photograph shows the white upper half of the granite tower painted that year.

The 9 November, 1906 issue of the Newport Daily News a photo shows a "Water Gathering Field" with 2 long sheds fitted with gutters and leaders which must have fed the cisterns, hence providing catchment water for the steam operated fog signal. Another early undated photograph (below) indicates a long (150-200 x 40 ft) sloping roof rain collection structure above the cistern field.

Photo from USCG Archives
Undated Photo (possibly 1921) Indicating Water Cistern Gathering Sheds and Fog Signal Building Located on 1749 Foundation Ruin

There is some confusion regarding the exact date that Beavertail's steam fog signals were no longer used operationally or for tests. The 1921 Corps of Engineers drawing below clearly show the water system cistern catchment sheds still in place and coal bins located next to the fog signal building.

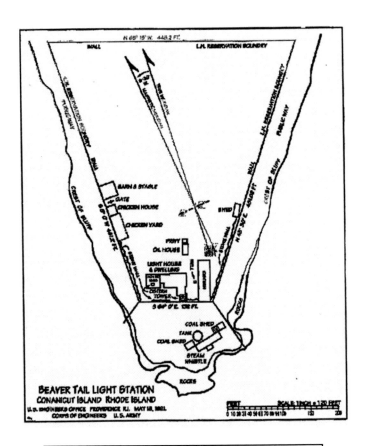

1938 The Great Hurricane

It was the Great Hurricane of 1938 that changed much at Beavertail. The storm literally carried away most of the fog signal building located on the old 1749 original lighthouse foundation. The sea demolished everything. Four feet of water entered the Keeper's and Assistant Keeper's 1st floor dwellings. The basements filled with saltwater and wreckage stood at the site of the fog signal building. The 1749 stone foundation, forgotten for over 80 years, was now exposed. The following year, the U.S. Coast Guard took responsibility of the Beavertail Light Station from the U.S. Lighthouse Service.

It was also the era where diaphone fog signals became popular replacing sirens. In 1939 a new brick fog signal building was constructed next to the granite light tower. It was equipped with dual oil compressor engines, twin compressed air reservoirs and two diaphones. The trumpet portions of the diaphones protruded through the south facing wall of the new building and the rear portions remained inside the building where they were protected from the weather elements. A secondary benefit was that the sound inside the building was slightly muted when men had to attend to duties while the fog signal was operative.

Diaphones emitted a two tone signal, one at a high frequency and the other at a lower frequency. The lower tone was often called the 'grunt' and the diaphone was designed to prolong the lower frequency sound because it carried at greater distance in air than the higher frequency tone. The two tones were accomplished by piston valves controlling the amount of air. As the valve slowed down, its action created a tone of much lower frequency. At times, mariners could only hear the full steady "grunt" low tone when the high tone was masked by other sounds; or the vessel was at a great enough distance from the emitted signal that the higher tone would be inaudible. Two or three different types of diaphones were in place nationwide. At Beavertail, the "Type F" diaphones in use were designed by the "Diaphone Signal Company" of Canada and built by "Deck Brothers - Precision Machinists" of Buffalo, New York.

It was not until well after WW II that the diaphone signal at Beavertail was discontinued. Siren experimentation continued as evidenced by installation reports in April 1962 that a siren compressor was replaced by a "Worthington" 7 ¼ x 7 ¼ unit driven by a 20 hp GM diesel.

Twenty years after WW II, automation of lighthouses had begun in earnest throughout the United States and by 1972 Coast Guard personnel were being reassigned to other duties. The fog signal building with its compressor engines and diaphones was now obsolete being replaced by automatic electronic tone generators. The old equipment was removed, except the overhead compressed air

126

tanks. The diaphone horn holes were sealed and the building abandoned. The building is presently occupied by the Rhode Island Department of Environmental Management, used as a small aquarium and a center for conducting visitor seaside naturalist programs.

Photo Courtesy BLMA
Fog Signal Building with Twin Diaphone Horns

Photo by Author
FA 232 Fog Signal

The replacement electronic fog signal unit was installed on top of the 1747 lighthouse foundation which bore a concrete cap. *(The cap was poured during World War II by the RI National Guard and used as base for observation equipment and a gun emplacement.)* Screened wire fencing similar to vertical wings were extended past the top of the cap on each side to discourage vandals and to protect the signal equipment. In addition, an automatic fog sensor device was installed inside the equipment control shed attached to the granite light tower. A small rectangular window in the shed allowed the strobe light of the sensor to flash seaward and if fog was present, a reflected signal back to the sensor was detected and measured. If a signal-returned measurement was lower than the set threshold of the detector, fog was present and the electronic fog signal was activated. For redundancy, a secondary fog signal was incorporated into the unit that operated at reduced power.

Sometime in the early 1990's the Coast Guard removed the fog horn signal from the 1749 foundation cap and installed a newer model "FA/232", 390 hz, 122 db loud horn manufactured by "Automatic Power Incorporated" to a location closer to the perimeter road and nearer to the granite light tower. The fog signal also contains dual true tone 300 hz resonator type diaphragms, acoustically coupled to electronically driven steel vibrators. This signal was enclosed completely with a rectangular wire mesh security fence and continued to be controlled by the strobe light sensor. Although the fog sensor malfunctioned often, the reliability of the fog signal was outstanding.

During the late summer of 2000, due to a malfunction caused by a direct lightning strike, the fog horn signal's controller inadvertently had activated the horn. The signal retained its programmed schedule of emitting a 3 second blast every 30 seconds, 24 hours a day, 7 days a week for the next three months. The Coast Guard, unable to find repair parts and in the interests of maritime safety, elected to allow the signal to operate rather than disabling the navigation aid.

Often, one hears of a story where individuals no longer heed or hear a constant irritant noise. This was borne out with the faulty continuous sounding fog signal. When custodian *Richard Shutt*

128

living in the Keeper's house 75 ft away from the signal, was asked why the Coast Guard did not fix that "noise", his reply was "what noise?". Likewise, the docents in the adjacent museum of the Assistant Keeper's house and the DEM naturalists in the old fog signal building readily adapted to the loud signal. After a few hours

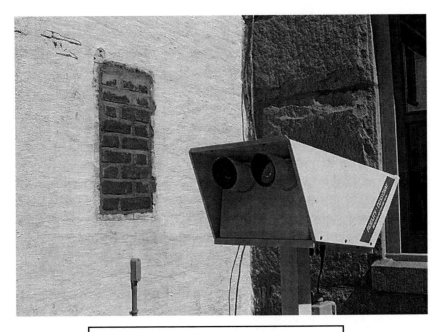

Photo by Author
Model VM 100 Particle Fog Sensor
and bricked up opening of previous
internally located sensor

on duty, they all totally ignored the 30 second interruption.
In 2006, the unreliable strobe light sensor inside the control shed was deactivated primarily because of unavailability of repair parts. A new atmospheric particle sensor ("Fidelity Model VM-100") was installed on the ground, outside the control shed. The new high accuracy sensor is microprocessor controlled with a xenon flash lamp and indicates by a digital readout the actual distance from the sensor to the detected fog.

Chapter 6

Charts, Light Characteristics and Pilots

While lighthouses, along with their enchanting picturesque locations hold the attention of the public, we, from time to time, forget how the user of these sentinels of the sea, the "navigator", applied his visual sightings to determine his location. The master of the ship needed an accurate position of his vessel when making a land fall or transiting along the coast. The ship's known position at any given time was paramount for the vessel's safe passage. Particularly at night, the accurate bearing and the distance from a light house provided a "position fix" on a chart. That position marked a point in time and a geographical assurance that the vessel was on a secure course. Visual sighting of lights allowed the navigator to pilot his vessel by confirming or correcting his dead reckoning plots from the light's range and bearing.

As the vessel proceeded on its projected course, the position fix was advanced as a function of time and estimated speed of the vessel. At any given point in time, the navigator could take a second, third or a series of bearings on the lighthouse and mathematically or by the use of navigation tables determine the new position. Estimated time of arrival or "ETA" to a new location was always based upon the last "position fix". "Position fixes" and ETA's were noted on track charts with a line drawn from one point to another. Where the position fix deviated from the previous ETA because of speed, wind direction and drift, course corrections were made or in the case of a sailing vessel, a new "tack" was executed to bring the vessel back on the course line.

Obviously, the accuracy of the charts and the information on them played an enormous role in the safe navigation of vessels along the coast lines and into harbors.

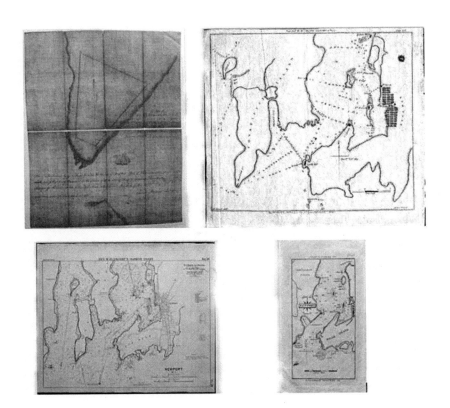

Early Charts of Beavertail Point and the Entrance to Narragansett Bay

Although Beavertail Light, at its very early existence, was the single most important navigation aid in Rhode Island. Its use by mariners was only as good as the accuracy of the charts at hand. Cartography was crude as were the instruments used to determine coordinates. Modern cartographers are amazed at the navigation accuracy that was achieved in the 17th and 18th centuries with charts of Narragansett Bay. Minimum features with insufficient details, were only available to ship captains. The charts evolved over two centuries as more terrain and bottom details were plotted.

Charts were frequently corrected and updated, and while Beavertail Light remained on its geographical location for more than 250 years, its light characteristics changed from time to time. This was more frequently done after 1850 as other lighthouses became operational in the vicinity. It was necessary for the navigator to correctly identify a lighthouse by either its light characteristic at night or by its physical shape and markings during daylight. From the sea, approaching Narragansett Bay via Rhode Island Sound, various lights were visible. On a clear night, the beams cast from lighthouses could be seen for many miles. Entering Rhode Island Sound within a sector of 20 miles to the west, north and east, the light or the "loom" of the light above the horizon from three, four or five lighthouses could be visible in addition to 3 lightships.

(Block Island SE Light, Block Island Sandy Point North Light, Point Judith Light, Beavertail Point Light, Martha's Vineyard Gay Head Light, Cuttyhunk SW Point Light and Sakonnet Point Light)

("Brenton Reef Lightship", "Hens & Chickens Lightship" (1866-1954) and "Vineyard Sound Lightship" (1844-1954). In 1954 both "Hens and Chickens" and "Vineyard Sound" lightships were replaced by "Buzzards Bay Lightship (1954-1961) and later by the "Buzzards Bay" tower.)

Different characteristics of lighthouses and lightships were necessary to distinguish one light from another.

As early as 1784, rotating reflector lamps were developed driven by clock type mechanisms to give a lighthouse its own chrematistics rather than just shining a constant light. By careful assignment of characteristics of each lighthouse or lightship, such as its on-off sequence, fixed, rotating, occulting, color and range, the navigator was given much added recognition information and the safety of the vessel was measurably improved.

Positive identification was achieved by providing a unique light characteristic to each light in view of the navigator and the uniqueness had to be different enough from any other light to prevent confusion. The characteristics included both the duration of the light, the time when it was on plus the interval between light and dark. This characteristic was always specified on charts and "light lists". Since timing of the characteristics was measured in seconds, it was not uncommon to have a stop watch on the bridge of a ship to be used to time the light and dark intervals and read each light characteristic to identify one from the other. The accuracy of the stopwatch provided precise confirmation as to the lights identity

132

from which he could then take a visual bearing enabling him to plot his position and/or correct his course on the chart. So important was timing that lighthouse inspectors arrived with calibrated stop watches to verify accuracy.

The charts specified each specific light as either "F" (fixed uninterrupted), "FL" (flashing), "LFl"(long flashing), "Q" (Quick flashing) or "Iso" (Isophase, equal intervals of light and dark) and the repetitive frequentness of the flash. To further provide identification, the colors of red, white and green and their durations are also used.

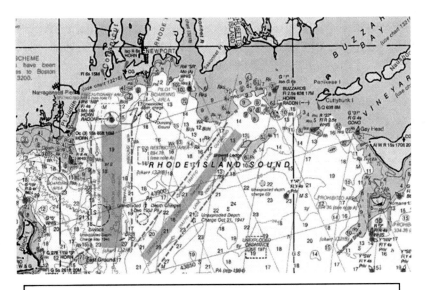

NOAA Chart 13218 - Approaches to Narragansett Bay

A word or two about the height of lighthouses here may clarify some misunderstanding and erroneous specifications of any given lighthouse. The range of a light is a function of the height of the light above the water and the height of the observer out at sea. Navigators use the first sight of the light from a lighthouse to confirm a bearing reference and secondly as a range estimate of the distance from the light itself. The published range of a light from the chart or the annual USCG light list was critical to establishing his position. That first sighting in conjunction with a bearing provided a highly reliable position fix.

Much confusion lies as to what reference point the height of the light is actually measured. For example, at sea level, a person 6 ft. high can see the horizon 3.3 statute miles away. Even the Coast Guard's method is not constant, although they now use the visible physical height of the structure enclosing the light rather than the height of the light source itself. This physical height as a daytime reference is most useful when the navigator uses a "statimeter", a navigation instrument that measures distance of an object when the observed height is known. He also has available to him various angular tables whereby taking vertical angle measurements by a sextant of the height of the lighthouse and knowing its stated height, the range of the light may be calculated.

Light Characteristics

As navigation aids improved and new aids established, a perplexing problem sometimes confronted the navigator. The light characteristic they knew and relied on changed and no longer was the friendly light a welcome beacon. Communications which told of changes were slow, sometimes taking months to document. In later years, changes were broadcast by radio using various modes such as teletype, voice, fax and digital means. While the changes came slowly, as soon as they took place, it was necessary to update charts and sailing directions. The Coast Guard issued monthly "Notices to Mariners" advising proposed changes in advance and confirming those that were implemented. But the responsibility remained with the navigator to note the change and correct his charts at the proper time when the change was officially made. Chart revisions followed showing all the corrections and changes requiring purchase of complete chart portfolios to replace out dated charts.

The following table describes and compares light characteristics of those approach lights. A sample taken from two charts 56 years apart indicates the progressive variations of these prominent navigation aids, all due to additional aids deployed as shipping increased and navigation safety mandated.

NOAA Chart 13218 Dated 1997 US Coast & Geodetic (Italics) Chart #1210 Dated1941	Characteristic (present)	Height above mean high water	Visibility (nautical miles)
Block Island SE Light	Flashing Green every 5 sec *Flashing Green every 3 sec*	261 *210*	20 *21*
Block Island Sandy Point North Light	Flashing White every 5 sec *Group Occulting 3 every 13 sec*	58 *58*	14 *13*
Point Judith	Group Occulting White 3 eclipses every.15 sec. *Fixed White*	65 *65*	16 *14*
Beavertail Point Light	Flashing White every 6 sec *Group Flashing 2 every15 sec*	64 *64*	15 *14*
Sakonnet Point Light	Flashing White every 6 sec with Red sector 195-350 degrees *Fixed White Alternating Green with Flashing Red 3 every 60 sec*	58 *58*	7 *14*
Martha's Vineyard Gay Head Light	Alternating White and Red every. 15 sec *Green Flashing (3) White and Red every 40 sec*	170 *170*	24 *19*
Cuttyhunk SW Point Light	Quick Flashing White *Fixed White*	63 *61*	8 *13*
Brenton Reef Lightship	*Occulting every 4 sec*		*13*
Hens & Chicken Lightship	*Occulting every 4 sec*		*14*
Vineyard Sound Lightship	*Occulting every 10 sec*		*14*

Light Characteristics Approaching Rhode Island Sound Noted from Two Different Charts Issued 56 Years Apart
(Not listed above are the associated fog signals or radio beacons)

Both Beavertail Light and the adjacent Brenton Reef Lightship went through many changes of light characteristics over their 257 year history. For example, Beavertail at various times in addition to showing a white and flashing white light, showed a fixed green, fixed green and white or a flashing green light. The color green was chosen to signify to the navigator that Beavertail Point was to be kept to his "port" (left) side on approaching from the sea. This was in accordance to the "International and Inland Rules of the Road" and conformed to the navigator's memorized "ditty" of "Red on the Right Returning", which meant keeping red navigation aids to "starboard" (right side) when returning from the seaward direction which conversely meant keeping green markers to port (left side).

During one period at Beavertail, ten (10) Plexiglas green light panels were in place. Two (2) of the panels facing the land mass were blackened out supposedly to keep the light from flashing into resident windows at night.

Colored sectors were also used for information. When the Brenton Reef light tower was dismantled in 1989, a red sector was added to Beavertail Light. The sector, similar to a pie shape if looked from above, warned a vessel proceeding from east to west to see Beavertail as a red light until such time as the vessel cleared the rocks at "Brenton Reef". When that safe transit was made, the light was visible as a white light enabling the navigator to judge when he could turn and enter the East Passage. Conversely, when the vessel was transiting from west to east viewing the white light of Beavertail until the sector turned red, the navigator then knew he was in a danger zone and had to make sure he was far enough to sea to avoid the dangerous reef.

The color appearance was accomplished by covering the lens or the glass lamp enclosure with a green or red plastic filter or green or red tinted glass sheet. The physical construction of the lens also could make the lens appear to flash. The center belly of the lens would incorporate one or more magnifier lenses termed a "bull's eye". When the lens was rotated, the "bull's eye" would project a beam while at the same time the prisms above and below the "bull's eye" continue to appear lighted only with reduced intensity.

Records of when and exactly why light characteristics or fog signals were changed are sketchy, incomplete or nonexistent. The table below lists both light and sound signals and the sources that were found. It should be noted that there is some confusion regarding the type of fog signaling equipment specified. For example, at one time the Lighthouse service classified "trumpets" as "sirens".

DATE AND SOURCE	LH OR LS	CHARACTERISTIC	SOUND SIGNAL
1856 USCG Historic Info. I	LH	3rd Order Fresnel lens Fixed white	
1857 Coast Pilot	LH	Tower 74 ft high Fixed White	
1855 Coast Pilot #1898	LH		Whistle
1879 Coast Pilot	LH	Fixed White	1st Order Daboll Trumpet 6sec blast ev 10 and 50 sec's
1880 Coast Pilot #905C	LH	Fixed White	Whistle
	LS	*2 Fixed White*	*Bell*
1898 Light List	LS	*2 Fixed White Two masts schooner, no bow sprit, black cagework. Hull straw color, black smoke stack and two whistles*	*Bell*
1899 Annual Report	LH	Flashing White 8 flashes at 2 sec, 15 sec dark 4th Order Fresnel lens	
1901 Coast Pilot #2481C	LH	Fixed Green & White	Siren
	LS	*2 Fixed White*	*Whistle*
1901 Coast Pilot 2481C	LH	Fixed Green & White	Siren
1905 Light List	LH	Eight white flashes, interval between flashes nearly 2 sec. interval between groups of flashes 15 sec	1st Class compressed air siren, 4 sec alternate silent intervals of 10 and 50 sec.
	LS	*2 Fixed White*	*Whistle*
1907	LH	4th Order Lens Installed	
1915 353.12-1915	LH	Flashing Green	Siren
	LS	*2 fixed White, 1000 cp each*	*2 Whistles 2 blasts every 30 sec & Submarine Bell*

137

1915 Light List	LH	9,100 cp, Gr FLW, 8 Flashes ev 30 sec, each flash 1.2 sec, 1 eclipses 15.5 sec.	1st Class siren, 2 blasts ev 68 sec.
1920 Light List	LH	9,100 cp, Gp FLW 30 sec, 8 flashes, 1 eclipse 16 sec.	
1930 Newport Daily News	LH	Light increased from 1700 cp to 37,000 cp	
1931 Coast Pilot 353.11-1930	LH	Group Flashing 2 every 15 sec, .03 sec flash eclipse 3.4 sec	Siren 2 blasts every 68 sec
	LS	*Occulting every 4 sec*	*Whistle & Submarine Bell*
1931 Light List	LH	240,000 cp, Gr FlW 15 sec, 2 flashes, eclipse 11 sec.	Siren 1st class air, 2 blasts ev 68 sec
1934 Coast Pilot 1210 3-1934	LH	Green Flashing 2 every 15 sec	Siren
	LS	*Occulting every 4 sec*	*Whistle & Submarine Bell*

The "Submarine Bell" (not to be confused with use for naval submarines) installed on the Brenton lightship was most effective, since sound through water would extend for many miles. While this phenomenon was very useful, it depended on ducting of the sound waves between temperature layers of the sea water to carry great distances. In most cases it worked very well and ships equipped with underwater microphones were no longer at the mercy of not detecting fog signals blown away by strong winds.

Beavertail Light Characteristic Changes

The compilation that follows, collected from available sources, indicates the light characteristic changes that took place over the years at both the Beavertail Light Station and the Brenton Reef Lightship. This listing is not inclusive. Almost all the changes were due to new lights (buoys and light stations) installed nearby or within visual range of each other or removed from service. The changes were made to help the navigator read and identify the specific characteristics of Beavertail Light (BL) and Brenton Reef Lightship (BR) to avoid confusion with other navigation aids in view.

1855
CP1898
BL "Light H", Whistle
WR , "bell"

1860
CP966C
BL "Beavertail Light"
BR "Brenton Reef Light Vessel

1880
CP 1905C
BL FW
Whistle
BR 2 FW, Bell

1899
Annual Lighthouse Board report
Fl W, 8 flashes at 2sec interval and 15 sec dark

1915
353.12-1915
BL "Beaver Tail Light" FLG
Siren
BR "Brenton Reef Light Vessel"
2 FW whistle, "(Submarine Bell Signals" 3-9)"

1930
Newport Daily News 2 Oct 1930
Instead of 8 flashes every 30 secs changed on Tuesday
Light increased from 1700 cp to 37,000 cp

353.11-1930
BL Gp F (2) ev 15 sec, 14 mi
Flash.03 sec, eclipse 3.4 sec, .03 flash, eclipse 11 sec
Siren
BR Occ ev 4 sec 12miWhistle, Submarine Bell Signals 3-9

1931
First Electric Light beacon installed

1934
1210 3-1934
BL Gr FL (2) ev 15 sec, Siren
BR Occ ev 4 sec, 12mi
Whistle, Sub Bell sigs 3-9

1937
BL Gp FL (2) ev 15 sec
Siren
BR Occ ev 4 sec ,12 mi

R Bn
Diaphone

1959
Chart #1210
BR Occ 4 sec 50ft 12 miles
Diaphone RBN 310
60m-10m + 30m-40m

1961
USCG Report 22 Dec
DL Gr FL G ev 15 sec
130,000 cp 1000w 1000 hr
Crouse Hinds Lamp

1963
1210
BL Gp FL G (2) 16sec, 14 mi
Siren
BR , Gp Fl (2) 10 sec ,87 ft
Horn R Bn 292 khz,15mi

1971
BL Gr FL G (2) 15 sec, Horn
BR Gp FL (2) 10 sec, horn 87 ft, 15 mi
R Bn 292 khz

1972
Light station automated

1973
3535-1973
BL Light Gp fl g (2) ev 15 sec   14mi
Horn
BR Gp fl (2) 10sec 87 ft
Horn, R. Bn 292khz

1977
Chart #13218
BL Fl G 5 sec
64 ft 12 miles

1983
Chart #1328
BR Gp Fl (2) 10 sec 87 ft 25 miles

1990
Reed's
BL Fl W 6 sec 15 mi
Horn 30 sec, obscured 175 – 215 degrees
No R Bn

140

1991
USCG
BL Type DCB 24 Plastic Lens Rotating Beacon Installed
Fl 6 sec

1995
BL Fl 6 sec 15mi
Horn, R Bn 310 khz

1998
Eldridge
BL Fl W ev 6 sec
Horn 1 bl ev 30 sec Ht 64 15 mi
No R Bn

2006
Notice to Mariners
BL Fl W ev 9 sec

For Beavertail Light, an interesting oddity took place beginning in 2004. Apparently the drive motor timing mechanism of the DCB -24 rotating beacon began slowing down. Nominal rotation speed since 1990 was a 6 second rotation corresponding to a 6 second flash but slower rotation was noted. Coast Guard personnel attempted, on a number of occasions, to correct the situation but either due to lack of parts or unavailability of a complete replacement of the entire drive motor, the rotation speed slowed even further. By late 2006 the motor speed stabilized at 9 rpm and the Coast Guard issued a "Notice to Mariners" report that Beavertail Light was now classified at a flashing rate of once every 9 seconds.

The Short and the Long of a Light's Range.

Determining the accurate range that a light is distanced from the vessel still remains somewhat of a mysterious mathematical calculation. Navigational charts and "Light Lists" all include the characteristics of the lights plus information as to the light's height above sea level and the distance that the light can be seen, but the published information is probable rather than precise. The prudent navigator must apply corrections available from nautical tables of conversion information to help him determine his accurate position from the light source.

All this sounds fundamental, but in reality, navigators for years have been perplexed by the variables, and in some cases, complex adjustments to parameters as they relate to determining their actual distance from a light. However well armed the navigator is with information from charts and light lists about the unique flash characteristics of a particular light, these adjustments skew his calculations.

Some fixed factors peculiar to each light do determine range and become part of the lights unique signature characteristic. These include the luminous intensity of the light source often identified by candelas, candlepower or lumens (seldom by the wattage or radiance of the bulb), the type of lens such as Fresnel, or parabolic mirror reflector beacon, and of course, the size and type of the light source such as incandescent, arc, short duration high intensity xenon strobe or more modern halogen. In addition to the lights intensity, the other fixed characteristic is the height of the light above sea level. This is where the curvature of the earth plays its important role as the "horizon" and limits light visibility to the observer as a function of distance based on the observer's location on the curved face of the earth.

Another complex phenomenon which occasionally enters the equation is the density of the air that cause light rays to refract or bend resulting in appearance of new image or mirage. When layers of cool air sit over the water, an object such as a lighthouse lying beyond the horizon, light rays from the object will curve down and make the object visible, thereby increasing the range. Depending on where the image is located, either above or below the object will also change its appearance.

For purposes of standardization, almost all charts and light lists add a factor of the height of eye of the observer to every light structure when the *nominal* distance of the light is stated. This factor assumes that the observer's eye is 15 ft above sea level. By adding actual height corrections of both the height of the light and the actual height of the observer from published curvature of the earth tables, the distance to the light can be more accurately calculated when first seen.

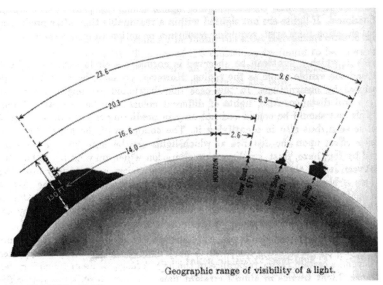

Geographic range of visibility of a light.

Bowditch Tables Vol II

Sounds simple enough, but other factors also come to play which modify the observation. Geographers, physicists, mathematicians and navigators have determined that there are really three different ranges that must be considered. The *"nominal range"* which is a function of the intensity of the light, the *"geographical range"* which is determined by the height of the light and not affected by the intensity although it must be bright enough to be seen at the full distance of its geographical range, and the *"luminous range"* which can be observed extending upward from the light's location.

A further correction is the optical refraction medium as light passes through different atmospheric densities. Add to this the complicated atmospheric condition of temperature inversion which increases range and conversely haze, fog, rain or snow which decreases range. Another small variable is the "dip of the horizon" which, other than use with celestial observations, can be considered inconsequential.

The *luminous range* under good meteorological conditions is longer than the *nominal range* which as a rule exceeds the *geographical range*. The *luminous range* takes no account of the height of the light or the observer and the curvature of the earth. It is derived from the *nominal range* and the current visibility conditions. Under certain conditions, the "loom" of a strong light far exceeds its stated *geographical range*. This is significant because the navigator sees the loom much before the actual light is observed.

Navigators use a "Luminous Range Diagram" to add corrections of meteorological visibility at the time of observation to estimate the range to the light.

As an example: When the *nominal range* is 15 miles as extracted from a light list or chart and the luminous meteorological visibility distance (from the diagram) is 11 miles, the luminous range is 16 miles. Conversely, if the meteorological visibility is down to 2 miles, the *luminous range* is only 5 miles.

The meteorological visibility distance used with the "Luminous Range Diagram" is derived from another table called the *International Visibility Code*. This code is a subjective estimate by the observer of the weather at the time of the observation and ranges from "dense fog" *(code # 0)* to "exceptionally clear" visibility *(code # 9)*.

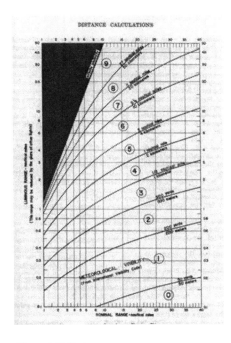

Bowditch Tables Vol II
Bowditch Range Graph

In summary…….. never bet on the exact range of any particular light, but if you're the navigator and its range is important to your safe passage, it is best to do all the arithmetic.

Coast Pilots

Coast Pilots are books that provide sailing directions and information about navigation aids in various geographical areas. They began as accumulation of notes provide by masters and navigators who had transited the area and were passing information to others to help those with less familiarity to make safe passage and enter a harbor The notes and writing were continually updated as new information was found and they gradually transformed into "Coast Pilots". Coast Pilots published by government agencies worldwide are available for almost any coast in the world and between their covers are details as to hazards, navigation aids, available services in a port and sailing directions from one port to another.

In 1796, *Edmund Blunt*, a Newburyport, Massachusetts businessman, published his first edition of the "American Coast Pilot" from the notations of a New England sea *Captain Lawrence Furlong*. *Blunt*'s editions unbelievably covered the entire east coast of the United States plus islands in the Caribbean Sea and extended down the east coast of South America. Some of his notations were collections of data from early Spanish and Portuguese explorers. While there were no charts included in the Coast Pilot, the publication included written sailing directions, navigation landmarks and latitudes and longitudes of principle harbors, including Newport along with astronomical tide tables. *Blunt's* Coast Pilot, supplemented with the crude charts were the "bibles" used by the navigators.

A hundred years later, the "*Stebbins Coast Pilot*" outlined specific point to point Narragansett Bay sailing directions for mariners and outlined the dangers of both underwater rocks and shoals. The *Stebbins* pilot book followed the "*George W. Eldridge Tide and Pilot Book*" of 1870. This was the first of the famous "Eldridge Coast Pilots" updated each year. Another reference with sailing directions was published by *John Bliss*. *Bliss* was a maker of nautical instruments and was most noted for manufacturing a "taffrail log" a device which measured the distance a vessel traveled. He died in 1857 but the ed until 1957. Over the years, the U.S. Coast Guard expanded and incorporated additional details for use by the navigator and annually publishes corrected light lists (characteristics of lighthouses and buoys) along the three coasts of the United States. These publications are now distributed by "NOAA", the National Ocean and Atmospheric Administration, and most every sea going vessel includes them in the navigator's library.

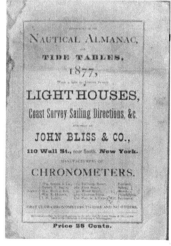

John Bliss 1877 Publication Covering Sailing Directions, Tide Tables, Lighthouse Locations and Light Characteristics.

Radio Beacons

When radio transmission came into being, it did not take long to recognize that a transmitted signal could accurately be detected by use of a directional antenna fixed to a receiver tuned to the frequency of the

146

emitted radio signal. Major lighthouses and all lightships were equipped with radio beacon transmitters. "Radio Direction Finding' (RDF) was the navigator's solution when in fog or with obscured visibility. The navigator would adjust his radio receiver antenna for a "null" or minimum signal from the transmitted station and use the relative bearing of the "null" to adjust his course to steer for the signal. The "null" measurement, rather than the maximum signal strength measurement, was much more accurate. Both detected audio and signal strength measurements were used. The human ear could detect a minimum discernable signal than a loud one and if a meter on the radio receiver was used, the dip of the meter needle at the null point was easily read.

Radio transmitter beacons operated at low frequencies (275-335 khz) continuously just below the AM commercial radio band. Groups of beacons, each with a distinct Morse code location identifier separated by only a few kilohertz, would be sequentially transmitted. The receiving ship would then wait until the signal he was seeking came on the air and then he would adjust his antenna to seek the "null" in the signal. If he missed the transmission or was not confident of the "null" reading, he would then wait for the sequential beacon repetition for another reading.

At the entrance to Narragansett Bay, the Pt Judith Light Station, the Brenton Reef Lightship and later the "Texas Tower" replacement were equipped with RDF transmitters. Pt Judith Light Station emitted the Morse code signal "P" (.--.) and Brenton Reef Lightship the code signal "B" (- ...) operated on 292 kilocycles. When the "Texas Tower" was removed, the radio beacon was transferred to Beavertail Point and the RDF antenna was located just behind the lighthouse structures. It retained the 'B" Morse code signal operated on 310 kilocyles (khz) until that too was replaced by new Narragansett Bay Entrance Buoy "NB' located 4 miles due south of Beavertail. The antenna still stands behind the Beavertail Keeper's house and is used periodically by ham radio operators on special weekend occasions commemorating lighthouses.

Buoy "NB" is equipped with a "RACON" (radar beacon) transmitter which responds with an image on a ship's radar screen when illuminated by the ships radar pulse operating on the same frequency.

There are no active marine RDF stations remaining in Narragansett Bay.

Marine Radio Communication

Wireless communications between shore and ship stations began in the early 1900's, primarily through the use of "Morse Code" by "spark gap" transmitters. The technology developed rapidly and by 1906 most large ships were fitted with transmitting and receiving equipment. Also an abundance of shore stations were broadcasting safety and weather information. 1906 was also the year that "SOS" was adopted at the "Berlin Radiotelegraphic Convention" as the official international standard for distress calls. In Rhode Island, the coastal wireless station communicating with ships was the *"Massie Wireless Station"* located at Pt Judith. *Walter Massie,* a contemporary of *Marconi,* built the station in 1907. It was used for communication with steamboats transiting between New York and New England. The original "spark gap" station operating on 300-350 khz was saved from destruction and moved in its entirety to the "New England Wireless and Steam Museum" in East Greenwich, RI and is the worlds oldest working wireless station in existence.

Telegraphy evolved into telephony (voice) and various modes of communication were adapted for ship to shore and ship to ship use. In the high frequency bands (HF) and very high frequency bands (VHF) specific channels are designated for marine use covering voice and digital data information including weather forecasts of coastal and high seas conditions worldwide.

Piloting and Pilots on Narragansett Bay

(Including notes from an unpublished manuscript "Piloting on Narragansett Bay 2004 by Edward Spinney)

An ancient and practical practice of bringing a vessel safely into a strange harbor where charts and navigation aids, such as lighthouses

148

were non existent, was by the practice of soundings. This was usually a weighted or leaded line marked in intervals of fathoms (6 feet to a fathom) thrown in front of the vessel by a crew member or by prodding the bottom with long marked poles. Both methods were time consuming and tedious, and at times a ship struck a rock or shoal while the line was being retrieved.

The entrance to Narragansett Bay provided its own traps to the unsuspecting vessel and even during daylight hours, there were treacherous rocks to avoid. The lighthouse at Beavertail provided a valuable reference and a variable bearing line as the vessel moved into the Bay, but provided little assurance unless other marks could be used to provided a cross bearing "fix" as to the vessels actual position. One method evolved advancing the single bearing by the vessel's estimated speed and taking a second bearing at a given time. Even with this navigational "fix", the position was an estimate only and the unknowns below the water were a constant worry. Here is where local knowledge of the bottom, tides and currents was worth the money paid.

The use of "local knowledge" always was preferred. This meant placing aboard a person, the "Pilot", who was familiar with the location of rocks, shoals and channels. The pilot would guide the ship master and helmsman to steer the vessel and avoid these underwater hazards which he learned existed from first hand experience. It was common practice to seek out a local indigenous native or fisherman and engage him to guide the vessel. In return, ship owners and captains were willing to pay handsome fees for safe guidance into port.

"Brenton Reef", a long rock shoal running southwest from Brenton Point, was notorious and along its side, south by east, stood "Seal Ledge", totally underwater waiting for any ship with a draft over nineteen (19) ft. "Newton Rock", off the southern tip of Beavertail Point where the lighthouse was located, lay offshore less than one half (1/2) mile from the point. Only when there was a high swell did it provide an advance warning of its danger. Over on the East Passage side another hidden danger was "Butter Ball Rock". While always awash, its proximity to Castle Hill with the deepest water in the bay, one hundred eighty four (184 ft), gave navigators a false sense of security. As a ship ventured further up the Bay before entering Newport Harbor, other obstructions had to be heeded. Off Conanicut Island lay "Kettle Bottom Rock" near the entrance of "Mackerel Cove" and the infamous "Dumplings", a series of small rocky islands off "Bull Point" were treacherous claws waiting for the unwary navigator. Further up were the shoals around "Rose" and "Dyer" Islands, the "Bishop Rock Shoals" and "Mitchell Rocks". The locations of all these hazards were the valuable knowledge of the local fishermen who saw piloting as a means to supplement their income.

There is no information how pilots were engaged during the late 18th century. Perhaps the ship owners or those who manned the "Watch House" at Beavertail would alert a fisherman to row or sail out and meet an incoming vessel. Block Island residents had an earlier opportunity to sight incoming vessels and often were able to get out to an incoming vessel offering services as a pilot. As shipping increased, local seaman saw the financial opportunity which developed into a very lucrative pastime supplementing their fishing income. There were no rules or regulations for piloting and it was the convention of ship masters that the pilot who "first came was the first engaged".

For over one hundred (100) years, pilots in Narragansett Bay were not organized. Early piloting was looked upon not as a profession but as a sideline business. Pilots were local fisherman or captains of coastal vessels who knew where the rocks, shoals and natural channels lay. Piloting services were unregulated, unorganized and operated as a quasi- business. Even in later years it was a freelance operation where any person could enter and offer services.

The business of actually getting the job to pilot a ship was usually a competitive race by local entrepreneurs to be the first to row or sail out to an incoming vessel. Often it was two rowers per "pulling boat" setting out from the Jamestown shore or Newport's inner harbor in both good and bad weather. Once reaching the incoming vessel, the pilot had to convince the Captain he was a qualified pilot and negotiate a fee. The pulling boat was then towed by the

150

incoming vessel. For vessels leaving Narragansett Bay, few took on a pilot, believing that they now knew the courses to steer and where the hazards lay. With open water in view, they were more comfortable in taking bearings and piloting the vessel.

In later years there was serious feuding between Block Island pilots and those on the mainland which eventually brought about Rhode Island piloting regulations. These piloting laws were not enacted by the Rhode Island General Assembly until 1867. Regulations included individual licensing by rigid qualification requirements and designation of geographical locations where a pilot could be expected to be stationed in order to board a ship. Fees were also established based on a formula defining the vessel to be piloting. It was only in later years that international signal flags or lights at night, denoting the ship was requesting a pilot, were flown from a yard arm or mast of the vessel. The striped blue and yellow international code flag "G" (George) became the "request for a pilot" when flown at the yard arm. After the pilot was on board, the vessel flew the red and white code flag "H" (How) signifying that a pilot was on board and the ship was under his guidance.

The work was both hard and sometimes hazardous since weather played a significant role. Narragansett Bay, with an ebbing tide against the strong prevailing southwest breeze, results in a rough chop mixed with rolling seas. Rowing two to five miles to intercept a vessel in these conditions is only for the very few. During winter, the famous "Northeaster" is experienced that makes the situation more precarious and dangerous. This excerpt from the Newport Daily News, January 10 1903, starkly reflects the risks.

> *This morning about 7 o'clock Captain C.H. King sighted a large tramp steamer flying her jack for a pilot. He hurried across the island (Conanicut) with his brother, Andrew T. King, and secured a rowboat at the ferry, started to row to the steamer. It was rough and cold work and the boat shipped considerable water, and the two men were soon completely cased in ice where the spray struck them and froze. They were fortunate enough, while off Castle hill, to be taken in tow by a Newport auxiliary sloop, and a mile and a*

half southwest of the lightship boarded the steamer, which
was an English tramp with about 5,000 tons of Welsh coal
for Providence. She was 22 days out from England and was
well covered with ice.

Today, Narragansett Bay pilots are equipped with computer charting (mapping) programs coupled to their personal GPS navigation instruments and hand held VHF marine radios which they carry aboard the vessels to be piloted. They are ferried to and off the vessels by fast sea-going motor boats operated by the "North East Pilots Association". Although experienced and supplemented with electronic aids, they also rely on lights, buoys and visual bearings to direct the ship safely into the channels and finally to harbor. The safety record of piloted vessels in Narragansett Bay is impressive although they do include a few mishaps and groundings. It is compulsory that a Pilot be aboard foreign and U.S. flagged vessels including naval ships and tugboats. Only those that have frequented bay waters often are exempt from piloting regulations as are the many private recreational and fishing boats.

There is an established boarding zone about 1.5 miles east of the Narragansett Bay Entrance Buoy "NB" south of Beavertail Point. Ships are directed to wait there for pilots to board. In most cases, the entering vessel or their local agent has contacted the "North East Pilots Association" by radio or telephone and advised them of their ETA. Based on this information, the pilot vessel plans on meeting and boarding the pilot onto the ship at that time within the prescribed boarding zone.

It is not uncommon to witness a pilot leaving a vessel departing Narragansett Bay when the vessel comes abeam of Beavertail Point. He departs the vessel either by a hull hatch/door near the waterline or by ladder onto the pilot boat which has maneuvered alongside.

Chapter 7

Shipwrecks and Groundings

The fundamental purpose of Beavertail Light is to save lives and property by preventing shipwrecks. How many it saved and how many wrecks were prevented will never be known. Thousands of vessels, both large and small, over the past 250 years have used the light; yet from time to time shipwrecks happened and life and property were lost. Narragansett Bay certainly had its share of shipwrecks and still experiences a few. However, with modern navigation aids the numbers have decreased dramatically. The discussion below provides some insight about earlier wrecks in the vicinity of Beavertail and, hopefully, helps the reader appreciate the results of those disasters.

To accurately estimate the total number of shipwrecks in and around Narragansett Bay is an impossible task. The coastline along the ocean and in Narragansett Bay exceeds 300 miles which is significant for the state that is only forty three (43) by twenty seven (27) miles in length and width. Even more difficult, is the estimation of how many vessels grounded or were destroyed prior to the light established at Beavertail. Records were not kept by the Colonial Government and since all vessels of that time were owned by merchants or ship masters, only family records would show or make reference to a loss. Furthermore, remains of wreckage, particularly wooden vessels, have long deteriorated and dissolved into the sea.

Most historians and diving enthusiasts agree that Rhode Island has more shipwrecks per square mile than any other state. Some reports claim over 2,000 wrecks, including colonial trading ships, ships of war and luxury passenger vessels from the 19th century, can be found in state waters. A few were abandoned derelicts that ship owners found too expensive to repair or overhaul and let them sink at their moorings. Little is know about the majority of them. Other sources say relatively few wrecks still remain. Reports of shipwrecks that occurred before 1874 are extremely rare. Those of more recent catastrophes are documented, as the U.S. Government and its agencies mandated that wrecks, collisions and loss be reported. It was a Congressional Act passed on 20 June 1874 where masters and owners were required to notify the Collector of Customs at the port of the vessel's documentation of any casualty of life, damage or loss of a vessel.

Over the years a number of private organizations and some individuals have documented details and locations of shipwrecks in and around Narragansett Bay. These organizational groups are made up largely of recreation divers and have provided much information of known wrecks that are accessible, some with related historical information. Notably, the "Hunting New England Shipwrecks" by *Dave Clancy* and his "Shipwrecks of Rhode Island" are sources which provide valuable data for both historians and divers wishing to explore wrecks. The "New England Shipwreck Directory" by *Dan Berg* supplements *Clancy's* information. On Conanicut Island, the "Jamestown Historical Society" has catalogued a few photos and the "Newport Historical Society" does contain early records of some shipwrecks.

Rhode Island's underwater archaeology program is administered by the "Rhode Island Historical Preservation and Heritage Commission" located in the old State House. The Commission maintains files on the location and condition of shipwrecks in Rhode Island waters and issues permits for underwater study.

Notably, the U.S. Coast Guard and the U.S. Customs Service, a department of the Treasury, along with the National Archives all contain information of shipwrecks. These are found in various "Record Groups". In 1907, when a Life Saving District was located in Wakefield, Rhode Island, a 12 page letter report listing "Wrecks and Casualties of Rhode Island and Fishers Island from 1752-1907" was filed but could not be found.

"List of Wrecks and Casualties, Coast of Rhode Island and Fisher's Island, 1752-1907." Includes date, rig, names of vessels, locality, type of casualty. (Letter dated March 11, 1907, from the Superintendent, Third Life-Saving District, Wakefield, Rhode Island, 12 pages, electrostats.

Most probably few wrecks actually remain due to rapid deterioration and breaking apart in storms. Availability of reliable records and actual findings of wrecks can only approximate the number of ships remains under water. For every shipwreck, there were probably hundreds of encounters where a vessel has gone aground, experienced damage, lost cargo or sustained injuries to its crew. The actual shipwrecks are positive proof of dangers from the sea. Wrecks forever have a mysterious attraction for exploration and intrigue. Rhode Island wrecks are popular dive locations and they are scattered from Block Island to the head of Narragansett Bay in the silt of the Providence River. The waters of the lower Bay contain much of the share of Rhode Island wrecks.

The actual cause of the thousands of wrecks and the thousands more of groundings can only be hypothesized. Inadequate, faulty or non existent navigation aids, including charts and sailing directions, are obvious causes for those early years. Weather contributed to both loss of life and property, but after 1800, when navigation aids were established, the cause was mostly weather and navigation errors.

Seamanship and local knowledge played a major role in completing a safe passage and those that erred or had limited knowledge ended up on the rocks When the spring and summer fog settled in, only soundings by a crew member in the bow of the ship, using a "lead line", provided some help to the navigator to keep the vessel with sufficient water under its keel as the vessel proceeded along its track. The lead line was of no help when the ship encountered abrupt underwater rock formations. Lighthouses, buoys (if existing) and land marks were invisible in fog. The other danger was tide, current, rain or snow with driving winds coupled with stormy weather which could drive a sailing vessel onto a lee shore.

As covered in Chapter 1, the hazards when entering Narragansett Bay were many but "Brenton Reef" on the East Passage and "Whale Rock" in the West Passage were the most notorious. Both locations were marked with navigation aids in the 19th century. A light ship, identified as "Brenton Reef" (one of a succession of four), was placed on station between Beavertail Light and the notorious reef in 1853 (see Chapter 8). In the west passage, southwest of Beavertail

Light, a lighthouse was constructed in 1882 on top of Whale Rock named because its shape resembled a whale's back. It stood until the Hurricane of 1938 when it was toppled with the loss of its Ass't. Keeper, *Walter Eberle.* All that remained was the round cast iron base. When Whale Rock is awash, its long low shape and the remains of the base resemble the turret of a submarine entering Narragansett Bay. It startles visitors when they first sight it immediately after entering Beavertail State Park.

Captain Cook's "Discover"

One of two very notable wreck sites in the area, separated by 167 years, are the remains of 13 ships of the British Navy scuttled in Newport harbor in July of 1778 as the French fleet approached and the British evacuated Newport. The purpose was to establish an underwater barricade around the entrance of Newport Harbor. One of the ships scuttled was the *"Discover"* (renamed the *"Lord Sandwich"* and refitted as a troop transport) used by the famous explorer *Captain James Cook* during his voyage to the Galapagos and the South Pacific Islands in 1768. This wreck with three others is under examination by the "Rhode Island Marine Archaeology Project" from a grant by the "NOAA Office of Ocean Exploration" and support from the "Rhode Island Sea Grant Program".

U-853 Submarine

The other wreck lies on the ocean floor due south of Beavertail Light. Three days before Germany officially surrendered in World War II on May 8' 1945, the *"U-853"*, a German submarine, torpedoed and sank the American flagged collier *"Black Point"* three (3) miles off Pt. Judith in view of Beavertail Light. Twelve (12) crew members lost their lives. On the following day, the U.S. Navy and U.S. Coast Guard depth charged the submarine, sinking the U-Boat with all hands aboard. Unfortunately, the U-853 never received the broadcast radio message on May 4, 1945 from its Submarine Command and Chief of the German Navy *Admiral Karl Doenitz"* to cease wartime hostility operations and return to their base. Its legacy remains as "the last German U-Boat sunk in World War II" which also sank the last merchant vessel in the Atlantic.

156

Unauthorized divers, sometime in 1946 or 1947, removed the deck mounted gun and cut off the two propellers. The gun was later found in a wooded lot in New Jersey and the two propellers were found on the property of the "Inn at Castle Hill in Newport".

Under International Law, the propellers are the property of the Republic of Germany and presently are in the custody of the Naval War College Museum in Newport.

Photo by Author
U-853 Propellers
Removed
from Sunken Hull

H.F. Payton

One shipwreck at Beavertail still leaves its visible mark after an incident which took place on 3 March 1859. The coastal schooner *H.F. Payton*, a two masted schooner with a cargo of 140 tons of large architectural granite stones, floundered against the rocks at Beavertail during a severe snowstorm. The ship broke apart and lost its entire cargo (except for a number of valuable chronometer time pieces) along the eastern shore of the peninsula. The vessel, departing from Boston, was on route to Alexandria (Washington DC) via Chesapeake Bay and the Potomac River where the cut stones, many carved with the fleur-de-lis, were destined to be used on a government building project. The 94 ft. *Payton* was built in Bristol, Rhode Island in 1854 and owned by a number of shareholders. Many of the stones, some as large as 8 x 4 x 2 feet, are still visible at low tide among the craggy natural rocks of the shore. *Note: A research paper written by P.J. Perkins details an extensive investigation as to the origin and destination of the stones and the schooner H.F. Payton.*

Steamship Rhode Island

One costly wreck that took place on the evening of November 6, 1880 was directly attributed to the inadequacy of the fog signal at Beavertail Light Station (See Chapter 5). The steamer *Rhode Island*, before it had entered Narragansett Bay in fog, had heard the Beavertail fog signal. The vessel then navigated up the west passage and 1 7/8 of a mile from the light station ran aground and sank on Bonnet Point. The steamer was a total loss, estimated at over $1,000,000. The master, crew and passengers interviewed by a Navy investigator claimed the signal failed because it was not heard. Further investigation determined that at the time of the disaster, the fog signal was operating, heard by other vessels and by officials in Newport. Only through extensive testing by the U.S. Lighthouse Board, it was determined that acoustical dead zones were found in Narragansett Bay and indeed the *Rhode Island* could not have heard the fog signal at the point where it went aground.

The Ballast Stone Mystery

Another mystery is of the vessel that floundered off the east side of Beavertail believed to have been caused during heavy fog sometime in the early 1900's. Beginning in 1939, immediately after the Hurricane of 1938, rectangular blocks of granite similar to paving

stones began appearing along the southern coast of "Hull Cove". "Hull Cove" is situated just north of Beavertail Point. Local residents began collecting the stones and used them to line sidewalks and driveways. In 1950 it was determined they were actually "ballast stones". Stones were fitted inside the bottom of

Photo by Author
Ballast Stones

sailing vessels to maintain stability of the ship to compensate for the heel of the vessel in strong winds. The stones were fixed deep in the bilges of the ship between the ship's members, its keel, ribs and planking. The large bronze rudder gudgeons were found by a local resident of Hull Cove in 1986. Over the years the wooden vessel deteriorated and the ballast stones remained in a heap in about 20 feet of water. After each major storm, the rocks and beaches were combed by the local residents and the stones collected .When the wreck location was found by divers in 1987, methodically the stones were collected and the site disappeared. But the earlier stones washed up by storms are vividly in place lining walks and driveways at many of the shore side homes at "Hull Cove".

Coal Barges

One famous wreck is that of the two coal barges that floundered on "Lucky Strike Rock" on Beavertail Point on 17 October, 1930. The incident involved the Tug *Julia Howe* towing three barges full of anthracite and losing two of them, the *"Howard Sisters"* and the *"Henry Howard"*. Both came ashore and the *Howard Sisters* broke up on the rocks, piling four feet of coal along the shore. There were rumors that the tug hauling the barges was deceived by residents who faked the location and caused the tug and barges to flounder on the rocks. When the word was passed that large quantities of coal were being washed ashore, Jamestown residents with bags, carts, wagons and wheelbarrows pillaged the coal and carted it away into their cellar storerooms to use in the forthcoming winter months. A major disappointment took place when the saltwater-soaked coal began to dry out leaving a stench of putrid 'low tide" in basements and cellars of the homes of the pillagers. The second barge, the *Henry Howard,* while on the rocks, had not broken up and some island residents unsuccessfully attempted to hijack its cargo.

Photo Courtesy of JHS
Scavenging Coal at Beavertail 1930

Photo Courtesy of BLMA
Captain Lawrence on the Rocks at Beavertail

The morning of 8 August, 1980 found the 78 ft. trawler, *Captain Lawrence,* on the rocks at Beavertail after a navigational error that ripped out part of her bottom when she hit "Newton Rock". The dramatic part of this incident was the rescue of two crew members by the Jamestown Fire Department and four others airlifted by a USCG helicopter.

Two men remained aboard trying to salvage the vessel but they too had to be rescued by boat as the vessel began to break up. What remained was salvaged and cut up by local residents for use as fire wood.

Tanker Mobil Light

On 4 September, 1946, after unloading her 100,000 barrels of oil in Providence, the empty tanker *Mobil Light* ran aground less than a mile north of Beavertail Point. Either she mistook Short Point as Beavertail Point and turned right, or inattentiveness by her master caused the grounding. Why the pilot on board left the ship before she was abeam of Beavertail was unexplained. It took two attempts with tugs to get her off the rocks apparently suffering little damage.

The Torpedoing of the USS Capella AK-13

While not associated with disasters around Beavertail Light, one of the most bazaar tales of ship wrecks off Conanicut Island is the incident of the U.S. Navy torpedoing and sinking one of its own ships in the anchorage off Jamestown. During World War II, a motor torpedo boat, "PT-59", stationed in the Melville training basin in Portsmouth (8 miles north of Newport) en route out of Narragansett Bay for training exercises, inadvertently launched a torpedo near Gould Island. The torpedo traveled 6 miles down the Bay, with PT-59 chasing it. It struck and exploded the stern of the anchored 4000 ton ship, the *"USS Capella"* (AK 13). The explosion was heard on Beavertail at the "Harbor Entrance Command Post". Every military complex on Conanicut Island went to a red alert status believing that they were under attack. Fortunately, the Officer of the deck of the *Capella* weighed anchor and with help from "PT-59" beached the vessel aground on Conanicut Island at "Potter's

Cove" before she sank. The following day the hole was temporary shored up, the vessel towed off the beach and escorted to New York for repairs. The Navy censored this event for over 50 years denying the incident ever took place. "PT-59" eventually saw action in the Pacific. "PT-59's" first commander in that theater of war was *Lt. John Kennedy* who had recently lost the "PT-109".

Photo from US Navy Archives
USS Capella AK 13

USS Severn AO-61

The afternoon of February 9' 1968 under clear skies and moderate seas, the U.S. Navy fleet oiler, the *"USS Severn"* loaded with 3,654,000 gallons of black oil, found herself perched on the rocks ("Newton Rock") directly in front of the lighthouse. It appeared as though it were going to enter the lighthouse itself. The cause of this grounding never was fully explained by the Navy. Fortunately, no oil was spilled. The cargo was off-loaded by smaller yard oilers. On the following day at high tide, Navy tugs towed the ship off the rocks. One observer stated the ship was heading south out of Newport when it suddenly turned completely around and ran up on the rocks. The Navy stated the ship was entering Narragansett Bay at the time of the mishap.

The *Severn* had a distinguished service record during WW II in the Pacific as a fresh water carrier and later was assigned to Newport as her home base.

USS Severn AO-61 on the Rocks February 1968

World Prodigy

One of the worse cases of an oil spill occurred on June 23, 1989 when the Greek registered oil tanker *"M/V World Prodigy"* ran aground on Brenton Reef. Its oil spill perplexed the environmentalists and brought to light the requirement of new preparedness techniques and equipment needs. This disaster also demonstrates that even with good navigation aids, good visibility and an experienced crew, the famous Brenton Reef still takes its toll of the unwary. The "*World Prodigy*" had passed abeam of the "Brenton Reef Tower" on one side and Beavertail Lighthouse in plain view on its port bow. The course was clear and direct to steer for Castle Hill light house, keeping the red entrance buoys on the right hand side. The ship's captain, who allegedly had not rested in over 30 hours, was distracted by paperwork and allowed the ship to pass on the wrong side of a buoy just north of Brenton Tower and the vessel impaled itself on the reef. At the Coast Guard hearing, the seaman at the helm of the ship refused to testify and there was no explanation why a pilot was not aboard.

Almost 300,000 gallons of heating oil was spilled. The incoming tide spread the oil into the lower Narragansett Bay and covered over 123 square miles. Marine life was killed, sea birds were coated with the oil, fishing grounds and some beaches, nearing the height of the summer season, were closed for two months. The spill also hit during a peak spawning period affecting eggs and larvae of fish and shellfish. The loss was both an environmental and economical disaster to the State of Rhode Island. The good news was the spill, which was light oil, helped by the warm sun, evaporated relatively rapidly.

Other Shipwrecks and Groundings

Shipwrecks and Groundings Vicinity of Beavertail Light
(Condensed excerpts from Wreckhunter.net & Jamestown Affairs)

Vessel	Type	Ft	Cargo	Date of Loss	Cause & Location	Depth
Minerva	*Brig*		*White salt ,linen*	*12/27/1804*	*Beavertail*	
Traveller	*Schooner*		*Corn*	*04/17/1809*	*Night approach All hands lost Brenton Reef*	

Minerva			Rum,wine rice, powder	12/29/1809	Evening approach 9 crew lost Brenton Reef	
Minerva	Brig Spanish			12/24/1810	Struck reef Brenton Reef	20 ft
Francis	Schooner		Sugar, raisins, salt	12/02/1815	4 crew lost Brenton Reef	
Two Cathrines	Schooner	100 ft	Salt	09/8/1821	Gale Dutch Island	
Maria Caroline			Cotton	11/21/1822	Broke up on rocks Bonnet Shore	
Amaranth	Schooner		Potatoes	12/ /1830	Gale	
J. Palmer				01/04/1840	Turned down offer of pilot. All hands lost. Beavertail	
Chicatabut			Corn	1840	Short Point	
Edward	Brig			1847	Beavertail	
H.F. Payton	Schooner		Granite Block Chronom eters	03/03/1859	Snowstorm Beavertail	
Target	Schooner	388 tons		02/ /1863	Caught in irons, ship stripped on rocks Mackerel Cove	
William James			Granite Blocks	03/ /1871	Grounded Mackerel Cove Kettle Bottom Rocks	
Rhode Island	Side wheel steamer	340 ft	Pass& freight	06/11/1880	Ran up on rocks in fog Off Bonnet Point,	10-30 ft
Bucco	Schooner			06/ /1889	Fog Lions Head	

Addie M. Anderson	4-Masted Schooner	184 ft	Coal	02/15/1889	Submerged rock. ½ mile NE of Whale Rock	50 ft
Lydia Skolfield	Square-rigged ship		Cotton seed oil	04/19/1891	Grounded in fog. Newport, Butter Ball Rock	30 ft
George W. Humphrey	Fishing Steamer			1910	Struck reef. Brenton Reef	25 ft
Cape Fear	Freighter	267 ft	Light	10/29/1920 19 killed	Collision with freighter City of Atlanta. ¼ mile off Newport Neck	180 ft
USS G-1	Sub-marine	161 ft		06/21/1921	Navy depth charge experiment. Off Taylor Point, Jamestown,	100 ft
Llewellyn Howland	Tanker	285 ft	Oil	04/21/1924	Grounded	30 ft
Eugenia	Schooner		Mackerel	06/30/1928	Night passage, Fog, Newton Rock, Total Loss. 1 mile SSE of Brenton	
Howard Sisters	Barge		Coal	10/17/1930	Lucky Strike Rock. Beavertail	
U-853	German Sub	232 ft		05/05/1945 55 killed	Depth charged by US Navy and USCG 12 mi South of Beavertail	130 ft
Mobillight	Tanker		Oil	09/04/1946	Beavertail	

Black Point	Collier	368 ft	Coal	05/05 1955 12 killed	Torpedoed by German sub U-853. 3¾ miles SE of Point Judith,	100 ft
Belleville	Freighter	434. ft		09/24 1957	Grounded in Fog. Just west of Seal Rock	30 ft
USS Severn	Tanker		Oil	02/09/1968	Grounded	
Mt Hope	Tug	118 ft		02/18/1968	Ran Beavertail aground in storm. South of Hope Island	20 ft
Capt Lawrence	Trawler	78 ft	Fish	08/08/1980	Grounded Beavertail	
World Prodigy	Tanker		Oil	06/23/1989	Grounded Brenton Reef	

B.W. Luther, the noted diver and author who documented wrecks scattered around the southern New England coast, has contributed much toward the identification of the shipwrecks in Narragansett Bay. Over many years, he has compiled information and the location of hundreds of vessels and has published charts of these marine disasters. His 1971 chart, "Marine Disasters of Narragansett Bay", includes the names of 272 ships that were lost including those around Beavertail Point and Brenton Reef.

Chapter 8

The Lightships and Light Tower off Beavertail Point

Brenton Reef

The dangerous reef of rocks and shoals called "Brenton Reef" off Brenton Point, Newport has for many centuries concerned seamen and their ships approaching Narragansett Bay. The reefs are located 2 miles due east of Beavertail Lighthouse and extend southwest about ½ mile from the land of Brenton Point. The reefs expose themselves only at very low tide and only when there is a heavy sea or swell. They are the hidden dangers which have taken both life and ships to their graveyard. Although Beavertail Light provided the beacon for navigators to make the initial land approach and marked the southern end of Conanicut Island, the reefs, which lay on the other side of the East Passage to the east of Conanicut Island, remained a hazardous threat to any shipping entering Narragansett Bay.

As shipwrecks and groundings continued on Brenton Reef, it was apparent that in addition to the lighthouse on Beavertail, a prominent navigation aid needed to be placed off the reef extending from Brenton Point. The solution was to strategically place a lightship where an approaching vessel into the East Passage of Narragansett Bay would follow a safe course between Beavertail Point and the anchored lightship, safely away from the underwater rocks of Brenton Reef.

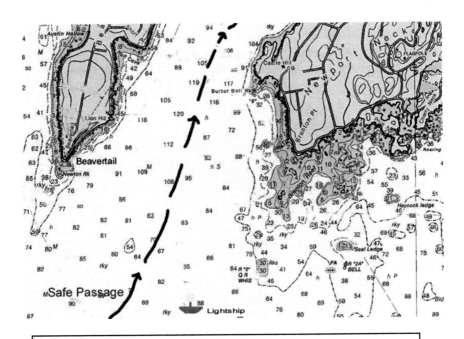

Safe Passage Between Beavertail Point and the Lightship

It was in 1851 that appropriations were made to build a "Light-a-Boat" to be placed off Brenton Reef to warn incoming ships of the hazard. A special vessel was constructed in Newport and launched in 1853. This two masted sailing vessel equipped with a single lantern of 8 lard oil lamps was designated "LV-14" and was the first of four (4) lightships to be assigned to Brenton Reef over a 110 year period. They were anchored in deep and safe waters where incoming vessels in transit could pass them close aboard and use the lightship as a point of entrance or departure in and out of Narragansett Bay. Each vessel bore the name "BRENTON REEF" or "BRENTON" on both sides of the hull. At times, another vessel marked "RELIEF", replaced the assigned vessel on station when the assigned vessel was required to proceed into port for maintenance, repairs or upgrading. In later years this was scheduled as an annual event.

Lightship History

Lightships were first conceived and used in England after continued disastrous voyages by ships carrying coal from Newcastle. Ships were floundering on the rocks and shoals on passages to the entrance of the Thames River to London. The first lightship named "Nore" was placed in service in 1732 by *David Aury and Roger Hamblin*, shippers who had lost vessels. They, in turn, levied tolls from other ships for maintenance of the "Nore" and the related costs needed to keeping the vessel on station. They later sold the rights to "Trinity House" the famous protector of British Commerce but continued to collect tolls for another 61 years.

By 1870, fifty-five (55) lightships dotted the Irish and British coasts. By comparison, the United States, at the height of its lightship fleet in 1939, maintained 30 stations. The total number of lightships eventually reached 43, which included 9 relief ships and 4 ships out of commission. By early 1980, all US Lightships had been retired and replaced by buoys or towers.

Lightships as well as lighthouses were under the direction of the Lighthouse Service within the Treasury Department until 1903. It was a service under the Commerce Department known as the Bureau of Lighthouses until 1939 when that service went out of existence and lightships and lighthouses were transferred into the US Coast Guard.

Brenton Reef Lightship Vessels

The early Brenton Reef lightships were wooden sailing vessels and the latter, "LV-102", a motorized special steel whaleback design painted bright red which was the color characteristic of more recent designs. She included a radio beacon transmitter and an underwater submarine signaling device. Only two ships of the LV 102 design were built. Her sister ship, the "Portsmouth" LV 101, is a museum now located in Portsmouth, Virginia.

Brenton Reef lightships were always in view from the mainland at Narragansett, Brenton Point in Newport and from Conanicut Island. They lay anchored less than two miles offshore Beavertail Point and with their painted hulls and name markings painted on each side, were easily identified. While the "Brenton" lightship was better known, there was a second light ship in Narragansett Bay located on the north end of "Aquidneck Island" where Mt. Hope Bay joins Narragansett Bay. This vessel was used to mark the "Hog Island

Shoal". She (LV-12) was on station from 1886 to 1901 and replaced by a "Sparkplug" lighthouse. In 1903, this vessel nearly, 70 years old, decrepit and un-seaworthy, was sold for $360.00.

Brenton Reef Lightships

Designation	Length	Period of Service	Disposition
LV 14	91 ft	1853-1856	Sold $615.00
LV 11	104 ft	1856-1897	Sold in 1925
LV 39	119 ft	1897-1935	Sank being towed to yard
LV 102 (WAL 525)	102 ft	1935-1962	Sold 1965. Used as crab processing vessel in Alaska. Final Disposition unknown

LV 39 after being sold, served as a floating clubhouse for the Peninsula Yacht Club in South Boston until 1975 when it was taken in tow to be delivered to a private Boat Yard North of Boston. The 100 year old vessel, built in 1875, was lost while it was in tow and sank off Bakers Island near Salem, Massachusetts. A fragment of it is on display at the Marine Museum in Fall River, Massachusetts.

Photos Courtesy of USCG Archives
Lightships LV 11 and LV 39

Lightship LV 102

Incidents of Record

LV 11

In 1890 Lightship (LV 11) was struck by the vessel CURLEW, a British registered ship. From 1863 to 1897, Lightship (LV 11) was painted WHITE with black letters "BRENTON REEF". The 1879 "Third District Light List" description identifies the hull color as "straw color".

LV39

In 1905 the Battleship USS IOWA struck and damaged the Lightship (LV 39).

During the period 1897 to 1913 Lightship (LV39) was also painted WHITE (straw colored) with black letters, "BRENTON REEF" plus the "NO 39" was painted on its side to identify the hull number .

1909 6 " fog whistle added, 12 " whistle retained

1911 Equipped with a submarine bell signal

1919 Equipped with a radio, discontinued 1923

1921 Lanterns and lantern houses removed, foremast replaced with tall steel skeleton light tower with acetylene lamp: no light installed on mainmast

PROPULSION SAIL, two-masted schooner rig, fore and main carried on Spencer masts

172

ILLUMINATING APPARATUS: 2 Lanterns, each with 8 Argand fountain burner oil lamps

FOG SIGNAL 12 " steam chime whistle, hand operated bell –When built, this was the first U.S. Lightship to be equipped with a steam fog signal.

LV 102
From 1913 to 1962, the lightship's hull was painted bright red with white letters spelling "BRENTON"

It had an unusual "fifth order" lens installed on the top of its single mast in a cylindrical housing from 1935-1955

After 1955 a new 375 mm lens lantern was installed

During the 1938 hurricane, LV 102 rode out the storm with all hands on board but dragged off station over one half mile.

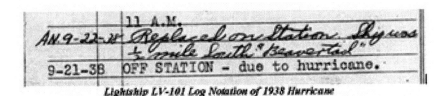

Lightship LV-101 Log Notation of 1938 Hurricane

Lightship Positions

While the Brenton Reef lightship was positioned at the entrance of Narragansett Bay, from time to time its position was slightly relocated, apparently at the whim of the service that was in charge.

1853-1889
41 degrees 25 min, North - 71 degrees 21.5 min West

1889-1942
41 deg 25.9 North - 71 deg 22.6 min West

1942 - 1962
41 deg 25.6 min North - 71 deg 22.6 min West

The Texas Tower was placed at:
41 deg 25.6 min North   71 deg 23.4 min West

Lightship Duty

Lightship duty was not a highly desirable position for a seafaring man. The turnover rate of officers and crew was very high. These were the ships that never sailed and were always exposed to the worst weather. The most prone to be hit or sunk by a passing ship. Ships intentionally steered for the lightship's position to visually confirm their own location. In fog they home in on the radio beacon. They then pass close aboard using the lightship as a point of departure to their next waypoint.

Life on a Lightship ranged from times of utter monotony to moments of sheer terror, especially when a ship was making a run for the lightship in poor visibility. The men on lightships anchored in position were in the most danger of being collided with, rammed, sideswiped or run over by large ocean going vessels. In August 1905, the "Brenton Reef Lightship, LV No. 39", was struck by the "Battleship Iowa", carrying away part of the lightship's stem and causing damage to her head stays. The danger increased when some lightships were equipped with radio beacons. Ships would tune their radio direction finders (RDF) directly on the signal emitted from the lightship. RDF was relied upon even more so in foggy weather. The ship was steered directly on the azimuth of the lightship's radio beacon. Since there was no range information, they had to keep a sharp lookout and veer off when the lightship came into view. In heavy fog, visibility could be limited to a few feet thereby establishing a dangerous situation.

On 15 May 1934, Lightship No. 117, occupying the Nantucket Shoals Station, was struck by the "RMS Olympic" in a dense fog and sank on station with the loss of seven crewmembers. Then again, on 6 January 1934, the United States Line "SS Washington" came within inches of ramming the new Light Vessel No. 117 on the Nantucket Station. The liner scraped the lightship's side, shearing off davits, a lifeboat and radio antennas.

An earlier incident happened during World War I when on 6 August 1918, Lightship No. 71, the first American lightship to be sunk by an enemy submarine, was lost on her "Diamond Shoals" station. Her crew took to their boats and reached shore without injury.

Don Goguen, MKCM (ret) was a Coast Guard crew member of the last lightship (LV 102) at Brenton Reef. Below he describes some of his experiences.

"I served aboard the Brenton Reef (LV 102) from Nov. 1959 to Apr. 1961. She was designated as WAL-525 at that time. She was built in 1916 or 1919 as I recall. This was my first duty station as a young 17 year old right out of boot camp. I was assigned to deck duties as a seaman apprentice. I did not care for the tasks of chipping and painting too much, but did qualify to stand watches on the radios and radio beacon, but can't remember specific equipment types.
An opening came up for a fireman in the engine room. I asked to transfer and learn the engineering rate. I can remember the power plant to a certain extent. The original plant was powered by steam and some of the deck equipment such as the windlass was converted to electric power. I don't know when the ship was converted to diesel.

The main engine was a Cooper Bessimer 6 cylinder diesel, direct reversible type. The engine was stopped and restarted by shifting the camshaft to run in the opposite direction for astern operation. The two DC generators were Hercules diesels and small converters were used for the AC equipment on board. We had few AC powered equipment for that reason. " Movie projector ", most important equipment next to the radar according to the captain. I was also the movie projector operator and got my butt chewed when the film broke. The generators were operated from 0600 to 2400 and the ships electrical supply came from storage batteries from 0000 to 0600. The batteries were charged during the day. The radar needed AC power, so if the fog set in during the night, we would have to go to generator power. This would also require the fog horn to be activated. Two International Harvester diesel air compressors were used for the fog horn. My normal watch was from 0600 to 1500 so if the fog set in between 0000 and 0600, I would be awaken to lite off the generator, air compressor and switch the electrical load. The other engineer and I would then stand six hours on and six hours off while the fog was in. I think the requirement for turning on the fog horn was if we could see Montauk Pt. on Long Island or not. Scary part of sitting in the fog was watching the big ships hone in on our beacon and see the blips on the radar as they came close by. Some times they got so close that the watch would alert the crew and we would get life jackets adorned.

The normal duty time spent on board was two weeks on and one week off. Not bad duty. The total crew was 14 and we usually had 9 on board at any one time. I rotated duty on board with two other engineers. I was stationed at Castle Hill Station when the ship was replaced by the tower. I think that was in1962, I'm not sure.

The only outstanding event I can remember was hurricane Donna in 1960. All lightships on the east coast were given the choice of staying on station or going to safer haven by the District Commander. Our BMC, who was in charge at the time decided to ride it out. The only other lightship to do so was the Portland as I was informed by our radio watch. We put both mushroom anchors out and ran the main engine ahead. We still got pushed four miles off station. Nasty little ride, green water breaking on the pilot house, made a sailor out of me. I tied myself to the engine room ladder so I could monitor the engine gauges and just ate crackers. The only time I moved was to fill the fuel day tank and make a head call. I volunteered to stay on watch because the ride was better low in the engine room.

Got a little rest when the eye of the storm passed by. The older guys said it was the eye, what did I know? We lost the radar antenna, both life boat covers and had one port hole staved in on the port bow. The crew patched the hole and mended two crewmen that were hurt by the storm. The storm got just as bad, if not worse after the eye had past. This time I watched sea water spray down the vent pipes into the engine room. A couple of seamen held a line around my waste so I could go out on deck and turn the vents. Anyone that didn't get a little sea sick in that storm is full of @#%&&&&. After the seas let up a day later, Castle Hill Station picked up the injured crewmembers. A few broken bones as I can recall.

Well that's about the only sea story I can remember from the days on the little red boat."

Don Goguen

Brenton Reef Tower

As the cost of operating, manning with crew and maintaining lightships on station continuing to rise, the U.S. Coast Guard was also faced with replacing the vessels, some of which were over 50 years old. Gradually all were phased out and fixed towers called "Offshore Light Towers" were placed, when practical, at some locations where light ships had previously anchored.

Brenton Reef Tower or the "Texas Tower" as it was nicknamed after the early oil rigs in the Gulf of Mexico, was constructed in 1961 on top of four 30 inch diameter red steel piles in 80 feet of water. The legs were driven 25 feet into bedrock. It was located 1 ½ miles southeast of Beavertail Light as a replacement for the lightship. It too had the letters "BRENTON" except it was painted on each of its four sides. Power for the unmanned tower was via an undersea cable from the Beavertail Light Station. It did retain an emergency battery backed up light in case of a power failure. Placed into automatic

176

operation in 1962, its characteristics were a 1.2 million candlepower, white light provided by a double ended type "DCE-36 Airport Beacon". It rotated, showing 2 flashes every 10 seconds, visible out to 16 miles.

The tower was also equipped with an automatic fog signal, sounding  a group of 3 second blasts every 60 seconds, when activated. The sound was baffled away from the Newport land area.

> *Photo from USCG Archives*
> **Brenton Reef Tower**

Some time about 1982, the Coast Guard declared they were considering discontinuing the use of the tower and solicited comments from users. Local fishermen and the recreation boating public objected, stating that it provided a valuable visible mark when entering Narragansett Bay. The decision was delayed on two separate occasions, but operational costs and extensive repair of the corroding under water legs were prohibitive. Over half a million dollars in repairs were estimated. Cracks had appeared in the visible areas of the legs and an underwater survey showed extensive corrosion. The tower continued to provide service until March 1989 when the Coast Guard declared the installation of the new 20 foot high Narragansett Bay entrance sea buoy had been placed further to seaward. They argued that improved electronic navigation aids available and the new buoy would provide the navigator safe approach into Narragansett Bay. The establishment of the sea buoy ended 138 years of marking Brenton Reef with a navigation aid.

A controversial environmental issue was raised when divers inspecting the legs of the tower found numerous lead acid batteries on the sea bed floor. Apparently, over the 30 year life period of the tower, Coast Guard maintenance personnel had been dumping dead batteries over the side. An investigation was undertaken and as a result, strict rules were adopted to prevent any recurrence at other Coast Guard sites. The tower was finally dismantled in 1992 with the remains dumped off the coast of "Shinnecock", Long Island in New York and made into an artificial reef for use as a fish haven.

Radio Beacon

Photo Courtesy Rick WX2T
Radio Beacon Antenna

The RDF radio beacon (type D) transmitting on the frequency of 310 kilocycles located on the Benton tower was transferred to the Beavertail Light Station. A vertical ground plane antenna was erected on the grounds behind the Keeper's house. Copper radials of # 8 wire, each 100 ft. in length were buried every 3 degrees from the antenna to act as an artificial ground counterpoise. The Morse code signal identifier "B", used previously for the identifier "Brenton", was retained and used for the identifier "Beavertail".

Point Judith Light Station's (P) radio beacon range was extended at the same time providing a radio coverage out to the Buzzards Bay entrance light. The range of the radio beacon for Beavertail essentially added 14 miles of additional range over the light. The radio beacon is no longer operational, but the radio tower still stands

178

and has been used by ham radio operators during special lighthouse commemoration events.

Sea Buoy "NB"

At the time Brenton Reef Tower was inactivated, a new Narragansett Bay entrance buoy, 20 feet high above the water was established further to the south at Latitude N41-23.1 and Longitude W71-23.3. This red and white sea buoy is designated "NB" for "Narragansett Bay Entrance". The buoy's characteristic is a four (4) second flashing light emitting the Morse code letter "A" plus a horn and a radar transponder beacon which transmits the Morse code letter "B" back to a ship when illuminated by the ship's radar.

The Narragansett Bay Sea Buoy "NB" is similar to this image

Brenton Reef is not void of navigation buoys. A series of 3 red buoys and 1 lighted red buoy round the southern and the western side of the reef leading up to Castle Hill lighthouse. All 4 buoys have audible gongs or whistles generated by wave motion providing a degree of warning in fog.

Chapter 9

The 1749 Foundation

The original stone and lime mortar foundation of the "Newport Light", as it was named in the mid 18th century, still stands. This statement is based on the assumption that two successive lights were built on the remains of the 1749 original light. In all three lights, the keepers never lived in the structure. Hence the term "lighthouse" is used only as an acronym for the building that housed the light.

This foundation is located a few feet to the south of the perimeter road which circles in front of the present lighthouse. It was buried and forgotten for over 80 years. The great Hurricane of 1938 revealed the foundation remains at the same time it destroyed the fog signal building that was built on top of it. For the past 70 years it remains neglected and exposed to the elements and ravages of the storms. Three less intense hurricanes have passed since the famous "Hurricane of '38" and each has taken further toll of the remains. Undercuts by wave action, freezing rain and salt spray have seeped deep into the stone structure, expanded and cracked the limestone mortar, loosening more of the original stones and toppling them back onto the adjacent rock ledges. In turn, during storms, heavy seas reach up onto the ledges and wash away those stones that have fallen. Today, a severe undercut on the southwest side threatens more collapse and further loss of the historic ruin.

The force of these storms also cut away at the base of the co-located land embankment and coupled with erosion from surface water such as rain and road drainage, the entire length of the embankment is in hazardous condition. Rock ledge beneath the sod is exposed and provides some preventive help in minimizing damage. The ledge material does flake and layers are exposed to water intrusion and the effect of freezing and expansion causes breakage.

Photo by Author
Site and Ruin of the 1749 Lighthouse

The ruin itself is simple in form and construction, comprised mostly of soft shale rock and lime mortar. When viewed, it becomes a humble edifice reflecting a story over 250 years old as part of early American development and the determination of its Colonial builders.

Peter Harrison the Architect

After the merchants and ship owners petitioned and convinced the Colonial Government in 1730 that indeed a lighthouse had to be established on Beavertail Point, it took another 18 years before they gave approval to a committee of six men to build one. Its design and construction was delegated to an established architect, *Peter Harrison* and his brother *Joseph Harrison*. *Peter Harrison* had never designed or built a lighthouse but he was greatly respected in colonial Newport. The new lighthouse was to be called "Newport Light" and in subsequent years it was also referred to as the "Harrison Light".

Harrison, at age twenty-six, had arrived in Newport from England ten years earlier, gifted with talent that many envied. He had commanded his own ship, gained knowledge of surveying and drafting and evolved into a self taught brilliant architect. His architectural feats were outstanding which later earned him the recognition as America's "First Architect". His designs in Rhode Island include Newport's *"Redwood Library"(still in operation) 1748-1750,* Thames Street's *"Old Brick Market Place" 1761-1762 ,* Newport's *"Touro Synagogue" 1760,* and in Massachusetts, Boston's *"Kings Chapel"1749-1750,* and the *"Christ Church"* in Cambridge.

Harrison's designs exceed over 200 buildings in New England reaching down into Colonial Williamsburg in Virginia. His allegiance, however, was to the "Crown" and his political affiliation and beliefs labeled him a "Tory". Loyal to his king, he eventually returned to England after the Revolutionary War.

Image courtesy of Redwood Library and Anthenaeum, Newport, Rhode Island

Peter Harrison

By Louis Sands copy after Nathaniel Smibert

Harrison had never designed a lighthouse previously and he built this one without detailed architectural drawings, representing a true vernacular structure. With both he and his brother being experienced seamen, most certainly their knowledge helped configure what was needed to satisfy a ship master with the overriding requirement being a light as bright and as high above ground as practicable.

The base of the tower was located about twenty (20) to thirty (30) feet above the high water mark. *Harrison,* with his advanced genius of applying practical engineering to designs that would endure environmental constraints, constructed the lighthouse as a round structure. He knew that severe wave conditions could be experienced at Beavertail Point and a structure with a curved face to the sea would provide less resistance to wind and wave forces.

Where he developed this idea one can only guess. The tragedy that occurred on the 27th of November 1703 at "Eddystone Rock" lighthouse, located 13 miles from Plymouth England, certainly must have influenced his design. Eddystone light built in 1699 was the first high seas light on the British coast. Its designer, *Henry Winstanley,* claimed it was indestructible. On the following morning of the "great storm" when daylight dawned, there were no signs of a lighthouse. The Rock was bare as it used to be. *Winstanley's* structure, with its designer, had been swept away forever. It became known as England's most famous lighthouse and a worldwide example for future designers to remember.

Why *Harrison* or the committee selected the site so close to the water's edge has not been postulated in either records or other written documents. The site sits at the very extreme edge of the seaward ledge rock about thirty (30) feet from the sea and at about the same level as the land to the north. During severe storms, the foundation experiences waves reaching up, perilously crashing onto the ledge, endangering the foundation itself. The safer course would have been to site the lighthouse fifty (50) or one hundred (100) feet further to the north where wave action is not as susceptible. From a navigational point of view, a safer location to the north would matter little. Perhaps at the time of the site survey, ample ledge rock stood as a buffer from the sea and was later destroyed by storm action. This is somewhat likely since the geological mass made up of mostly shale ledge appears today somewhat different from the photographs taken before the Hurricane of 1938.

The 1749 wooden lighthouse constructed on the stone foundation was started on 8 May 1749 and completed 6 months later on 9 September 1749 The lighthouse had a diameter of twenty four (24) feet at its base and is the same diameter as the current foundation ruin. The top of the lighthouse was thirteen (13) feet in diameter with a height from the ground to the top of the cornice of fifty eight (58) feet. Above that was a lantern gallery of eleven (11) feet in height and eight (8) feet in diameter. This height gave the lighthouse a theoretical range of fifteen (15) miles, taking into account the height above water and the height of the observer. During one period of construction, thirty eight (38) men were employed. These men were employed for 3 days "at the raising". There are no further references as to what was raised. It has always been assumed the wooden tower was built from the ground up. In 1753, changes were made to the lantern and in August of that year, an allocation of "48 squares of glass, 2 gallons of rum and 3 pounds of sugar" were accounted "for raising a mast".

The Fire of 1753

It is not known how and why a fire on 23 July, 1753 destroyed the entire wood frame lighthouse three years after it was constructed. Spilled oil, a fallen candle, flaring lamp wicks, a lighting taper, inattentiveness, lightning or another source could have been the cause. There is no known record as to the cause. The lighthouse constructed of timbers and sheathed with boards and internal wooden stairs, either burned up or burned down as may fit the description. In any case, it was considered a total loss. Three (3) years earlier the light was reported, "much out of repair" and there was a danger of the lantern itself falling because of wood decay. A report signed by *Josiah Arnold,* a committee member, and *Charles Spooner,* one of the constructors, recommended that more windows be installed to allow more air into the structure "to keep the wooden work dry".

As noted in Chapter 1, *Abel Franklin,* the first Keeper at Beavertail, continued to keep a light with an ordinary lantern mounted on a pole until a new structure could be constructed. In August of 1753, the General Assembly authorized *Jonathan Nickols, Daniel Jencks* and *William Reed,* as a committee, to build a new light. This second light was to be built of stone and brick on top of the remains of the old light and the foundation ruins we see today. Again, *Peter Harrison* was engaged to design this new light, and *William Reed* contracted to build it. There was considerable discussion regarding the material to be used, although from the experience with the wooden tower, all were in agreement that brick would be best. *Reed* was fortunate to have the building supplies close at hand. With mutual consent of the Colonial Government, he used local stone and bricks salvaged from the remains of material used for building "Fort George". This fortification was located on Goat Island in Newport harbor and had been completed during the same year.

The lighthouse was constructed and placed in operation successfully. Charts and maps of the era show "Newport Light" prominently on Beavertail Point. Sometime later, the brightness of the light had deteriorated. Complaints were lodged by sailors and inference by inspectors were made that the structure itself had not been maintained. The light at times was weak and also exhibited erratic failures resulting in shoddy performance. In 1760, the General Assembly was forced into remedial action by these reports of unreliability and trouble with the light. *Peter Harrison* again was appointed, along with *Reed* and *Capt. Josiah Arnold,* in 1760 to *"put the lighthouse in good repair".*

For the next 15 years, the light and the tower, while being maintained, had only a change of two (2) different keepers *(Able Franklin and John Bowers).* Shipping had increased dramatically and outages were not tolerated although little had been done to improve the lamp system right up to the Revolutionary War. When the British with their six thousand (6000) troops evacuated Newport and Jamestown on 16 October 1779, they removed much of the lantern works, set fire to the tower, most likely the internal stairs and woodwork of the structure. This was done to prevent use of the light by the French Navy standing offshore and American Patriots now armed with sloops of war and small frigates. Nothing is recorded as to the disposition of the co-located keeper's house.

Elizabeth Hemick, in her "History of Jamestown and Early Days Around Narragansett Bay" states an excerpt from an early record.

> *"Again, the question of how a stone and brick lighthouse burned down raises the issue of the light's construction. The British in the Revolutionary War set fire to it and the flames so shocked the walls; especially about the Windows, that, notwithstanding they are four feet and half thick at the bottom and a half feet thick at the top, our Masons have not since been able to make them tight and secure against the impressions of storms of rain."*

A short time after the British left, repairs were made and the light again became operational but it continued with outages and unreliable performance. Duty rates were increased in 1783 to eight (8) pence a ton to pay for repairs and a *Caleb Gardner* was ordered to repair the light and also construct a road down to the lighthouse. The records read *"the road to be built shall be free to all persons with horse and carriage".* During August of 1785, one hundred and fifty (150) pounds was allocated to "repair and put in order the lighthouse at Beaver Tail". The task was given to *Thomas Rumreill.* During the same year, "Light Money" assessments were increased for all vessels entering Newport to help defray the added cost.

The structure amazingly remained in service until 1856, a total of over 100 years. It was now time for a new lighthouse. During an 1851 inspection, it was stated, *"the tower was the worst yet seen, greatly out of repair and both inside and outside in wretched condition".* Yet it stood as a tribute to *Harrison* as this was possibly the only structure that Harrison created without architectural drawings. This report stipulated the replacement of the light with the present structure now on site and coincided with the new U.S. Lighthouse Board's upgrading of lighthouses throughout the country. When the granite light tower was built in 1856, followed shortly after with a new Keeper's House, the *Harrison* light stood in the way of the granite light tower and was demolished by leveling it to the top of its base foundation. There is one reference that states, *"A few days later (after the new granite tower was constructed) the old brick tower was blown up)"*. The foundation was slightly below the adjacent ground level of the new light and, therefore, was covered over with fill and dirt built up to the same level of the terrain around the new light.

Further Use of the Filled Land

Over the next 80 years, the land over the covered foundation was used for various purposes, primarily for installation and test of experimental sound signals related to fog. Chapter 5 details these experiments and describes various equipment configurations used at Beavertail. Some early photographs also show small buildings constructed over the foundation ruin and next to it, but the site was used predominately for a large steam whistle building with a coal shed on each side sitting adjacent on top of the ruin fill. Water tanks and collecting cisterns to feed water into steam boilers were located nearby the light tower.

The Hurricane of 1938

The original foundation was forgotten and remained lost for eight (8) decades until the aftermath of the "Great Hurricane of 1938". That storm caused much havoc and damage to all of Rhode Island. At Beavertail, a tidal surge flooded the two keeper's houses with four feet of water. The ruin must have had six (6) to eight (8) feet of water rushing over it and tons of water pounding onto its rock ledges. The hurricane washed away the walls of the existing fog signal building and left much of the equipment sitting atop the foundation ruin, twisted torn and unsalvageable. The restless waves, having reached up and over the filled area, dissolved the dirt and washed all of it away exposing the old stone foundation.

The following year a new "Fog Signal Building" with two large diaphone extending from its south side horns was constructed on higher ground and sited to the east of the granite tower. It remains today as the Rhode Island Department of Environmental Management's naturalist and aquarium center.

One year later, 1939, Europe was at war and the U.S. Government was preparing defenses to protect its military assets. Coast Artillery installations have always been a priority to protect the U.S. Navy and its ships in Newport. Large "Endicott" era coastal gun batteries had been deployed in the area as early as 1896. When America entered the war in 1941, new threats had been recognized and Beavertail Point took on a more military role. The 1749 stone ruin foundation, now visible from the effects of the hurricane, was capped with concrete. Electrical cables with conduit were extended to the cap for a mobile gun and a twelve (12) inch diameter searchlight emplacement. A cast block of concrete was also laid on the circular cap to support a sensitive long range optical range finder which required a stable platform to minimize vibration from movement and wind buffeting.

The exposure of the 1749 ruin by the 1938 hurricane caught the interest of the Jamestown Historical Society (JHS), and they immediately recognized it historical importance. The Society's President, *Peyton Hazard,* in 1941 began a series of letter requests to the U.S. Coast Guard to memorialize the ruin with a plaque. Because of the priorities of WW II, the request was curtailed. Again in 1946, *Hazard* contacted the Coast Guard. JHS finally received approval to place a wood oak carved tablet fastened to the concrete cap. *Rdm. W. N. Derby,* Commander of the 1st Coast Guard District, in his letter to JHS stated that *"the old tower foundation is no longer of value as a required part of present day activities of the light station and will not justify further Coast Guard expenditures".* This statement was premature as 30 years later the still standing "Fog Signal" building was decommissioned. The building with the two (2) diaphone trumpets was abandoned. Its oil engines, compressors and related equipment removed and an automatic electrical reed diaphone fog signal was installed on top of the foundation where the commemorative tablet stood. Also in his letter of approval, recognizing its historical value, *Rdm. W. N. Derby* authorized the Jamestown Historical Society to *"perform other maintenance as you may wish to undertake to preserve the remains of the foundation".*

For the cost of $35, the now famed *John Howard Benson* of Newport was commissioned to make a new commemorative tablet encased in concrete. *Benson* had bought an old Newport colonial tombstone and grave stone cutting business in 1927 from the renowned *John Stevens* family. The carved oak plaque was recessed into a concrete form and *Elizabeth Davis,* who chaired the JHS Committee, had it mounted on top of the concrete cap in 1948, but within one year it was vandalized. *Benson* recommended a more durable plaque made of slate costing $200 carved by one of his apprentice students should be considered as a replacement. JHS voted to proceed and in 1951 an engraved dark gray slate plaque was in place reading;

"FOUNDATION OF THE ORIGINAL
BEAVERTAIL LIGHTHOUSE
ERECTED IN 1749
THIRD LIGHTHOUSE TO
BE ESTABLISHED
ON THE ATLANTIC COAST"

Photo by Author
2ⁿᵈ Historical Plaque Commissioned by Jamestown Historical Society in 1951

Forty years later in 1991, Hurricane *"Bob"* hit New England and its eye traveled directly over Conanicut Island. The slate monument was broken from its mountings and tossed up onto the northerly embankment of the foundation ruin. In 1992, the JHS Board debated on how the monument could be replaced but no further action took place. When the Beavertail Lighthouse Museum Association opened a museum in the Assistant Keeper's house in 1993, JHS granted the loan of the slate plaque as an artifact for public display.

A post card photograph clearly indicates that an electric fog horn signal system was located on top of the ruin about 1990. The Coast Guard mounted the fog signal on the concrete cap above the ruin and extended two long arms of wire fence on the north side to prevent vandals from climbing up onto the cap. Later, an upgraded system was procured and located on the edge of the perimeter road thirty (30) feet away protected by a surrounding wire fence. This present system actually contains two separate signals, one of lesser amplitude used as a backup in case of failure of the primary signal horn. The ruin was left abandoned with only its concrete cap, and being the furthest seaward point on Conanicut Island, has become a favored viewing perch by visitors.

Saving the 1749 Ruin

Twelve years later at the 2005 BLMA annual membership meeting, *James Wermuth,* a Newport based preservationist, early architectural excavation expert and historian of *Peter Harrison's* works, addressed the membership about his concerns regarding the remains of the original foundation. *Wermuth* posed the question, "What possible value of what appears as a pile of rocks could such a ruin be?". It had no aesthetic or practical use appeal. The answer, of course, was its valuable design serving as a reference to *Harrison's* other contributions to Colonial architectural history, and in fact, the foundation remains as evidence of the 3rd oldest lighthouse in America. The structure was designed and built unlike any existing architectural order of that time, thereby adding to its uniqueness. *Wermuth* proposed, as a minimum, that the remains should be documented archeologically before it is all washed away and asked BLMA to assist him.

BLMA volunteers, *George Warner, Varoujan Karentz and Linda Jacobson*, over a period of scheduled sessions, assisted *Wermuth* to scribe a compass rose on top of the concrete cap, mark azimuth coordinates, measure diameters, height, and then photograph a 360 degree full height panorama detail of the stone configurations. During the documentation sessions, another but smaller circular foundation was found nearby due north and about twenty five (25) feet in distance from the rim of the original ruin. With only a portion of it showing, it is estimated to be twelve (12) feet in diameter. Construction appears similar to the stones of the 1749 ruin and only conjecture can classify its purpose since there has been no documentation unearthed describing it. Possible uses could have been the foundation of a fog signaling device, such as a bell or perhaps the foundation of the earlier brazier fire or watch tower. One early undated drawing refers to a fog signal near the location that was destroyed by a hurricane. Alongside that ruin is another foundation most likely of a later period that appears to be partially made of concrete and resembles a footing for a small building. Only five (5) to six (6) feet of that exposed footing shows and only by exploratory excavations can better definitions be made.

The late winter storm of 2005 further undercut the southwest portion of the foundation and toppled stones onto the ledge below leaving a section of the concrete cap overhanging in space. In the spring of 2006, the DEM inadvertently sledge hammered the overhanging section off in the interests of safety since the concrete cap is used by visitors to Beavertail to sit and view the ocean.

According to *Jeremy D'Entremont*, New England's most prominent lighthouse historian, states in his book, "The Lighthouses of Rhode Island", a large bell weighing six hundred (600) lbs. was installed at Beavertail in 1829 on a twelve (12) foot brick tower for use as a fog signal. A request has been made to the Coast Guard to allow a few test borings to help identify and gather more information. An alternative or supplemental non-invasive geophysical survey using a microwave reflective ground imaging technique is also being considered. The survey would also cover a wider area of the grounds and detect other archeological deposits and buried man-made features.

There has been no consensus as to how to preserve or stabilize the 1749 remains other than to agree that the remaining stones will fall to the fate of the next major hurricane and most likely destroy the remains. Options considered included building a protective revetment wall in front of the ruin, removing the ruin stone by stone and reconstructing it elsewhere on the light station property safe from the sea, or removing a few of the stones and establishing an exhibit nearby with interpretive signage that tells of the location and history of the original lighthouses. Opinions expressed by others include doing nothing and letting nature take its course.

With its fate undecided, *Harrison's* work and a visible piece of 259 year history may indeed disappear.

Note: GPS coordinates

1749 Ruin
Latitude   41 degrees 26'.944 N
Longitude   71 degrees 23'.957 W

Unknown small ruin
Latitude   41 degrees 26'.950
Longitude   71 degrees 23'. 956

Chapter 10

The Organizations

Beavertail State Park, Rhode Island Parks Association, Town of Jamestown and the Beavertail Lighthouse Museum Association

The public involvement with Beavertail Light cannot be separated from Beavertail State Park. The light station property and the park are abutting properties. From a visitor's point of view, Beavertail Light Station is located at the end of the state park. There is no physical distinction of Jamestown, state and federal property. Only a perimeter wooden" post and rail" fence around the light station property separates the Federal property from the state park, although the fence as the actual property line is believed to be in error.

Four (4) distinct organizations are actively associated with the park and the light station: "U.S. Coast Guard", Department of Environmental Management of the State of Rhode Island, "Town of Jamestown" and the "Beavertail Lighthouse Museum Association". Although separate entities and jurisdiction by federal and state agencies are involved, the interests of the Town of Jamestown, RI Department of Environmental Management (administers of the state park) and the non profit Beavertail Lighthouse Museum Association are all entwined.

The romance with lighthouses is worldwide. Thousands are enthralled by lighthouse stories coupled with vivid pictures of exhilarating scenes of the seascape surroundings. It has always been recognized that lighthouse locations, sitting at land ends, are on the most striking and most beautiful real estate views imaginable. Their breathtaking vistas and history captivate all. Local and regional advocates supporting lighthouse preservation formed into national organizations and together, thousands of people have banded together. All were preservation oriented and chartered themselves to save these historical lights. When the U.S. Coast Guard commenced a program to "automate" their lighthouses throughout the United States, fuel was added to the "preservation fire" because the buildings that housed the keepers of the lights were no longer needed and they were allowed to fall into disrepair.

While the story of Beavertail's lighthouses begins in the 1740's and continues under various government authorities, including the U.S. Lighthouse Service and later by the U.S. Coast Guard, in more recent times, other organizations and agencies became involved in its care. The involvement and concern was brought about by the Coast Guard's gradual neglect and abandonment of the buildings no longer needed to sustain the newer automated light in the granite tower. As a result, concerned private citizens and advocacy groups organized themselves as "preservationists" recognizing the historic significance and the need to save Beavertail's buildings and grounds. Collectively they undertook a stewardship role committed to securing the site for use by future generations.

Actually, over a period of a few short years during the 1980's and early 1990's, a number of events transpired involving both public and private groups. All were motivated by the same objective, to provide public site accessibility and preservation of the historic buildings. The Rhode Island "State Parks and Recreation Department" of the Division of Environmental Management (DEM) took an active and early role, although all the organizations involved were mutually aligned toward preservation with emphasis on public recreational and educational use.

The property, owned by the Federal Government on which the lighthouse sits, was defined on May 16, 1921 by a "U.S. Army Corps of Engineering" drawing showing the light station site boundary as 448.2 feet north, 481.02 feet east, 132 feet south, 481.2 feet west with a public right of way (ROW) outside of the boundary. This only includes the fenced-in area. The lighthouse is located in Lot #1, Plat #13 in the town of Jamestown Tax records showing it as 7.35 acres (the total area) and the owner as the U.S. Government.

194

Land and building assessment worth in 2007 totals $6,226,214. The property used to be on Lots 1, 2 and 3. Lots 2 and 3 were merged with Lot 1 in 1993. The address is 800 Beavertail Road and the structures are erroneously listed as comprising 2,600 square feet in total.

Fort Burnside

Prior to World War II, only the Coast Guard light station and a few National Guard observation posts were the only structures located on the lower southern end of the Beavertail peninsula. Fishing was the prime recreation for local residents as it had been for many years and a few fishing shacks were scattered about. As early as 1754, the "Newport Colonial Lighthouse Committee" granted a public "Right Of Way" (ROW) to provide access to the rocks around the lighthouse for fishermen. This access remained open until just prior to World War II. Beginning at the entrance of the present park boundaries, all the properties to the south were placed "off limits" to the public, including the perimeter road around the light station grounds and remained so until 1946.

During the period from 1939 to 1946, including the World War II years, the present site of Beavertail State Park was occupied as a military defense facility known as "Fort Burnside". It was part federal property and part leased from local land owners. The fortifications extended down to and around the light station grounds where optical range finders, high intensity searchlights, artillery and machine gun emplacements were installed. Manned primarily by the 243rd Coast Artillery of the Rhode Island National Guard, it served as the eyes and ears protectorate of Narragansett Bay. Fort Burnside was fortified with guns and controlled under water detection devices, mine fields, submarine nets and a communications control station. The control station, still standing a short distance north of the light station, was manned by both Army and Navy personnel. The facility was identified as the "Harbor Entrance Command Post" (HECP). It controlled all military, commercial marine and fishing vessel traffic entering and leaving Narragansett Bay. On the north side of Fort Burnside, along the west side of Beavertail Road, the "Massachusetts Institute of

Technology" (MIT) operated a highly classified naval development radar facility. This complex experimented and trained carrier based Navy aviators in nighttime fighter intercept tactics and carrier control operations.

By 1946 at wars end, Fort Burnside was essentially abandoned. The U.S. Navy then took administrative control of the property to use for radio communication purposes. The property was re-identified as the "NAVCOM Transmitter, Naval Communications Station Beavertail Point (N-RI-467)". The U.S. Navy maintained a very low frequency radio communication transmitter control facility in the HECP building. A few hundred yards away, a six hundred (600) foot high guyed antenna tower was installed with massive antenna tuning coils installed in an adjacent building.

Other than the remnants of two 3 inch gun revetments and an ammunition storage bunker ("Whiting Battery") which are still visible on the east side just north of the light station and the HECP concrete command center, all evidence of any military occupation is gone. *(The HECP in the middle of the park is mostly hidden by foliage but noticeable today by a communications and radar towers. The concrete building built under the guise of a farmhouse to mislead the enemy is under custodial care by the RI DEM and is considered a candidate for a historical site.)*

Automation

Starting in World War II and following on during the postwar periods, the Coast Guard in earnest began reducing the need and dependence of lighthouses. New navigation technologies had emerged such as LORAN and SHORAN, both providing electronic ranging information from shore station transmitters with great accuracy, and today, with worldwide coverage by the satellite Global Positioning System (GPS). In the 1960's, a major automation project called the "Lighthouse Automation and Modernization Program" (LAMP) was initiated further limiting the need for lighthouse personnel. By the late 1960's, fewer than 60 lighthouses in the country had keepers. By 1990, all had been automated except Boston Light. In addition, a major Coast Guard reorganization established a new "Short Range Navigation Division" comprised of localized "Navigation Teams" who provided periodic preventive maintenance and immediate response to unmanned lighthouses if any outages or other discrepancies occurred.

This major program undertaken by the Coast Guard improved navigation aid reliability and achieved significant cost savings at the same time. Improved lighting, elimination of oil lanterns, labor saving use by electricity, electronic controls for remote status monitoring of both the light beacon and the fog signal systems were installed and routed to the central monitoring locations. These locations gathered the status data from a number of geographically separated light stations including the state of automatic redundant light beacons and backup fog signaling equipment. This further reduced the manpower and logistic support needs at a light station, thereby achieving additional cost reductions of light station operations. Equipment failures and status of redundant switching apparatus were readily apparent by alarm systems at these navigation aid support stations. When fault alarms were received, Coast Guard repair crews could determine the urgency, and as needed, dispatched to correct the failure or defer the maintenance.

Automation alone was not the single reason for abandonment of fixed facilities. New lights, improved sea buoy reliability and vastly advanced visual aids technology allowed consolidating lights. The by-product was less frequent maintenance, more reduction of personnel and improved safety at sea. At the light stations there was no longer any need to have "lighthouse keepers" on site. The living residences were no longer required along with the costly upkeep of maintenance, utilities and grounds keeping. By 1990, automation had caught up with the last light station in Rhode Island with housed keepers. The awesome brick "South East Light" on Block Island, which housed the only 1st order Fresnel lens ever installed in a Rhode Island lighthouse, joined the others as an unmanned station. The light on Little Brewster Island in Boston Harbor, "Boston Light", notably the first lighthouse in the colonies, was the last in the nation to be automated. The light was electrified in 1948 and shortly after, the clockwork mechanism that rotated the lens was replaced by an electric motor. The original Fresnel lens remains in place today, its white flash visible for 27 miles. On April 16, 1998, that light also was no longer attended, although other on site duties are performed by personnel. The automated light at Point Judith, six (6) miles southwest of Beavertail, is the only light in Rhode Island where Coast Guard personnel reside nearby. The light stands on the property of the U.S. Coast Guard station which responds primarily to search and rescue operations.

As the automation process progressed, the USCG abandoned even more of its buildings except leaving structures which housed the light itself. In many locations, where the light was incorporated as part of the building, the total structure itself was abandoned, equipment removed and unmanned maintenance-free standing towers or poles were erected with replacement modern reliable light beacons set on top of them. At other locations where improved aids were commissioned, nearby light stations became obsolete and were no longer required. The Coast Guard removed the lighting equipment and abandoned the site. Abandonment meant just that; personnel were moved out and reassigned and empty buildings fell into disrepair. Some were demolished but most just suffered erosion and decay at the mercy of the elements. Many were vandalized, some were sold and taken over as residences by private owners.

In Rhode Island, during the 250 years of the state's lighthouse history, 30 lighthouses had at one time or another been in existence. In addition, five (5) different lightships at two (2) lightship stations, "Hog Island Shoal" (1) in the upper bay and "Brenton Reef" (4) and one light tower (Brenton Reef) were operated over a 136 year period *(see Chapter 8)*. As of 2006, only twenty one (21) Rhode Island lighthouses remain standing and from those, only thirteen (13) are active navigation aids. Six lighthouses are privately owned and the remaining have been removed or are in ruin with some visual semblance of their foundations.

At Beavertail, the only structure the Coast Guard maintains is the granite light tower where the revolving light beacon is housed, sixty four (64) feet above sea level and its attached automation switching equipment room, plus the remote fog signal system. The light was automated in early 1972 and for a short time following the

198

changeover, the keeper houses were occupied as temporary housing for Coast Guard personnel. Petty Officer *John Baxter* with his wife and children lived in the Keeper's house. *Baxter* and Coast Guardsman *George Light,* who resided in the Assistant Keeper's house, were the last of the Coast Guard inhabitants. They both were eventually assigned to the Coast Guard lifesaving station at Pt. Judith.

There has been little if any preventive maintenance of the 1856 granite tower since 1980. Its electric and electronic active navigation equipment is attended to by repair crews dispatched from either the Coast Guard station at Woods Hole, Massachusetts or the "Navigation Aids Support Group" in Bristol, Rhode Island. For the next few years, the empty buildings at Beavertail continued to deteriorate. Unattended, vandalism was evident to the extent that on one occasion in 1975, the light itself was shot out by gunfire. It remained unlit for several days and cost $1700 to make repairs to the light and broken windows. Buildings were desolated with peeling paint, broken windows and roofs needing replacement shingles. The grounds showed neglect with overgrown grasses and weeds. It was time for public sentiment to enter the picture and step up to save the site.

Beavertail State Park and the Aftermath of World War II.

This was the period when public interest began to peak about the properties vacated by the military. Administrations in Washington were anxious to close down and remove excess military installations and property off their accountability records and sales of property added new dollars to Treasury funds. Real estate developers and some land owners also smelled opportunity to build on prime waterfront property. As early as 1940, twenty two (22) tracks of residential land were laid out and mapped with seven (7) streets along the east shore north of the light station property. These tracks were never developed and the land was absorbed by the government. The bridge linking Conanicut Island to the mainland had opened increasing off-island accessibility to Beavertail. Meanwhile, conservationists were becoming proactive environmental preservationists, foreseeing the need of establishing land trusts to save open spaces. Many immediately saw the beauty of Beavertail and its draw as one of the state's outstanding scenic destinations.

The property was still under the control of the government and the Navy had been using a part of it as a communication site. In December of 1955, a meeting was held between Jamestown representative *Dr. Gobeille* and *Rear Adm. Ralph C. Earle*, commander of the Newport Naval Base, about opening the Beavertail area year round. The area had been closed by the Navy since World War II except for a few summer months when it was opened with the town and the Navy each furnishing a guard to police the area. There was much support of this idea and local residents from civic organizations pledged their cooperation to maintain order and prevent vandalism.

In Jamestown, a "Beavertail Recreation Committee" was formed and began investigating buying the land from the U.S. Government, but at the same time, the state interceded. The "State Division of Parks and Recreation", under the Rhode Island Department of Environmental Management, convinced Jamestown officials that the costs associated with maintaining a large park would be prohibitive to the local community. DEM stated the inclusion of any Jamestown ceded property into the state's park system would be more beneficial to all of Rhode Island's citizens. Town officials concurred and an agreement was prepared. The crescendo of interest built to a point where other conservationists and preservationists were caught up with urgency and imagination of a public park and convinced local political and government administrators, along with their congressional representatives, that Beavertail must belong to the public.

U.S. Senator *John Chafee,* a past governor of Rhode Island and at the time a senior senator with a conservationist's conviction, picked up the torch. He, along with U.S. Senator *Claiborne Pell*, U.S. Representatives *Claudine Schneider* and *Fernand St. Germain, Robert Bendick* of the RI State Department of Environmental Management visited Beavertail and were briefed by Jamestown officials and state recreation administrators. *Chafee* immediately recognized the threat of possibly losing the last remaining prime

200

recreation area in Rhode Island to private interests. Through his dedicated efforts in Congress and liaison with federal agencies in concert with the other Rhode Island congressional members, Beavertail State Park was to become a reality.

Transfer of Property

The first parcel of property transfer from the government took place on July 11, 1973, eight (8) years before Beavertail State Park opened. That is when the U.S. Government ceded, with a quitclaim deed, twenty (20) acres to the Town of Jamestown. This was based upon an application submitted by the town on November 30, 1972 in accordance with the "Federal Property and Administrative Services Act of 1949" which encouraged municipalities to apply for unused federal lands.

This parcel referred to as Parcel "A" was located at the south eastern portion of the yet to be Beavertail State Park. The twenty (20) acres was formerly a portion of the Naval Communications Station, designated as "N-RI-467". The land transfer was conveyed in perpetuity for use as a public park or for public recreation purposes and formally accepted by *Albert. B.Gobeille,* Jamestown Town Council President.

During this same period, some very significant proposals and discussions were under way by the Town of Jamestown with both the U.S. Coast Guard and the U.S. Department of Interior. These proposals were spearheaded by *William V. Gurney Jr.,* Jamestown's Director of Parks and Recreation who, recognizing the transfer of the twenty (20) acre parcel was only the predecessor of other property. Knowing that the lighthouse property was a tremendous visitor attraction and because it was in such disrepair, months of negotiation with the Coast Guard and the U.S. Department of Interior resulted in an agreement to provide a live-in caretaker to reside in the lighthouse Keeper's house. This agreement was initiated in June of 1977 and a few months later *Peter Anderson* was selected by Jamestown's Administrator as the first custodian.

Anderson and his family were allowed to live in the residence at no charge in return for work to be performed that ranged from maintenance of buildings and grounds to acting as *Park Policeman*. During winter months, "he was to make and paint picnic tables, signs and paint trash barrels". The Town Recreation Department also procured a "radio equipped Jeep" for park patrol purposes. In a few short months, improvements became apparent as lawns were mowed and trimmed, litter curtailed and visitors were complying with keeping Beavertail free and clear of litter. Many breathed a sigh of relief that the valuable historic buildings were being cared for.

Further interest for the establishment of a large state park resulted in planning by the state and the town as described previously. These planning initiatives coupled with support from preservation groups resulted in the U.S. Government, on April 16, 1980, ceding a second "Quitclaim Deed" of about one hundred fifty eight (158) acres to the State of Rhode Island. This too was ceded in perpetuity under similar terms for use as a public park or for public recreation. The property was accepted by Governor *J. Joseph Garrahy* and is later referred to as Parcel "C" on Jamestown planning maps.

The January 14, 1980 Agreement

Earlier, the Town of Jamestown, under an agreement dated January 14, 1980, leased the original deeded twenty (20) acre Parcel "A" to the State of Rhode Island for a period of forty (40) years (renewable), thereby combining the two properties into one hundred seventy eight (178) acres.

As early as 1978, a master plan for Beavertail State Park was developed to include new roads, bicycle paths, parking areas, a ranger naturalist station, public restrooms and a visitor interpretive center.

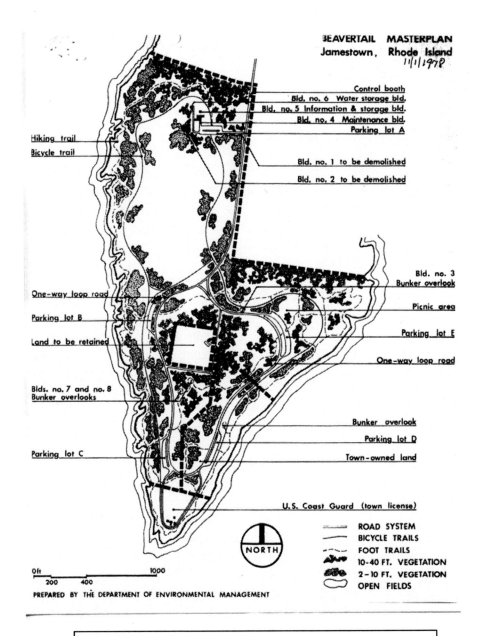

BEAVERTAIL MASTERPLAN
Jamestown, Rhode Island
11/1/1978

Control booth
Bld. no. 6 Water storage bld.
Bld. no. 5 Information & storage bld.
Bld. no. 4 Maintenance bld.
Parking lot A

Bld. no. 1 to be demolished

Bld. no. 2 to be demolished

Hiking trail
Bicycle trail

Bld. no. 3
Bunker overlook

Picnic area

One-way loop road

Parking lot E

Parking lot B

Land to be retained

One-way loop road

Blds. no. 7 and no. 8
Bunker overlooks

Bunker overlook

Parking lot D

Parking lot C

Town-owned land

U.S. Coast Guard (town license)

NORTH

ROAD SYSTEM
BICYCLE TRAILS
FOOT TRAILS
10-40 FT. VEGETATION
2-10 FT. VEGETATION
OPEN FIELDS

0 ft   1000
200   400

PREPARED BY THE DEPARTMENT OF ENVIRONMENTAL MANAGEMENT

Concept of Beavertail State Park envisioned in 1973

The combining of these property acquisitions established the ground rules for Beavertail State Park "in such a way to allow the people of the state to observe and enjoy its natural features".

203

The agreement included the rules and plans for the creation of the state park outlining the user needs and requirements for preserving the fragile ecological, scenic and historical aspects of Beavertail. Maps and proposed development plans, including overlooks, nature trails and a visitor center, were drawn up but the concept almost immediately ran into difficulties which had to be addressed. There was concern regarding endangered plant species, vehicular traffic, parking, sewage and trash disposal, wildlife habitat and total visitor capacities. Before any further work was done, DEM had to modify the plan when the state began cutting back on new projects and requested monies were reallocated to higher priority projects. Funding gradually dried up and the complete envisioned Beavertail State Park program never materialized.

The initial agreement also provided for establishing a consulting "Beavertail Advisory Committee" made up of five (5) members that would include three (3) to be chosen by the Town of Jamestown, one (1) appointed by DEM and one (1) chosen jointly who was not a local resident but knowledgeable of environmental protection and preservation practices. The Advisory Committee continues to meet semi annually in May and October to address current issues and recommend actions or solutions to improve the park.

The seven (7) acres outside the state park containing the Beavertail Light Station remains in federal hands under jurisdiction of the U.S. Coast Guard

(DEM's role at Beavertail State Park and their interest of preserving the light station for the public benefit is noteworthy. The park, open 7 days a week, without entrance fee, is managed by its Chief of Parks and Recreation, "Larry Mouradjian" and "Robert Paquette", the Regional Park Manager. "Brian Gallager", the Park Supervisor maintains the property with help from other DEM employees. Mouradjian has been instrumental and a key player in every aspect concerning Beavertail State Park from its early inception and is the advocate who continues to recognize that the light station should be folded into the parks property authority to guarantee its long term preservation.)

The Rhode Island Parks Association and Bay Island Parks

At the same time Beavertail Park planning was underway, further enthusiasm by visionary preservationists created an organization identified as "The Rhode Island Parks Association", a coalition of interested people and organizations dedicated to the idea of preservation and public use of state properties and historical sites. Its purpose was to supplement state and federal efforts in achieving projects where government funding fell short. *Laurel L. Bowerman* was the president of the non profit group. There was much early movement with a campaign to gain supporting membership by soliciting membership at a $10.00 fee plus $3.00 discounts on state park passes, a 10% discount on association products, a subscription to the association newsletter and special invitations to "members only" events at state parks.

The association comprised an impressive list of dignitaries for its Board of Directors and Trustees, including *Antoinette Downing, Senator Claiborne Pell, Governor Edward DiPrete, Dr. Robert McKenna, Robert Weygand, Sarah Gleason, William Hawkins and Robert Bendick among others.*

In 1994, the State DEM experienced budget cuts that forced one third of the seasonal staff to be laid off, severely limiting the upkeep and staffing of new programs. There was serious consideration of closing off Beavertail Park and Fort Wetherill as stated by Bill Hawkins, chief of the state Parks and Recreation Division at the time. The Providence Journal's feature story on March 16, 1994 showed a photograph of the Light Station and a caption that stated "Eroding Support of Beavertail Park is one of the several recreations sites too be abandoned by DEM".

As the plans for the new Beavertail State Park began to unfold (before the financial crisis), an even greater vision developed by the DEM Division of Parks and Recreation. It was called "Bay Island Parks". This inspiration collected the islands of Narragansett Bay, including the nearby "Dutch Island", into a state-wide accessible public park concept. The plan included nine sites in Narragansett

Bay. Over 2,300 acres were designated to be part of Bay Parks System. The sites were located on "Aquidneck", "Conanicut", "Prudence", "Patience", "Hope" and "Dutch" Islands. The idea was not only visionary and bold; it too captured the public's imagination and support.

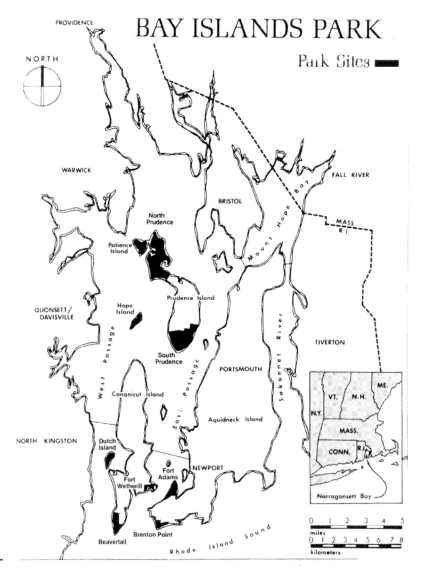

Beavertail Point was envisioned to be the headquarters complete with a Visitor's Center using the abandoned USCG Assistant

Lighthouse Keeper's residence. The Bay Island Park concept was short lived only because the dreaded deer tick "Lyme Disease" had broken out. Many of the islands in Narragansett Bay (a few uninhabited) had aggressive populations of deer and DEM had wisely curtailed and discouraged public visitation. In addition, severe funding restraints discouraged any new programs to be undertaken by the DEM.

Beavertail State Park opened in 1981 to the delight of local and state citizens. By 1989 the state had spent $300,000 on landscaping, roadwork and exterior restoration of buildings. During the period the government controlled the property, only a single road ran down the center of the peninsula. The shoreline was undeveloped. New roads were opened around the perimeter of the park and public parking spaces constructed that allowed overlooks on both sides of the peninsula. If one wished, they could drive around the perimeter of the park without leaving the vehicle to enjoy the vista or park and spend the entire day. At the time, the state estimated it would spend an additional $11,000 a year on maintenance and utilities. Much more needed to be done and the Park Association "believed that individuals, businesses and other groups would be willing to support a State Parks Project with such clear benefit to Rhode Islander's". Progressively, interpretive signs, a few walking trails and clearing of brush opened up more land for visitors to enjoy Narragansett Bay and the spectacular views that Beavertail afforded. The light station at the end of the peninsula became a destination point where visitors walked, sat and fished on rock ledges. Indeed, even with the limited funds, Beavertail State Park with the Beavertail Light Station became the jewel of scenic beauty in the State of Rhode Island. Some say it is the most scenic photographed and artistically painted location in the state.

The Assistant Keeper's House and the Beavertail Museum

When the negotiations with the government first began, park officials had their eyes on the vacant Assistant Keeper's house. As early as the 1970's, the RI DEM had used the Beavertail Light Station Assistant Keeper's house as a local office for its naturalist. It is somewhat unclear when and under what authority the U.S. Coast

Guard gave permission to RI DEM for its use. *(The six room house was originally built in 1898. It housed the extra helper and his family assigned to the light station because of the maintenance work overload of new fog signal equipment.)* After the last Coast Guard inhabitant was reassigned, the building became unfit for public use because its interior had deteriorated when the heating system was removed.

On July 1, 1983, the U.S. Coast Guard issued a license (DTCG-Z71101-83-RP-019L) to the Town of Jamestown to use the licensed premises comprising of four buildings for public outdoor recreational purposes, educational and historical displays, other activities and services or part of the above for a period of five (5) years to be renewed every five (5) years. Excluded from the license was the active navigation aid granite light tower and fog signal device. It was this license that provided the authorization to establish the museum and maintain the property and grounds.

On Sunday, October 16, 1983, a celebration was held at the Light Station marking the completion of both landscaping and exterior renovations. This date also was the formal announcement that a plan was laid for the inclusion of a museum in the Assistant Keeper's house. The event was marked by the attendance of *Adm. Richard A. Bauman*, Commander of the Coast Guard District, *Jerry McIntyre*, President of the Jamestown Town Council, *John F. Doyle* chairman of the Beavertail Committee, and State Representative *Norma Willis*.

At about the same time, the Rhode Island Parks Association had begun discussing the establishment of an aquarium and a naturalist program in the fog signal building with the "University of Rhode Island's Graduate School of Oceanography". The details as to how DEM and the Town of Jamestown arrived at a mutual understanding for the use of the fog signal building under DEM operation and management are vague. In 1991 the RI Parks Association did receive a $4500 grant to restore the fog signal building.

Over the subsequent years of operation, the DEM summer naturalist/aquarium program conducted out of the fog signal building was educational, popular with the visiting public and highly successful. A children's "touch" shell fish pool was added and native fish species filled a number of aquarium tanks. In its early years, *Missy Englehard* conducted nature walks and established an outdoor tidal pool exploratory program that became a popular visitor attraction. More recently DEM summer employee naturalists, under the direction of DEM's Goddard Park operation, have managed the program including stocking the aquarium tanks and maintaining the salt water circulation pumps.

While Beavertail State Park had opened in 1981, it was in 1983 that the RI Parks Association began planning to renovate the Assistant Keeper's house for a museum with exhibits concerning natural and nautical history. Under the promotional slogan "Join Us in the Light Brigade", the renovation of the Beavertail Lighthouse Assistant Keeper's House into a museum was the first initiative of the group. *Laurel Bowerman,* the president, pleaded for help. *"A building that saved hundreds of lives shouldn't be left to die"* she said. Under the supervision of the "Stand Corporation" of Warwick, RI, the restoration contractor, volunteers were solicited to undertake carpentry, painting and general labor tasks. A membership program was initiated at $10.00 to include a $3.00 discount at other state parks and 10% discount on RI Parks Association products. Two association members, *Pat Beausoleil and Sarah Gleason* were actively involved in obtaining artifacts for display in the museum. A fund raising program was initiated. The Association estimated that the total cost for the rehabilitation would be $49,167 but revised that figure eventually to $85,000 for the work including the museum exhibits.

A building that's saved hundreds of lives shouldn't be allowed to die.

Rhode Island Parks Association
Beavertail Lighthouse Renovation Project.

First
Promotional
Poster to save
Beavertail Light
1983

By April of 1987, only $2,930 had been raised. The Association had planned a dedication for June 1988. On August 30, 1988, the RI Historical Preservation Commission obtained a $5,600 (matching) federal grant to be administered by the Rhode Island Parks Association to rehabilitate the Assistant Keeper's quarters. In the grant request, the Commission stated that the owner of the property is the U.S. Coast Guard and that the RI Parks Association would be the sub grantee, explaining further that "the Town of Jamestown leases the Beavertail facility from the Coast Guard, and the Rhode Island Parks Association sub-leases the facility from the Town of Jamestown". This grant was conditional upon approval of all parties involved including, the State's Historical Preservation Officer (SHPO), the Coast Guard, the Town of Jamestown and the RI Parks Association.

At the time, DEM had an award winning traveling exhibit highlighting Rhode Island's lighthouses. When the tour was completed, the exhibit would be permanently housed in the Assistant Keeper's house. The traveling exhibit, titled "The Light Must Be Kept Burning: Rhode Island Lighthouses, Past, Present and Future", was to be the heart of the museum. Funded by a grant from the RI "Committee for the Humanities", it started its journey throughout Rhode Island in May of 1985 and was exhibited in Newport, Narragansett, Block Island, Westerly, East Providence, Woonsocket, Barrington, Bristol, Warwick, and for 2 months at the Rhode Island Historical Society in Providence. *Stuart Parnes*, an exhibit designer from Mystic Seaport, later to be the Executive Director of the Chesapeake Bay Maritime Museum, served as a consultant. The project, according to co-director *Sarah Gleason*, was the first project jointly funded by two state agencies, DEM and RI Historic Preservation Commission, later known as the "RI Historic Preservation and Heritage Commission". *Gleason,* author of "Kindly Lights (1994)" a book about southern New England lighthouses, shared leadership with *William McKenzie* throughout the creation of the museum. In 1998, a grant of $1000 was awarded by the RI Historic Preservation Commission to adapt and install the lighthouse traveling exhibit into the 1ˢᵗ floor spaces in the Assistant Keeper's house.

As the "Join Us in the Light Brigade" promotion gained momentum, the signature parties and other Jamestown organizations provided enthusiastic support. The Coast Guard belatedly further refined the license agreement on May 22, 1989 that the Town of Jamestown "assume the cost of continued maintenance and repair of the property and preserve the architectural and historical integrity of the property". The project was undertaken by dedicated volunteers and supporters who envisioned the benefit to the public of telling the story and history of the light station.

Monies were to be collected by membership, gifts, naming opportunities and product sales. Two years after the start of the campaign and one year after the federal grant was received, the "Grand Opening" took place on Sunday, June 25, 1989 at 2 PM, under the auspices of the Rhode Island Parks Association and its Executive Director, *Patricia Beausoleil*. Although it was three months later, in September of 1989, the formal letter of agreement to establish the museum was endorsed by the RI Historical Preservation Commission, the Coast Guard, RI Parks and Recreation Division and the Town of Jamestown.

The entire first floor of the Assistant Keeper's house had been renovated, exterior walls repaired, new vapor barriers installed and plastering completed. In October of 1988, as a donation, the "International Asbestos Removal Company" removed all the asbestos and carried out the demolition necessary to begin the project. The renovation included new electrical wiring and fixtures provided by "Massachusetts Gas and Electric" with donated services by "IBEW Local 99" apprentices under supervision of the "Columbia Electric Company" of Cranston, installation of a new gas fired heating system donated by the "Providence Gas Company", new flooring, some basement floor reinforcing posts and mounting of most of the exhibits. A small gift shop was operational on the stairs leading to the second floor.

That Sunday marked the first day and the opening announcement stated that the museum would be open to the public Wednesday through Sunday until Labor Day. There were a host of major benefactors who provided financial support in addition to the local businesses and historic and preservation organizations. (*See inclusion*)

Inclusion:

DONATIONS TO THE BEAVERTAIL LIGHTHOUSE MUSEUM BENEFACTORS: Paul& Mary M.Boghossian Memorial Fund, Prospect Hill Foundation, Providence Journal Rhode Island, Committee for the Humanities, Rhode Island Historical Preservation Commission, Rhode Island Marine Sportfishing Alliance, Mr.& Mrs.Christopher Siegwart, Sharpe Family Foundation, Stanley-Bostich Company, Town of Jamestown, Norman Beretta, Betsy Bessinger, Jeanne Bunkley, COLORLAB, Columbia Electric Company, Barbara Cunha, Design Plastic Studio, Duffy & Shanley, James Gibbs, International Asbestos Company, Marybeth Lamotte, New England Coatings Association, Ken Parris, June Webb, Providence Gas Company, Rhode Island Department of Environmental Management, Evelyn Rhodes, Craig Richardson, Stand Corporation, Dawn and Paul Sullivan, Jody Sullivan, T.& J. Container and the United States Coast Guard.

Other Organizations included: Bay Voyage, Calico Cat, Early,Cloud &
Company Everett Associates, F. DiZoglio & Sons,Inc, Gustafson
Design, Island Realty, Ken's East Landing, Jamestown Distributors,
Jody's of Jamestown, John Picerne,Inc., Meredith & Clarke Inc, Mid-
Bay Framery, Patron Protective Systems, Pocasset Seafood, Ryan's
Market, Secret Garden, Stearns Farms, The Anchorage,Inc., Upper Deck
GiftShop, Wickford Gourmet Food, D.A.R. Friends of the Sakonnet
Lighthouse, Jamestown Golf and Country Club, Jamestown Junior
Women's Club, Jamestown Lion's Club, Jamestown Rotary Club,
Jamestown Yacht Club, Mount Hope Bridge Authority, Mystic Seaport
Museum, Newport Historical Society, Quononoquott Garden Club, Rhode
Island Historical Society, and Rose Island Lighthouse Foundation

Beavertail Lighthouse Museum Association (BLMA)

In 1992, the private Rhode Island Parks Association disbanded
under the constraints of being under funded. Some of its members
and others, dedicated in the idea of the museum and recognizing the
importance of keeping the public interest in the museum, planned to
form a new group to save the work of the previous organization.
Jamestown Administrator *Frances Shocket* and former Town
Administrator *Robert Sutton,* encouraged the public to attend
planning meetings. *Hugh Bucher,* a member and volunteer of the
Parks Association, had begun to take on administrative duties from
the original volunteer coordinator *Henry Armburst.* With other
devoted members, *Bucher* and his wife *Ann* held a number of
organizational meetings calling themselves "The Friends of the
Beavertail Lighthouse" and from those meetings the new steward of
the museum, the "Beavertail Lighthouse Museum Association
(BLMA)" was created.

The BLMA incorporated itself in July of 1993 with only thirty (30)
members and elected *Hugh Bucher* President, *Linda Warner* Vice
President, *Charlotte Head* Secretary and *Marion Pierce* Treasurer.
Within a few short months membership had increased to one
hundred ten (110) and from there the organization just kept growing.
Funding came from membership dues and sales of memorabilia sold
on site. Members benefit from a 10% discount within the museum
gift shop which was first located on the steps leading to the second
floor of the Assistant Keeper's house. It has since been expanded
and moved to the rear room of the house. In 1994, it was estimated
that over 5000 visitors passed through the museum. New additional
artifacts have been found over the succeeding years, and *Robert*

Dennis of Middletown, an ex Coast Guard sailor, donated thirty three (33) hand crafted models of Narragansett Bay lighthouses he had made over the years. *Dennis* had served on the USCG "SHRUB", a buoy tender, operating out of Bristol from 1936-1939. *Joe Bouchard,* a BLMA Board Member, also contributed a series of models he crafted. The museum's center piece artifact is a fourth (4th) order Fresnel lens on loan from the Coast Guard. This specific three (3) foot high beehive shaped lens was the last that had been in service at Beavertail. In 1991 it was replaced by a rotating aero type beacon.

The museum under the auspices of the BLMA was opened to the public on weekends from Memorial Day through the 8th of June and then daily from 10:00 AM to 4:00 PM until Labor Day in September. From that day, a weekend schedule was resumed until Columbus Day in October. That schedule essentially remains the same each summer. With the increase in visitors growing each year, extended daily schedules from June to October are under consideration. Admission into the museum has been free to the public from the day it opened and remains so today.

In 1997, an estimated 10,000 visitors toured the museum where 50 volunteer docents rotated around two shifts each open day. The site's popularity has since risen with the state park and the lighthouse museum considered a major visitor destination. Over 25,000 people were counted passing through the museum doors during its 2007 short open season. The BLMA is often called upon to provide special historical educational tours for visiting schools, and for public and private organizations. Local, state, nationwide and international tour groups are accommodated.

The BLMA, as a community service, annually provides two financial college scholarship awards to high school student applicants. The scholarships are funded from the proceeds of gift shop sales and donations to the BLMA during the year.

Another idea which took hold was a winter "Holiday Season Open House". Beavertail Light with its rotating white light beacon, the museum decorated in winter greens and all the lighthouse windows fitted with candle lights, is a spectacular sight. The first winter open house was held in December 1993. BLMA President *Hugh Bucher,* dressed in an authentic Keeper's uniform, greeted guests and visitors. The Open House included a Winter Nature Walk conducted by *Missy Englehard,* the DEM naturalist, who ran the summer program and a prize raffle of donated items. Since then, "Winter Open House" has been conducted every year.

Hugh Bucher

Also at that time, the BLMA undertook a $12,000 fund drive to re-roof both keeper buildings with red shingles replicating the light station's roof coloring of an earlier era. The fund drive was named after *Henry Armburst*, the first volunteer coordinator. A grant from "The Champlin Foundations" for $13,000 was also received to supplement the roof work under a contract placed with the "B. N. Goldstein Roof Restorations Company". A second Champlin grant in 1996 was used to create a gift shop in the former kitchen and to repair some windows. In 2005, BLMA received a matching $18,000 grant from the Rhode Island Historic Preservation and Heritage Commission to replace deteriorated storm windows in both keepers' houses and the granite light tower. A supplement from the Town of Jamestown for $6,000 to replace storm doors and bulkheads was also received and the work was accomplished by the "Abcore Restoration Company" of Narragansett.

From time to time, per request of the BLMA, the granite light tower has been infrequently opened to the public. Coast Guard personnel would temporarily deactivate the rotating beacon in the lantern room in the upper level of the tower. Visitors would then be allowed to climb the internal cast iron circular stairway up through a floor hatch into the lantern room. Just below the lantern room, at a height of fifty five (55) feet above the ground, a door hatch allowed access to the external catwalk surrounding the lantern room. This catwalk provides a 360 degree panoramic view of Beavertail Park, Narragansett Bay, the rocks below and breathtaking ocean views. By 2006, years of neglect and deterioration of the iron work railing around the catwalk and upper gallery made it unsafe and visitor access was curtailed.

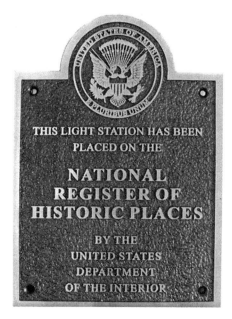

Although the Light Station site was listed in the National Register of Historic Places on December 12, 1977 by the Jamestown Historical Society, it had neglected to provide a historic marker to that fact. It was not until 2006 that BLMA commissioned a bronze plaque be cast to be mounted at the entrance to the museum to enlighten visitors of the importance of the site.

The Keeper's House

(Since 1977, the Keeper's House has been under custodian care administered under an agreement/license from the Coast Guard by the Town of Jamestown. A custodian living on site is vital to minimizing vandalism.)

Immediately after assuming responsibilities of maintaining the site as specified in the 1983 license, the Town of Jamestown established

216

a set of guidelines for qualifications for a caretaker/custodian to reside in the Keeper's quarters. The custodian was allowed to live in the residence free of any rental fee. Utilities such as electricity, heating fuel and telephone were paid by the custodian. In return for the free rent, he was required to perform a minimum of twenty (20) hours maintenance related work. The first town appointed custodian, *Peter Anderson,* filled the position beginning in 1977 for the next 16 years. In 1993, the second custodian, *Clayton Carlisle* and his family replaced him and the third, *Richard Schutt,* a single person, commenced the duties in 1999. The custodian also has use of the two car garage and the old oil storage shed.

It was under *Schutt's* tenure that another faction in Jamestown picked up interest in the residence for use as a "fill-in" to meet other obligations, namely government mandated "Affordable Housing". Ignoring objections from the Beavertail Advisory Committee, the BLMA and Coast Guard Administrators in Washington, Jamestown officials in the fall of 2006 took steps to evict *Schutt* from the premises and appoint a family with 4 young children under the guise of meeting "Affordable Housing guidelines". A new custodian selection point system was established to select the candidate, significantly favoring a low income Jamestown resident with a family. A $300 a month (refundable) rental fee was proposed to be paid to the town by the custodian.

In February of 2007, a new concern of possible lead contamination of the soil and paint on the windows from years of lead paint deposits was raised that could be detrimental to children. At that time, a hold was placed on having a family move into the premises. Overriding Jamestown intentions of using the Keeper's residence as a revolving housing unit, the "USCG Commander of the Civil Engineering Unit", *J.J. Metcalf, in April of 2007* informed Jamestown officials that the Coast Guard was in the process of reviewing usage of licensed properties and that type of occupancy is not allowable.

Beavertail Light Station's Future

The future of the 259 year old light station is dependant upon those who have the foresight and dedication to provide the resources and protective measures to preserve the historic buildings and property features for public use. It is not the role of a single group of interested people or that of a single organization. Considerable effort, planning and funding by many are required to establish an endowment to meet the clear objectives of preserving the site.

While it appears that only four organizations have interest in Beavertail Light Station, (BLMA, DEM, Town of Jamestown and the Coast Guard), in reality, there are a total of ten. Four are associated with the State of Rhode Island. These include the "Division of Parks and Recreation" under the "Department of Environmental Management", the "Division of Tourism" under the "Economic Development Corporation", the "RI Historic Preservation and Heritage Commission" and the "Coastal Resources Management Council".

Three federal agencies concerned are comprised of the "U.S. Coast Guard", the "General Services Administration", and the "National Park Service" under jurisdiction of the "Department of Interior". The others are: two private non profit organizations, the "BLMA" and the "Jamestown Historical Society", and one municipality, the "Town of Jamestown".

Each of these organizations has set rules and guidelines, and each has different charters but all look at the light station as an asset. However, it was the BLMA, who after 11 years of operating the museum seriously began to address questions about the future of the light station, its preservation and on site operations.

Early in 2003, under the direction of President *Linda Warner,* the BLMA formed a "Long Range Planning Committee". Its purpose was to identify key issues regarding the operations of BLMA, the future of the light station and make recommendations to the BLMA Board. The Executive Officers and the Board of Directors fully realized that their museum's popularity was increasing and Coast

Guard contribution toward repair and maintenance of the site had dwindled. The Town of Jamestown, while sympathetic to the repair and preservation needs, had become reluctant to fund major repairs and was also burdened with other municipal obligations. It was time to establish a new plan and to set directional goals for the organization, keeping both educational and preservation priorities in focus.

The new "Long Range Planning Committee" was chaired by *Richard Sullivan*, a longtime member and officer of BLMA. After a series of meetings by committee members *Charles Auld, Don Barrows, Allen Bestwick, Joe Bouchard, Jim Filkins, Varoujan Karentz, Frank Meyer, Charles Osenton and Charlotte Richardson*, recommendations were made to the BLMA Board of Directors at their September 23, 2003 annual membership meeting.

> *"There is consensus that acquisition of the entire lighthouse site, including the Keeper's and Assistant Keeper's Quarters, granite tower, fog horn building and original foundation is the priority long range goal. The Long Range Planning Committee (LRPC) is in agreement that the most achievable objective on route to acquisition is the expansion of the museum's educational exhibition space into the Keeper's Quarters, the fog horn building, the building adjacent to the granite tower and the tower itself. This expansion aligns with BLMA's objectives of education and preservation".*

> *'That the BLMA take steps to create a plan taking full responsibility for the Light Station site at some future date and to petition the appropriate federal, state and local agencies of BLMA's intentions. This responsibility will include operation and maintenance of grounds and buildings.*

The BLMA board and membership endorsed the recommendations and the Long Range Planning Committee was absorbed into a new "Site Acquisition Committee" chaired by *Varoujan Karentz*.

Within a year, a "Notice of Intent" had been formulated and conceptual plan for ownership, operation and management of the light station site was published. The conceptual plan was forwarded as information to federal, state and local agencies and followed up with briefings. The plan dovetailed into the Coast Guard announcement that it was gradually "excessing" lighthouse properties from its inventories in conjunction with the U.S. National Park Service (NPS) program of transferring light stations over to municipalities and nonprofit organizations. The transfer of these properties was taking place under a congressional law titled the "National Historic Lighthouse Preservation Act of 2000". The Act encouraged saving historic light house locations and structures for public educational use. Over the next few years, more than forty (40) lighthouses were transferred. Beavertail Light Station was to be included in this program but a date of release had not yet been set.

In 2005 and 2006, the Coast Guard had slowed down its site transfers because of environmental cleanup issues on many of its land sites. Problems of hazardous lead paint in buildings, in the surrounding soil and how best to remove the contaminants were the prime concern and since the Coast Guard acknowledged they were responsible for the clean up, methods and procedures to be used had to be studied.

When Beavertail is "excessed" by the Coast Guard and turned over to the U.S. Government Services Administration (GSA) for disposal and hence to the National Park Service (NPS), the BLMA application to the NPS will include a "Memorandum of Agreement" that provides the State of Rhode Island to become the property transferee (owner), the Town of Jamestown as a partner to provide some related maintenance services, and the BLMA to undertake the operation and management of the expanded museum. An alternative interim possibility exists that will allow the expanded museum to operate under BLMA management by an amendment to the existing Coast Guard license.

In anticipation of the site's eventual transfer, the BLMA, under a matching grant from the "U.S. National Trust for Historic Places", undertook a professional site study of the light station and its best use for an expanded museum and availability for the general public. The study and engineering evaluation, undertaken by "Newport Collaborative Architects" firm of Newport, was completed at the end of 2006 and provides a "Master Plan" for the use of the site after the transfer from the government. The architectural company was noted for its past experience in development planning for many of Rhode Island's historic places including a number of lighthouses.

The architectural study recommended two (2) phases. The first phase is centered on the creation of a center of attraction for visitors behind the fog signal building, expanding the museum into all the buildings including the light tower, retaining the fog signal building as an aquarium managed by DEM, adding a small theater and additional exhibits into the Keeper's quarter, and modifying the two (2) car garage into a gift shop. The 2nd floors of both keepers' houses would be used for livable quarters; one, for a custodian, and the other for probable use as a "Living Experience" rental unit by visitors. The 2nd phase would consider the construction of a "Visitors Interpretation Center" at a location in the state park north of the present site. The center would highlight historical information of all lighthouses of Narragansett Bay, and the historical military significance of Beavertail during World War II. The concept would also move the aquarium to this new location and the fog signal building would revert to housing historical fog signal development exhibits for which the light station contributed much to the U.S. Lighthouse Service in its early years. Any changes that affect the landscape require both review and approval to meet with "Open Space" ordinances, development plan processes, and permitting requirements of the Town and the Rhode Island's Coastal Resources Management Council.

Cost estimates were also prepared by both the "Abcore Company" and the "Newport Collaborative Architects" to refurbish, restore and stabilize all the buildings on the site. The serious deterioration of the 1856 granite tower and its iron work was of major concern as well as the basements of both keepers' buildings. Estimates range into the hundreds of thousands of dollars.

In November of 2007, four competitive grants were received by the BLMA. One from the "Champlin Foundations" in the amount of $227,000 was to completely repair and restore the granite light Tower. The "RI Historic Preservation and Heritage Commission" provided a matching grant of $50,000 to begin undertaking repairs to the two keeper houses. "BankNewport" provided a matching grant to replace the deteriorated post and rail perimeter fence surrounding the light station property and the fourth grant was provided by the "US National Trust for Historic Places" to begin an underground radar imaging survey of Beavertail's 1749 foundation.

BLMA Officers and Board Members

As with any nonprofit organizations, its Board of Directors and Executive Committee, all whom are volunteers, determine the success and or failure of any organization. The BLMA has a distinguished record and exemplary reputation in the community. Its hierarchy organization is comprised of volunteers from throughout Rhode Island, and reflects the statewide interest for preservation of the light station. *(See Appendix V for a listing of Officers and Board Members.)*

Memorials

While it has not been the policy of the BLMA to solicit funds nor encourage naming opportunities, there does exist a number of memorial plaques on site which pay tribute to past members and those who have provided a significant service toward the preservation of the light station.

Flag Pole:

Plaque at base of flagpole states it was dedicated to *Jimmie Smith* "dedicated member of the "Jamestown Beavertail Committee". Whose efforts helped in the formation of the State Park.

Door of Assistant Keeper's Quarters:

Plaque on door states "Restoration of the door and knocker in memory of *Donald C. Mattera* by family Members"

Tree Planted in Rear of Keeper's House with Plaque:

"In Memory to *Rebecca Jamison Carlisle* Sept 1995". She was the wife of caretaker/custodian *Clayton Carlisle* who was killed in a tragic automobile accident.

Stone Tablet Commemorating the 1749 Original Lighthouse:

This tablet was placed on top of the 1749 foundation ruin and was washed off by Hurricane "Bob" in 1991. Now temporally located in the BLMA museum.

National Historic Place Plaque: to be placed in 2008

Granite Bench in Front of Assistant Keeper's House:

Plaque states "1-17-95 In remembrance of *Rebecca Jamison* the *Jamison* family"

Afterword

While this book, within its relatively few pages, reviewed glimpses of happenings at Beavertail Light Station over the past 250 years, it is hoped the reader gained some new insight about those who made the light possible, of the people who lived and how they worked there. More importantly, it is hoped that it provides the reader a better appreciation of the lights contribution to the thousands of vessels and their crews who used the light to make safe passage.

The time has arrived to consider the next 250 years and how this historic facility can be secured for future generations. The importance of Beavertail light as a navigation aid is now less subdued and is rapidly reaching its obsolescence due to alternative modern electronic navigation methods. Once its use becomes part of the past, it joins other lighthouses and light stations nationwide in becoming a historic artifact. The site will be turned over to the public for their enjoyment, education, use and preservation. The "US National Park Service" has opened this door with its "Historic Lighthouse Preservation Act". The non-profit "Beavertail Light House Museum Association" has voluntarily accepted the preservation and educational stewardship role, although at times stumbling over interferences caused by bureaucratic well intentioned hurdles.

That stewardship role is not an easy path. It takes much volunteer effort and funding to preserve the site, its buildings and with it, its history. It has become a major visitor and tourist destination, an educational engine for school children who, like sponges, soak up the keeper's way of life and stories of development that the site beholds. Coupled with "Beavertail State Park", the light station at the southern end of "Beavertail Point" herds in thousands of people a year to enjoy a seaside holiday unsurpassed anywhere in Rhode Island.

Herewith, remains an obligation and a challenge to every person who has ever visited Beavertail. It is making a commitment to help save this historic site and all that it means for the next century and beyond.

Become part of it.

Appendix I

Reference Sources

Appleton's *pages (726-727) Steam Signals*

Beavertail Lighthouse, Manuscript , *Date and Author Unknown*

Beavertail Sound Signal Study, *2005-06, Lanette Macaruso*

Bowditch, An Epitome of Navigation, Volume II

Bowditch, The American Practical Navigator HO 9

Bulletin of JHS. A short History of Beavertail Light *William Gilman, Low August 1936*

Carnegie Hero Fund Commission , *2006, Capt George Manders Medal*

Chapman's: Piloting and Seamanship

Correspondence from Doug Bingham President Lightship Sailors Association, *May 2000*

Defenses of Narragansett Bay in World War II, 1980, *Walter Schroder*

Department of Commerce Lighthouse Service Records, Waltham, MA.

Development Grant Agreement RI Preservation and RI Parks Assoc. *dated 13 October 1989*

Early American Hurricanes,. American Meteorological Society, *Boston, Ludlum, D. 1963*

Early Days Around Narragansett Bay, *Elizabeth Helmick, JPL 974.561*

Early Rhode Island, Grafton Press 1910, *William B Weeden. A.M .Pirates, Ship Counts*

Famous American Lighthouses, *Spring 1995*

Frank Meyer Report, *Beavertail Ownership Relationships dated 25 January 2004*

History of Jamestown 1949- *Colonial Council minutes*

History of Jamestown and Newport, *H. S. Visitors Guide 2004*

History of Jamestown on Conanicut Island, *1949, Walter Leon Watson*

Internet Web Site www.nightbeacon.com , *light characteristics*

IRS letter *re; RI Parks Association Project Statement dated 8 September 1986*

Jamestown Affairs, *Meriden Press 1966, Sue Maden & Patrick Hodgkin , Shipwrecks*

Jamestown Affordable Housing Committee *Memorandum dated 8 May 2002*

Jamestown Press, 1 *September 2005- Conanicut Island Land Trust, Russell Clarke*

Jamestown Press, *12 November 1993- Sue Madden, Patrick Hodgkin, Shipwrecks*

Jamestown Press, *17 March 1994, Closing of Beavertail Park*

Jamestown Press, *4 June 199,- Lighthouse Museum Seeks Support*

JHS Newsletter *Spring 1992 ,1749 Marker*

Lease Agreement Town of Jamestown and State of Rhode Island *dated 14 January 1980*

Letter- *4/15/2001 - Don Goguen, MKCM (ret), LV 102 Lightship*

Letter Report Land Transfers, *25 January 2004, Frank Meyer*

Letter, 27 April 2000, *Joesph MacDougald ex watch officer HECP Fort Burnside Beavertail*

Letter, Sandra Driscoll ,*Aug 2006, Re: BMl, E. Donahue*

LH 974.561 *Helm, slavery*

Lois Sorensen Family Genealogy Records 2003

Longitude, *Dana Sobel, 1995 Walker Publishing*

Meteorological Dairy, David Melville , *Newport Historical Society, gas lighting*

Narragansett Bay Pilots , *Manuscript (undated) Edward Spinney,-piloting*

Narragansett Bay Shipwrecks *1971 B. W. Luther*

Narragansett Bay: A Friend's Perspective , *Sea Grant URI ,Stuart O. Hale*

National Park Service, Lighthouse Keepers in the Nineteenth Century

Newport Daily News, 17 October 1983- 4th order lenses in Lighthouse

Newport Daily News, *9 November 1906, water gathering field*

Newport Daily News 13 Oct 1905, telephone connection to Beavertail

Newport Daily News, *20 October 1930-,Coal Barges ashore on Conanicut Island*

Newport Historical Society, *Card Catalog file 2007*

NOAA Coast Pilot,- 2000 , Navigation Hazards

Notorious Triangle- *Jay Coughtr , slavery*

NY Times, notes , *ship disasters*

NY Times, 6 November, 1880, SS Rhode Island

Providence Journal March 2006 Series, *Unrighteous Traffick, slavery, G .Carbone*

Quick Claim Deed United States of America and State of Rhode Island *dated 25 January 1980*

Quick Claim Deed United States of America and Town of Jamestown *dated 11 July 1973*

Reeds Nautical Almanac and Coast Pilot

Rhode Island Parks Association, *Final Report Letter dated 11 Oct 1989*

Rhode Islander Magazine, *August 1946 Mickey Radar Site*

Rhode Islands First Light House, *Bulletin of NHS #39 Summer 1970, Richard Champlin*

RI at the End of the Century *Vol 111, Edward Field*

RI Records 1780-1783

RI State Archives

Rushlight, December 1998-, *David Melville gas illumination experiments*

Sail Magazine, *September 2004 ,Chris Roman, Weather and Sea*

Sea Classics Friendly Fire, *August 2001,Anthony S. Nicolosi, USS Capella*

Stebbins Coast Pilot, 1901

The Beavertail Stones, Sept 2003, *P.J Perkins*

The Harbor Entrance Command Post, *April 2000 , Varoujan Karentz*

The Keeper's Log, Vol. VIII, *NO.1,* Fall 1990, Wayne C.Wheeler,

The Keeper's Log, Vol. XI, No.3, Spring 1995, Gleason, Sarah,

The Lighthouses of Rhode Island, *2006 , Jeremy D'Entremont*

The Lightships at Brenton Reef, *2000 , Varoujan Karentz*

The Slave Trade- *1997, Hugh Thomas*

Town of Jamestown Letter to US Dept of Interior *dated 1 Nov 1977*

US Coast Guard Historians Office *2001*

US Lighthouse Board Report, *1894 Fog Signal Experiments*

US Navy Station Newport, *http://www.nsnpt.navy.mil/history.htm*

USCG Atlantic Coast Pilot and Light List

USCG Agreement, *Z71101-0001-92, 25 Oct 1991, lens loan*

USCG Allowance *Report, Feb 11 1952 , lens manufacturer*

USCG Historic Light Station Information *Web Site 2001*

USCG Letter, *M. Brite dated 19 April 1994*

USCG letter, *Rdm. W. N. Derby dated 4 Sept 1946*

USCG Library, New London, CT

USCG License DTCG-Z71101-83-RP-019L

Wireless and Steam Museum, *Ericsson Engine, Robert Merriman notes, 2005*

Wreckhunter.net website, Shipwrecks in Narragansett Bay

1421 The Year the Chinese Discovered America, 2003,–*Mendes*

Appendix II

Narragansett Bay Lightships
(Source USCG Historian Records, Washington DC)

VESSEL DESIGNATION: LV 11

YEAR BUILT: 1853
BUILT AT: Baltimore (MD)
BUILDER: Tardy & Auld
APPROPRIATION: $15,000
CONTRACT PRICE: $13,462
DESIGN: Wood- white oak; copper & iron fastened; 2 masts with day marks at both mastheads
LENGTH: 104'0", BEAM: 24'8", DRAFT: 9'10" TONNAGE: 320 gross
PROPULSION: Sail- schooner rig; fore and main carried on Spencer masts
ILLUMINATING APPARATUS: Lanterns, each having 8 constant level oil lamps
FOG SIGNAL: Hand operated 1050 lb bell, plus "horn and gong"

CONSTRUCTION NOTES - MODIFICATIONS - EQUIPMENT CHANGES & IMPROVEMENTS:
LV 11-
1855: Rebuilt at New York Navy Yard $11,000 after being blown ashore-
1856: Lamps fitted with reflectors-
1865: Repairs after being driven on rocks; new false keel, part of main keel and
     bottom planks replaced, forefoot and rudder repaired recaulked and coppered,
     both masts repaired - $8,000-
1870: Standing rigging replaced with iron wire - $1,040
1876: Rebuilt and re-rigged, "frame and planking decayed" - $21,620.76
1891 and 1905: repairs for collision damage
1912: Illuminant changed from oil to oil/gas
1919: Equipped with radio; discontinued 1922
1920: Lanterns, lantern houses and Spencer masts removed; equipped with lens
     lanterns capable of using either oil or acetylene

STATION ASSIGNMENTS: LV11
1854-1855: Nantucket New South Shoal (MA)
1856-1897: Brenton Reef (RI)
1897-1902: Relief (3d District)
1902-1925: Scotland (NJ)
(1901: Jul 3-Dec 19, sent to 4th District for "temporary service as Relief ")
(Prior to 1867 when No.11 was assigned, official records identify this vessel by the name of the station on which it was serving)

HISTORICAL NOTES: LV 11-
1854: Jun 15, placed on Nantucket New South Shoal, (MA)-(lst Nantucket lightship)-
1855: Feb, broke adrift and blown ashore at Montauk NY, salvaged & repaired-
1856: Placed on Brenton Reef, (RI)
1865: Oct 19, parted chain and blown ashore on rocks during westerly gale, crewman reported "badly injured"-
1890: Nov 26, in collision with British steamer CURLEW
1891: Nov 23, fog bell characteristic changed to ring 10 sec, silent 30 sec
1897: Nov 4, Withdrawn (replaced by LV 39) and transferred to 3d District as RELIEF

1901 Jun 30, towed to 4th District for "temporary service as Relief"
1901: Dec 19, returned to 3d District, still in Relief status
1902: Dec 2, placed on Scotland,(NJ)
1903: Mar 10, in collision with schooner
1905: Mar 14, Apr 12, May 29, in collision with scows under tow
1912: Apr 10, in collision with mud scows under tow
1925: Oct 30, when removed from Scotland station, was reported to be the oldest vessel (72 years) in the Lighthouse Service and possibly the   oldest vessel in any US Government agency at that time.

RETIRED PROM LIGHTSHIP DUTY: 1925 AGE: 72

SUBSEQUENT DISPOSITION: LV 11-
Sold 1927?

COMMANDING OFFICERS: LV 11
1854-1855: Samuel D Bunker, Keeper
1886-1888: David H Caulkins, Keeper
1888-1893: Edward Fogarty, Keeper
1893-1898: Edward Fogarty, Master
1905-?: Thor Olsen, Mate
1916-1918: Emil C Ness, Mate
?-1916: John N Veseth, Mate
?-1917: Ernest W Borgstrom, Master
1918-1919: Uno Taplo, Mate
1918-1920: John Anderson, Mate
1920-1925: John N Veseth, Mate

1852: Said to have been named LEDYARD when launched-
1856: Third inspector Ludlow stated "very slightly built and will answer best
    for use on an inside station"-
1856: Rebuilt $11,000
1856: Second lantern installed (apparently on jigger mast)

STATION ASSIGNMENTS: LV 14
1853-1856: Brenton Reef (RI)

VESSEL DESIGNATION: LV 14

YEAR BUILT:	1852
BUILT AT:	Newport (RI)
BUILDER:	?
APPROPRIATION	$15,000 (1851)

 DESIGN: Wood - white oak & yellow pine; copper & iron fastened; 2 masts (foremast higher) day marks on both
LENGTH: 91' (loa), BEAM: 22', DRAFT: 9', TONNAGE: 159 gross
PROPULSION: Sail - "sloop rigged"
ILLUMINATING APPARATUS: Single lantern with 8 lard oil lamps
FOG SIGNAL: Bell and horn, hand operated

CONSTRUCTION NOTES - MODIFICATIONS - EQUIPMENT CHANGES & IMPROVEMENTS:
LV 14-
1856-1872: Cornfield Point (CT)
1872: Relief (CT) - laid up

HISTORICAL NOTES: LV 14
1853: Mar, placed on Brenton Reef (RI)

1856: Dec, placed on Cornfield Point (CT) after rebuild
1866: Rammed by a New London steamer in heavy fog; considerable damage
1868: Mar 18, broke adrift, towed to New London, resumed station Mar 20
1872: Withdrawn from station - condition "so bad as to render her unworthy of
    further repair"; placed in Relief status and laid up

More notes:
RETIRED FROM LIGHTSHIP DUTY: 1872 AGE: 20
SUBSEQUENT DISPOSITION: Sold at public auction, New London (CT) 1872 - $615.00
SISTER VESSELS: None

VESSEL DESIGNATION: LV 39

YEAR BUILT: 1875
BUILT AT: Pelham (NY) (City Island)
BUILDER: David Carl
APPROPRIATION: $50,000
CONTRACT PRICE: $42,200
SISTER VESSELS: None
DESIGN: Wood- white oak & locust; copper & galvanized iron fastened; 2 masts, day marks on both; smokestack forward of mainmast; 2 aux. steam boilers, steam pump and steam fog signal machinery
LENGTH: 1196" (loa); BEAM: 26'9"; DRAFT: 12'6"; TONNAGE: 387 gross
PROPULSION: Sail-schooner rig; fore and main carried on Spencer masts
1919: Equipped with radio; discontinued 1923
1921: Lanterns & lantern houses removed, foremast replaced with tall steel
    skeleton light structure with acetylene lamp, no light installed on mainmast

STATION ASSIGNMENTS: LV 39
1875-1876: Vineyard Sound (MA)
1876-1877: Five Fathom Bank (NJ)
1877-1897: Relief (MA)
1897: Relief (NY)
1897-1935: Brenton Reef (RI)

HISTORICAL NOTES: LV 39-

1875: Nov 16, stationed on Vineyard Sound (MA)-
1876: Jun 14, relieved Five Fathom Bank (NJ) (replacing LV 7 which returned to
    Staten island for repair)-
1877: Jun 19, returned to 2d District, and assigned Relief duty-
1879-1882: Remained at Woods Hole Depot except while under repair
1883: Nov-Feb, relieved Vineyard Sound
1884/83: Remained at Woods Hole (apparently seldom used. due to rotten condition)
1886: Aug 28-Oct 16, relieved Vineyard Sound; Dec 30-Mar 11 1887, relieved
    Pollock Rip
1887: Extensive overhaul, rotten timbers and planking replaced
1888: Sep 18-?, relieved Pollock Rip
1889: Jul 25-Oct 3, relieved Vineyard Sound
1890: May 26- Jun 30, relieved Vineyard Sound
1891: Aug 9-Jun 28. relieved Vineyard Sound; July, boiler & machinery repairs
1892/3: "supplied with new riding stopper prior to going on Nantucket. New South
    Shoal" as relief vessel
1894/95: Remained at Woods Hole during both years
1895: Oct 1-Jan 15 1896, relieved Great Round Shoal

More notes: LV 39-

1896: Jan 15-Feb 18, relieved Pollock Rip; May, repaired: Jul 5 ã Jul 30, relieved Boston; Aug 14-Jan

24 1897, relieved Vineyard Sound
1897: Jun 12, transferred to 3d District, towed to Staten island by AZALEA; relieved Fire Island LV 58 from Jul 15 to Sep 2; then assigned to   Brenton Reef (RI) taking station Nov 4, 1897
1905 Relieved for repair "having been continuously on station since 1899"
1905 Aug, struck by battleship USS IOWA, carrying away part of lightship's stem and causing damage to head stays
Remained assigned to Brenton Reef station until 1935

RETIRED FROM LIGHTSHIP DUTY: 1935; AGE: 60

SUBSEQUENT DISPOSITION: Reported by Boston Globe to be in use as floating restaurant at Gloucester, MA in 1960's: observed in use as Coast Guard Auxiliary clubhouse, Boston, MA in 1967; sank in 1975 (age 100) while being towed to a shipyard at Beverly, MA; not salvaged

COMMANDING OFFICERS: LV 39
1897: (Jun-Aug) Jacob C Flinkfelt, Master
1898-?: Edward Fogarty, Master
?-1917 Charles A Hawkins,Mate
1917-1919: Karl M Larsen, Mate
1919: Fred J Worth, Mate
1919-1922: Martin Berg, Mate

ILLUMINATING APPARATUS: 2 lanterns, each with 8 Argand fountain burner oil lamps
FOG SIGNAL: 12" steam whistle, hand operated bell
(First US lightship to be equipped with steam fog signal when built)
CONSTRUCTION NOTES - MODIFICATIONS - EQUIPMENT CHANGES & IMPROVEMENTS:
LV 39-

1879: Recaulked and boilers overhauled
1882: Hull and boiler repairs at New Bedford; extensive rot
1887: Rotten timbers replaced at New Bedford; also repaired 1889,1891,1893
1897: Extensive repairs prior to being transferred to 3d District
1899: Jul 25-Mar 8, 1900, extensive overhaul and refit
1905: Brought in for repair, having been continuously on station since 1900
1909: 6" fog whistle added; 12" whistle retained
1911: Equipped with submarine bell signal
1922-1923: Harold White, Mate
1923-1927: Theodor Anderson, Mate
?-1927: Charles Steijen, Master
1927-?: Theodor Anderson, Master
1927: John B Kelley, Mate
1927-1929: Frederic Sundloff, Mate
1928-?: August E Gustafson, mate

VESSEL DESIGNATION LV 102

YEAR BUILT: 1916
BUILT AT: Wilmington (DE)
BUILDER: Pusey & Jones
APPROPRIATION: $125,000
(Appropriation. Oct 22, 1913 for Southwest Pass light vessel)
CONTRACT PRICE: $110,065
SISTER VESSELS: LV 101 / WAL 524
DESIGN: Self propelled; steel whaleback hull; single large dia. tubular lantern mast forward; steel pilot house/bridge at foot of mast; small jigger mast aft

LENGTH: l0l'10" (loa); BEAM: 25'0"; DRAFT: 11'4"; TONNAGE: 360 tons displ
PROPULSION: One 200 HP Mietz & Weiss 4 cylinder 2 cycle direct reversing kerosene engine
driving 4 bladed propeller; speed 8 knots

ILLUMINATING APPARATUS: 500mm 5th order lens with 6 flash panels and kerosene
lamp revolved by weight driven clockwork; large cylindrical lantern; 24,000cp
FOG SIGNAL: 6" air siren; mushroom type horn on deck; compressor driven by two
40 HP kerosene engines; submarine bell; hand operated 700 lb bell
space
CONSTRUCTION NOTES - MODIFICATIONS - EQUIPMENT CHANGES & IMPROVEMENTS:
LV 102
Launched Nov 27, 1915; sea trials Dec 13, 1916; delivered Edgemoor DE Jan 1917
1917: Lamp changed to Incandescent oil vapor (IOV)
1919: Equipped with radio
1931: Equipped with radio beacon
1932: Illuminating apparatus electrified
1935: Fog signal changed to 10" plus 6" air whistles
1945: Fitted with detection radar
1944: Re-powered with Cooper-Bessemer 315HP diesel engine
1955: Original lantern housing and 5th Order lens removed and replaced with
        duplex 375mm lens lantern, 13,000 cp
1963 USCG lists vessel at 11'9" max draft, 393.9 tons; air diaphragm horn
        (Leslie 17" typhoon); CR-103 radar; other characteristics in line with above
Radio and visual call sign NMGR (1940-1963)

STATION ASSIGNMENTS: LV 102 / WAL 525
1917-1918: Southwest Pass (LA)
1918-1933: South Pass (LA)
1933-1934: Relief (MA)
1935-1962: Brenton Reef (RI)
1962-1963: Cross Rip (MA)
(1918: Southwest Pass unusable due to silting; station discontinued and LV 102
        transferred to South Pass
1933: South Pass station discontinued
1942-1945: During WWII, remained on Brenton Reef station; no armament
        provided

HISTORICAL NOTES: LV 102 / WAL 525
1917: Jan 10, departed Edgemoor (DE) Lighthouse Depot for New Orleans
1917: Feb 24, placed on Southwest Pass (LA)
1918: Moved to South Pass
1926: Apr 18-21, while docked at Pensacola, FL during hurricane, stern stove in and
        plating severely damaged by colliding repeatedly against the bow of LV 81 which
        was tied up astern. Both vessels hauled and repaired
1933: Transferred to 2d District; assigned as Relief while being overhauled
1935: Placed on Brenton Reef (RI) until 1962 than moved to Cross Rip (MA)

More notes:

RETIRED FROM LIGHTSHIP DUTY: 1963; AGE: 46
SUBSEQUENT DISPOSITION: Decommissioned at Boston Oct 25, 1963; towed to Portland, ME for
storage awaiting final disposition; sold Mar 2, 1965; then used as crab processing ship CROSS RIP in
Seattle, WA.. Listed in Merchant Vessels of the US 1970 as fishing out of Ketchikan, AK, named BIG
DIPPER

COMMANDING OFFICERS: LV 102 / WAL 525
1916-1918: Albert C Scull, Master
1917-1918: Henry Olsen, Mate
1918-1919: Henry Olsen, Master

1918: Horace Gager, Mate
1919-1920: Dennis Morrissey, Mate
1919-1922: Frank Murphy, Master
1920-1921: Adolph Nordberg, Mate
1922: Henry Olsen, Mate
1922-1927: Henry Olsen, Master
1922-1927: William H Clements, Mate
1927-?: William H Clements, Master
1939-?: Norman Gray, Master
1962-1963: CWO Edward Godlewski, CO

Appendix III

The compilation below are from reports forwarded to the 3rd Lighthouse district located in Newport, RI and subsequently passed along to the US Lighthouse Board who annually provided a formal report to the Secretary of the United States Treasury under which the Lighthouse Service was organized. The chronology of activities reported to the Lighthouse Board give a perspective of the changes and activities at Beavertail Light Station (RI) from 1873 to 1905.

1873   Considerable Repairs were made to the Daboll trumpet fog signals operated by the 24 inch Ericsson caloric engines. The duplicate engines were also repaired one at a time.

1874 $8,000 were expended for better accommodations (the Keeper's quarters were   completed in 1858)

1876   *Beavertail Light Ship #11.* $21,620 was expended for repairs to include new ship frames, hosepipes, rails and rigging.

1883   Daboll Trumpet Fog Signal repaired operated by 24 inch hot air engine.

1884   Dwelling repaired. Installed two 10 inch steam whistles with duplicate boilers and a large water cistern for collecting rain water. It was quoted ; "the new signals will meet every want of the navigation"

1885   *Brenton Reef Lightship #11.* Hull is in good condition. Deck leaks, bell frame rotten, foremast decayed.

        Beavertail Lightship #11. New canvas, paint and medicines placed aboard.
        Lighthouse fog signal was operated for 504 hours, 67,456 pounds of coal consumed.

1889   Purchased land for $3500. Re-pointed tower and replaced and refitted lantern glass.

1897   *Brenton Reef Lightship #11.* 12 years on station. Needs thorough repairs before
        winter.

Hog Island Shoal Lightship #12. Vessel is old. No spare vessel is available. Needs $500 to repair. Received new main, jib, boat sails, cooking gear and stores.

Lighthouse fog signal was operated for 593 hours, 46 tons of coal consumed.

Light Station Addition (Assistant Keeper's house) completed.

Hog Island Shoal Lightship #12. Vessel not seaworthy and weak. $70,000 estimated to   replace. A fixed lighthouse can be constructed for $35,000.

1901   Two 13 hp oil engines for fog signal to be installed. Light characteristic changed to flashing white. 8 flashes at 2 second intervals then dark for 15 seconds. Lens size changed from 3rd order to 4th order.

1902   Fog signal changed from 10 inch steam whistle to second class siren. Automatic duplicate 13 hp oil engines with two air tanks, two sirens and auto signals. Complaints that signal is not sufficiently loud enough. Added two large trumpets and sound deflectors on roof to deflect signal seaward.

Changed color of tower to white.

1903   Changed fog signal to conical siren by long continued experiments and tests. "Signal now seems to meet requirements of navigators."

1904   *Brenton Reef Lightship #39.* Built in 1875, 387 tons on station. Has chime fog and whistle signal. Two steam whistles (6 and 12 inches) Signal used for 614 hours. Consumed 89 tons of coal.

Light station. 2nd class siren, oil engines and compressed air. Signal used 583 hours and consumed 949 gals of fuel.

1904   Inspected the 2nd class siren in duplicate, worked by oil operation for 497 hours and used 873 gal. of fuel.

1905   Inspected the 1st class compressed air siren in duplicate, worked by 13 horsepower oil engines. Siren signal in operation for 120 hours and used 1032 gal. of fuel.

Appendix IV

Excerpts from the annual U.S. Lighthouse Board Reports to the Secretary of the U.S. Treasury regarding Beavertail Light Station and Brenton Reef Lightship (fiscal years ending in June)

1874
$8000 expended for better accommodations

1876
Lightship #11 $21,620 expended for repair of frames, rails, hause pipes and rigging

1873
First class Daboll Trumpet operative by 24 inch Ericsson caloric (heat) engines in duplicate. One engine at a time, need considerable repair.

1878
Lightship, no repairs required

1880
Fog signal repaired

1881
Installed two 10 inch steam whistles with duplicate boilers with large cistern for collecting rain water. System will meet every want of navigation. Dwelling repaired.

1882
Lightship #11 hull is good. Deck leaks and bell frame rotten. Will last a year. Foremast decayed

1888
Lightship, new canvas, paint and medicine aboard.
Lighthouse, fog signal 504 hours of operation, 67,456 pounds of coal consumed

1897
Lightship #11 now 12 years on station, needs repairs before winter.
Hog Island Shoal Vessel #12, vessel is old, no spare vessel, needs $500 to repair. Good for one year. Received new main, jib, boat sails, cooking gear, and stores.
Lighthouse, fog signal 593 hours, consumed 46 tons of coal

1898
Keeper's addition completed.

Hog Island Shoal vessel not seaworthy. $70,000 for replacement. New light can be built for $35,000

1899
Two 13 hp oil engines for fog signal will be installed. Light characteristic changed from 3rd order fixed to 4th order flashing white, 8 flashes at 2 sec interval then dark for 15 sec.

1900
Fog signal changed from 10 inch steam to second class siren, automatic with duplicate 13 hp oil engine, two air tanks, two sirens auto signal. Complaints received "not sufficiently loud". Added large trumpets and deflector on roof to deflect sound from trumpets to seaward. Changed color to white on tower

1901
Changed to conical siren by long continued experimental test. "Seems to meet requirements of navigators"

1889
$3500 allocated to buy land, tower re-pointed, lantern glass refitted

1903
Lightship #39 on station. Built in 1875, 387 tons, has chime whistle and fog signal. Two steam whistles, 6 inch and 12 inch, operated 614 hours and consumed 89 tons of coal
Lighthouse, 2nd class siren, oil engines and compressed air. 583 hours, consumed 949 gals of oil

From the Northeast U.S. Archives Record Center Waltham, MA, Aug 2004

Crouse Hinds lamp changer 1000 w T-20 1000 hour rated

22 Dec 1961 gr flash ev 15 sec 130,000 cp

Radio beacon 100 ft radials #8 wire every 3 degrees plus 8 ft. ground rod

1955, Sept. 2 Fence 30 ft., 4ft high to keep children from falling down the bank

1950 Asst. Keeper's house, Copland fridge and Capital coal burning furnace

"Watch Books "Dept of Commerce Lighthouse Service"

1926 Record of absences
1880 Record of passing vessels
1882-1886 10 inch steam whistle
1904 Siren 2nd order
1905 1st class Siren oil fired steam

Appendix V

Beavertail Lighthouse Museum Association (BLMA)
Executive and Board Members
1993-2007

1989
Henry Armbrust
1st Volunteer Coordinator

1993
President, Hugh Bucher
Vice President, L. Warner
Treasurer, Marion Pierce
Secretary, Charlotte Head
Board, ...June Webb, David Clem, Velma Moore, Pat Beausoliel, Ann Bucher, Bob Zartler, Alden Walls.

1994
President, Hugh Bucher
Vice President, Linda Warner
Treasurer, Marion Pierce
Secretary, Alden Walls,
Board,.... June Webb, David Clem, Ann Boucher, Patrica Beausoleil, Charlotte Head, Robert Dennis, Nancy Logan.

1994
President, Hugh Bucher
Vice President, Linda Warner
Treasurer, Marion Pierce
Secretary, Alden Walls? Lotte Head
Board,... Charlotte Head, Nancy Logan, Robert Dennis, Velma Moor, Pede Manchester, N. Walls

1995

1996
President, Anthony Faria
Vice President, June Webb
Treasurer, W. Craig Armington
Secretary, Alden Walls Jr.
Board,... June Luedke Webb, David Clem, Robert Dennis, Nancy Logan, Charlotte Head, Fred Clarke, Diane Faria

1997
President, Charles Auld
Vice President, Hugh Bucher
Secretary, Linda Jacobson
Treasurer, Richard Sullivan
Board,.... Donald Barrows, Ann Bucher, Brenda Johnson, Frank Meyer, Linda Warner, Susan Warszawski

1998

238

1999
President, Eric Armour (less than full year)
Vice President, Charlie Auld
Treasurer, W. Craig Armington
Secretary, Charlotte Richardson
Board,....Jean Boschen, David Clem, Linda Turillo Levesque, Susan Warsawski, Richard Sullivan, Jim Munro, Peter Frazier, Hugh Bucher, Robert Dennis.

1999
President, Charlie Auld
Vice President, Hugh Bucher,
Treasurer, Richard Sullivan
Secretary, Charlotte Richardson
Board,...Jim Munro, Don Barrows, Peter Frazier, Linda Levesque, Susan Warsawski, Bob Dennis

2000
President, Charlie Auld
Vice President, Hugh Bucher
Treasurer, Richard Sullivan
Secretary, Linda Jacobson
Board,....Linda Warner, Frank Meyer, Don Barrows, Brenda Johnston, Ann Bucher, James Munroe.

2001
President, Charles Auld
Vice President, Hugh Bucher,
Secretary, Linda Jacobson,
Treasurer, Richard Sullivan,
Board,....Don Barrows, Ann Bucher, Brenda Johnston, Frank Meyer, Linda Warner, Susan Warszawski

2002
President, Linda Warner
Vice President, Hugh Bucher
Secretary, Linda Jacobson
Treasurer Richard Sullivan
Board,... Laura Brasil, Alan Bunner, Agnes Filkins, Frank Meyer, Susan Warazawski

2003
President, Linda Warner
Vice President, Alan Brunner
Secretary, Linda Jacobson
Treasurer, Richard Sullivan
Board,..... Joe Bouchard, Laura Brasil, Agnes Filkins, Patricia Lucas, Frank Meyer, Emily Wild

2004
President, Linda Warner,
Vice President, Joe Bouchard
Treasurer, Richard Sullivan,
Secretary, Linda Jacobson
Board,.....Don Barrows, Brenda Johnston, Varoujan Karentz, Richard Koster, Pat Lucas, Frank Meyer

2005
President, Linda Warner,
Vice President, Joe Bouchard
Treasurer, Richard Sullivan,
Secretary, Linda Jacobson
Board,.....Don Barrows, Brenda Johnston, Varoujan Karentz, Richard Koster, Pat Lucas, Frank Meyer

2006
President, George Warner
Vice President, Richard .Sullivan
Treasurer, Richard Koster
Secretary, Charlotte Richardson
Board,.... Guy Archambault, Joe Bouchard, Brenda Johnston, Varoujan Karentz, Frank Meyer, Bill
Sprague, Lanette Maracuso

2007
President, George Warner
Vice President, Richard .Sullivan
Treasurer, Richard Koster
Secretary, Charlotte Richardson
Board,.... Guy Archambault, Joe Bouchard, Brenda Johnston, Varoujan Karentz, Lanette Maracuso,
Joan Vessella

2008
President, George Warner
Vice President, Richard .Sullivan
Treasurer, Richard Koster
Secretary. Paula Florentino
Board,.... Guy Archambault, Joe Bouchard, Varoujan Karentz, Lanette Maracuso, Charlotte
Richardson, Joan Vessella

240

ISBN 978-1-4196-8847-8

90000 >

9 781419 688478

1604256

Made in the USA